LITERARY CRITICISM AND CULTURAL THEORY
OUTSTANDING DISSERTATIONS

edited by
William E. Cain
Wellesley College

A ROUTLEDGE SERIES

OTHER BOOKS IN THIS SERIES:

A COINCIDENCE OF WANTS
The Novel and Neoclassical Economics
Charles Lewis

MODERN PRIMITIVES
*Race and Language in Gertrude Stein,
Ernest Hemingway, and Zora Neale
Hurston*
Susanna Pavloska

PLAIN AND UGLY JANES
*The Rise of the Ugly Woman in
Contemporary American Fiction*
Charlotte M. Wright

DISSENTING FICTIONS
*Identity and Resistance in the
Contemporary American Novel*
Cathy Moses

PERFORMING LA MESTIZA
*Textual References of Lesbians of Color
and the Negotiation of Identities*
Ellen M. Gil-Gomez

FROM GOOD MA TO WELFARE QUEEN
*A Genealogy of the Poor Woman in
American Literature, Photography and
Culture*
Vivyan C. Adair

ARTFUL ITINERARIES
*European Art and American Careers in
High Culture, 1865–1920*
Paul Fisher

POSTMODERN TALES OF SLAVERY
IN THE AMERICAS
From Alejo Carpenter to Charles Johnson
Timothy J. Cox

EMBODYING BEAUTY
*Twentieth-Century American Women
Writers' Aesthetics*
Malin Pereira

MAKING HOMES IN THE WEST/INDIES
*Constructions of Subjectivity in the
Writings of Michelle Cliff and Jamaica
Kincaid*
Antonia Macdonald-Smythe

POSTCOLONIAL MASQUERADES
*Culture and Politics in Literature, Film,
Video, and Photography*
Niki Sampat Patel

DIALECTIC OF SELF AND STORY
*Reading and Storytelling in Contemporary
American Fiction*
Robert Durante

ALLEGORIES OF VIOLENCE
*Tracing the Writings of War in Late
Twentieth-Century Fiction*
Lidia Yuknavitch

VOICE OF THE OPPRESSED IN THE LANGUAGE
OF THE OPPRESSOR
*A Discussion of Selected Postcolonial
Literature from Ireland, Africa and
America*
Patsy J. Daniels

EUGENIC FANTASIES
*Racial Ideology in the Literature and
Popular Culture of the 1920's*
Betsy L. Nies

THE LIFE WRITING OF OTHERNESS
Woolf, Baldwin, Kingston, and Winterson
Lauren Rusk

FROM WITHIN THE FRAME
Storytelling in African-American Fiction
Bertram D. Ashe

THE SELF WIRED
*Technology and Subjectivity in
Contemporary Narrative*
Lisa Yaszek

THE SPACE AND PLACE OF MODERNISM
The Little Magazine in New York
Adam McKible

THE FIGURE OF CONSCIOUSNESS
*William James, Henry James, and
Edith Wharton*
Jill M. Kress

THE WASTE FIX

Seizures of the Sacred
from Upton Sinclair to *The Sopranos*

William G. Little

Routledge
Taylor & Francis Group

LONDON AND NEW YORK

First published 2002 by Routledge

2 Park Square, Milton Park, Abingdon, Oxon, OX14 4RN
605 Third Avenue, New York, NY 10017

Routledge is an imprint of the Taylor & Francis Group, an informa business

First issued in paperback 2020

Library of Congress Cataloging-in-Publication Data

Little, William G., 1961–
  The waste fix : seizures of the sacred from Upton Sinclair to the Sopranos / by William G. Little.
     p. cm. — (Literary criticism and cultural theory)
  ISBN 0-415-94053-2 (hardback)
  1. American fiction—20th century—History and criticism. 2. Waste (Economics) in literature. 3. Auster, Paul, 1947—Views on waste (Economics) 4. Postmodernism (Literature)—United States. 5. Sinclair, Upton, 1878–1968. Jungle. 6. Refuse and refuse disposal in literature. 7. Leyner, Mark—Views on waste (Economics) 8. Consumption (Economics) in literature. 9. DeLillo, Don. White noise. 10. Sopranos (Television program) I. Title. II. Series.
  PS374.W36 L58 2002
  813'.509355—dc21

                                                    2002004961

ISBN 13: 978-0-415-94053-5 (hbk)
ISBN 13: 978-1-138-98693-0 (pbk)

To my father,
who taught me the virtues of wasting my time otherwise

Contents

Acknowledgments   ix

BACKFIRE I: WASTE EXPECTATIONS   1

Chapter One: Naturalism's Shambling Figure   13

1. Joint Anxiety   13
2. Shit Fits   17
3. Blank Posturing   28
4. Sham(ble) Fiction   41

BACKFIRE II: MELVILLE'S (UN)FLINCHING FAITH   55

Chapter Two: Nothing to Go On: Paul Auster's Cracked Case   65

1. Catching a Break   65
2. Nothing Doing   69
3. Absent-Minded Hunger   74
4. Firing Blanks   80

Chapter Three: (Mis)Spelling Disaster: Faith in *White Noise*   93

1. Dis-astrologic   93
2. Garbage Disposal   97
3. Void Where Prohibited   103
4. Trash Recollection   113

Chapter Four: Figuring Out Mark Leyner: A Waste of Time   117

1. The Rush of Scandal   117
2. The Warped Writer   120
3. The Art of Dispatch   122
4. Putting Off   129

BACKFIRE III: HITTING ON *THE SOPRANOS*   141

Notes   157
Bibliography   167
Index   173

Acknowledgments

I wish to thank the following people for their support and encouragement during my work on this book: Stephanie Browner and Steve Pulsford, for their friendship; Patrick Brantlinger, Jonathan Elmer, Istvan Csicsery-Ronay, and Mark Taylor for their valuable feedback during various stages of the writing; Ray Hedin, for his kind and unwavering mentorship. Above all, I wish to thank my father, H. Ganse Little, Jr., whose intellectual passion and critical rigor I admire. Without the fire of his mind as backing, I would not have been able to launch this project.

THE WASTE FIX

BACKFIRE I

Waste Expectations

Waste is a religious thing.

Don DeLillo, *Underworld*

It has become something of an accepted practice to describe the modern American landscape as a spiritual and cultural wasteland.[1] Such an exercise relies heavily on a depiction of America as the site of numerous unsettling spectacles: unbridled materialism; suburban sprawl; psychic hotlines; Hollywood special effects; schoolyard killing sprees. This lament, in turn, is based in large measure on a conviction that the nation has been reduced to a wasted state through an addiction to spectacle. According to this argument, America is both wired to the screen and wired by the screen, with the result that so-called real virtues have been abandoned in favor of the vacuousness of virtual reality. America, the theory goes, is getting wasted on the drug of image, and those images which deliver the most intense fix or generate the biggest boost are images of devastation, violation, and radical expenditure. America is in a fix because it is fixated on a perpetual exhibition of the atrocious: the terrorist blast; the twister swath; the celebrity 'crash'; the professional wrestling ring; the private web cam; the violent video game; the shopaholic's prime time confession.

Yet running parallel to the claim that the nation is in a shambles is the persistent assertion that deliverance from the wasteland of the virtual is at hand. According to this latter expectation, the path out of the wilderness is marked, paradoxically, by the virtues of waste. In one respect, the notion of waste expressing virtue folds neatly into Thorstein Veblen's famous concept, mapped out in *The Theory of the Leisure Class*, that what structures consumer culture is a "fundamental canon of conspicuous waste" (91). This canon establishes as virtuous the figure who spends time and money unproductively. Such gratuitous expenditure, exemplified by rampant con-

1

sumption of leisure activities and material goods, confers on the spender the seal of esteemed virtue because it signifies what Veblen calls "pecuniary distinction," the highly prized ability to be able to afford being useless, prodigal, wasteful: "From the foregoing survey of the growth of conspicuous leisure and consumption, it appears that the utility of both alike for the purposes of reputability lies in the element of waste that is common to both. In the one case it is a waste of time and effort, in the other it is a waste of goods. Both are methods of demonstrating the possession of wealth, and the two are conventionally accepted as equivalents" (85).

In another respect, however, Veblen's insights into consumer culture's honorific treatment of waste represent but a partial treatment of America's investment in waste. Specifically, he neglects to recognize that the national commitment to making a virtue of waste is fired, historically, by a problem of religious expectation which, as the sociologist Max Weber claims, constitutes nothing less than the ideological backdrop to the rise of modern capitalism. In *The Protestant Ethic and the Spirit of Capitalism*, Weber argues that early Calvinist doctrine places a unique burden on Protestant reformers by leaving unresolved individual anxieties about how to get a fix on the certainty of election. As Weber formulates it, Calvin responds to such anxious expectation by offering the idea of "expectant faith":

> He [Calvin] rejects in principle the assumption that one can learn from the conduct of others whether they are chosen or damned. It is an unjustifiable attempt to force God's secrets. The elect differ externally in this life in no way from the damned; and even all the subjective experiences of the chosen are . . . possible for the damned with the single exception of that *finaliter* expectant, trusting faith. (110)

Since Calvin's explanation does not adequately fix the problems presented by the doctrine of predestination, early Calvinist thought develops the notion that one can generate conviction about one's salvation through what Weber calls "a type of Christian conduct which served to increase the glory of God" (114). This good conduct does not eliminate expectancy altogether, but it eliminates the debilitating, draining, wasting effects of expectancy. In other words, such conduct insures waste-free expectancy: "Thus, however useless good works might be as a means of attaining salvation, for even the elect remain beings of the flesh, and everything they do falls infinitely short of divine standards, nevertheless, they are indispensable means, not of purchasing salvation, but of getting rid of the fear of damnation" (115).

What Veblen overlooks is that modern rituals of material consumption bear traces of redemption-bound expectancy. Specifically, the canon of conspicuous waste emerges out of the Puritan conviction that wealth, insofar as it is acquired and reinvested for the sake of God's glory, is actually a mark of virtue: "Wealth is thus bad ethically only insofar as it is a temptation to idleness and sinful enjoyment of life, and its acquisition is bad only when it is with the purpose of later living merrily and without care. But as a performance of duty in a calling it is not only morally permissible, but actually enjoined" (Weber 163). For the modern consumer, wealth is a virtue because it allows one to spend time wastefully. For the Puritan, wealth is evil *only* insofar as it tempts one to spend time wastefully, only insofar as it distracts one from unwavering service to God. As Weber puts it: "Waste of time is thus the first and in principle the deadliest of sins" (157). To get out of the fix time creates, Puritanism endorses what Weber calls "methodically rationalized ethical conduct" (125), a systematic, regularized mode of existence defined by devotion to worldly work assigned by God for the worship of God: "For everyone without exception God's providence has prepared a calling, which he should profess and in which he should labor. And this calling is not, as it was for the Lutheran, a fate to which he must submit and which he must make the best of, but God's commandment to the individual to work for the divine glory" (160). The believer gets out of temporality's waste fix through acceptance of a "fixed calling" whose virtuousness is measured, paradoxically, by the accrual of material profits. The virtue attached to conspicuous waste is thus a secularized version of the virtue attached to the elimination of waste. Consumer culture's waste expectations take the shape Veblen describes only when, for complicated socio-historical reasons, the religious expectations informing waste-free expectancy fade into the background.

The Puritan legacy of waste stigmatization suggests that the modern virtu-alization of waste cannot be adequately understood apart from what Mary Douglas dubs "the filtering mechanism" at work in every society. In her anthropological study *Purity and Danger*, Douglas outlines how every means of organizing experience—social, medical, epistemological, religious, etc.—creates structure and establishes order through complex processes of discrimination which result in the formation of categories, the drawing of boundaries, the imprinting of pattern, the bestowal of names. By necessity, these acts of separation yield elements that don't fit easily into the constructed schema, differences that can't be readily reduced to the same: "Any given system of classification must give rise to anomalies, and any given culture must confront events which seem to defy its assumptions" (37). Douglas frequently refers to this fugitive stuff as dirt and illustrates how a system's confidence depends on its ability to distance itself from such unsettling matter by defiling it as contaminated filth or hazardous waste: "Dirt is the by-product of a systematic ordering and classification of matter, in so far as ordering involves rejecting inappropriate elements. . . . [O]ur pollution behaviour is the reaction which condemns any object or idea likely to confuse or contradict cherished classifications" (35–36). Every system expects a lot from waste because only by rejecting, spitting out, or expectorating what it labels as waste can a system confirm its identity as clean and proper.

With these expectations in mind, I wish to take the initial step of suggesting that American consumer culture makes a virtue of waste not simply by valorizing conspicuous consumption but, more broadly, by philosophically constructing waste as that which, treated properly, will deliver the modern individual from the temptations, uncertainties, and drags of a scene characterized by rapid proliferation of the virtual. From progressive muckraking to postmodern recycling, from municipal mandates to medical research, the culture has exhibited an obsession with branding—i.e., isolating and, depending on the case, stigmatizing—various strains of waste (e.g., idleness, overwork, depression, attention deficit, artificial additives, obesity, cable glut, corporate tie-ins, political incorrectness). Guiding this obsession is the expectation that waste is something which, converted to good use, will restore individual and community to a state of prelapsarian unity. As illustrated by the mass market success of products ranging from Slim·Fast to steroid supplements, from tofu to Tai Bo, some of contemporary culture's most intense, anxious speculations on and in waste are intertwined with expectations about fashioning an individual subject whose integrity or whole-someness depends on mastering waste through rituals of manic expulsion and/or manic incorporation. Whether filtering it or flaunting it, encapsulating it or acquiring it, shedding it, shredding it, or showing it off, we pump waste full of great expectations. While the culture's fetishism of waste may be a measure of certain collective anxieties, it is also a measure of how wild is the hope for recovery.

A case in point is the contemporary rage to Reduce, Reuse, Recycle, an imperative whose virtues are, at best, debatable. A 1996 *New York Times Magazine* article titled "Recycling is Garbage" actually asserts that large scale recycling does not make sense from either an economic or a scientific standpoint:

> Mandatory recycling programs aren't good for posterity. They offer mainly short-term benefits to a few groups—politicians, public relations consultants, environmental organizations, waste-handling corporations—while diverting money from genuine social and environmental problems. Recycling may be the most wasteful activity in modern America: a waste of time and money, a waste of human and natural resources. (24)

Why have these reclamation projects been so widely adopted when they may be more detrimental than beneficial? The *Times* article suggests that it is because such conversion fantasies are ultimately infused with spiritual expectations: "Americans have embraced recycling as a transcendental experience, an act of moral redemption. We're not just reusing our garbage; we're performing a rite of atonement for the sin of excess. Recycling teaches the themes that previous generations of schoolchildren learned from that Puritan classic, 'The Pilgrim's Progress'" (26). The piece concludes with the claim that conscientious disposal at the curbside is simply a variant of conspicuous consumption: "The muckraker has forgotten that there is more to life than hoarding natural resources. His recycling has become the most primitive form of materialism: the worship of *materials*" (53). In the quest to escape the virtual through a redeeming experience of the authentic, we make up our waste products—our paper, plastic, and glass—to be just like nature's raw materials. Philosophically speaking, the virtue of these artificial substances is that they can be melted or pulverized to a point where they cease to signify. Purged of their function as mimetic objects, they become, paradoxically, virtual embodiments of the real thing.

In an essay titled "From Salvation to Self-Realization: Advertising and the Therapeutic Roots of Consumer Culture," the critic T. J. Jackson Lears traces these ritualized waste-processing strategies back to a "crucial moral change" taking place at the turn of the twentieth century, a change initiated by "a shift from a Protestant ethos of salvation through self-denial toward a therapeutic ethos stressing self-realization in this world—an ethos characterized by an almost obsessive concern with psychic and physical health defined in sweeping terms" (4). According to Lears, this still-flourishing ethos emerges in response to anxieties about an experience felt to be ever more alienating, aleatory, agnostic, and, above all, unreal. In other words, America's modern virtu-alization of waste is linked, from the outset, to fears of entrapment in a wasteland of the virtual:

> In all, the modern sense of unreality stemmed from extraordinarily various sources and generated complex effects. Technological change isolated the urban bourgeoisie from the hardness of life on the land; an interdependent and increasingly corporate economy circumscribed autonomous will and choice; a softening Protestant theology undermined commitments and blurred ethical distinctions. . . . [T]he feeling of unreality helped to generate longings for bodily vigor, emotional intensity, and a revitalized sense of selfhood. (10)

In place of the Logos of divine Authority, the logic of authentic subjectivity. Consumer culture's discourses on the virtues of waste dramatize an evangelical effort to narrativize a figure and, as I will argue, to figure a narrative in which no polluted other remains to haunt the firmly self-possessed individual.

In this context, my book poses the following questions: What are the remains of a system that claims to homogenize all heterogeneity by keeping waste under such a watchful eye/I? What role does literature, in some quarters considered an all but irrelevant or wasted medium, play in attending to these remains? Through interdisciplinary engagement with a series of twentieth-century American fictional texts, I propose the idea that perhaps the greatest hazard facing American consumer culture is not its perceived status as a virtual wasteland but rather its reluctance to hazard philosophical inspection of such a remainder, a form of waste neither fully conspicuous nor totally inconspicuous. I argue that the culture's determination to virtu-alize waste in pursuit of transcendent self-realization is governed by a massive campaign to repress, bury, or leave unexamined an Other kind of waste which cannot be neatly seized by thought. This irreducible remainder is not quite the same as conspicuous waste because, as Veblen indicates, the latter is an expression of purposelessness seized on for purposeful, thoughtful ends: "It would be hazardous to assert that a useful purpose is ever absent from the utility of any article or of any service, however obviously its prime purpose and chief element is conspicuous waste" (101). Closely resembling conspicuous waste—indeed, its spitting image—this radical refuse gives consumer culture seizures of anxiety because it lays waste to the expectation of acquiring redeeming virtue through comprehensive waste management. Such profoundly unsettling excess challenges the binary oppositions—useful/useless, being/seeming, clean/dirty, inside/outside, self/other—on which the culture's waste treatments depend. A shadowy alternative to the supposedly 'real' waste from which models of virtue are constructed, it might otherwise be labeled *virtual waste*.

Since virtually nothing can be expected of virtual waste, one may feel there is hardly any virtue in trying, however haltingly, to speak about it. Put another way, one may be tempted to spit at the idea. Such an act of defilement would make sense in light of Mary Douglas' claim that every culture seeks to protect the integrity of its ordering systems by denigrating as polluted whatever highlights the fragility of system boundaries. Indeed, she argues that serious threats to system are most often ritually signified as threats posed to the physical body by its own material byproducts, its own expectorations: "Any structure of ideas is vulnerable at its margins. We should expect the orifices of the body to symbolise its specially vulnerable points. Matter issuing from them is marginal stuff of the most obvious kind. Spittle, blood, milk, urine, faeces or tears by simply issuing forth have traversed the boundary of the body" (121). However, she goes on to argue that while cultures establish rules of avoidance with regard to the marginal, they also tend to invest this dangerous otherness with tremendous religious power: "To talk about a confused blending of the Sacred and the Unclean is outright nonsense. But it still remains true that religions often sacralise the very unclean things which have been rejected with abhorrence. We must, therefore, ask how dirt, which is normally destructive, sometimes becomes creative" (159).

With expectation, then, that my project is bound to be hit, from some quarters, with the usual kind of critical spray (is bound, in other words, to backfire), I intend to pursue Don DeLillo's declaration, in *Underworld*, that "Waste is a religious thing" by exploring, within the context of the twentieth-century American landscape, Douglas' tentative connection between waste and the sacred. To do so, I turn to fiction, in part because Douglas' question of how that "which is normally destructive, sometimes becomes creative" is intimately bound up, from the beginning, with questions of *plotting*. I say "from the beginning" because the creative aspect of waste is evident in the plots of numerous creation myths. As the historian of religions Mircea Eliade illustrates, many of these stories describe how the cosmos gets conceived out of an unbounded scene of chaos or formlessness: the infinite void; the black waters; the endless night. In these myths, the world is founded from and on a vast waste, a ground frequently figured as a dragon which must be bound, dismembered, or brought under foot:

> [T]he dragon is the paradigmatic figure of the marine monster, of the primordial snake, symbol of the cosmic waters, of darkness, night, and death—in short, of the amorphous and virtual, of everything that has not yet acquired a "form." The dragon must be conquered and cut to pieces by the gods so that the cosmos may come to birth. It was from the body of the marine monster Tiamat that Marduk fashioned the world. Yahweh created the universe after his victory over the primordial monster Rahab. (48)

According to Eliade, the cosmogonic gesture of conquering or fixing "virtual" waste yields a plot of fully meaningful, "sacred" space and time, a plot marked off from undifferentiated, "profane" time and space. He argues that numerous rituals in archaic societies—the construction of a house, the celebration of a new year, the recitation of a creation myth—are undertaken with the aim of reproducing this original plot: "For all these palaeo-agricultural peoples, what is essential is periodically to evoke the primordial event that established their present condition of humanity. Their whole religious life is a commemoration, a remembering" (101). In spatial terms, ritual imitation of a divine fix on "virtual" waste may entail the architectural fixing in place of a central post designed to replicate the *axis mundi*, the sacred "cosmic pillar" charged with the power of organizing habitable space, supporting the sky, and providing a means of passage "from one cosmic region to another" (37). In temporal terms, ritual imitation of a divine fix on "virtual" waste may entail becoming transfixed by mythic recitation of the *illud tempus*, the sacred "time of origins" charged with metaphysical and ontological plenitude:

> But since ritual recitation of the cosmogonic myth implies reactualization of that primordial event, it follows that he for whom it is recited is magically projected *in illo tempore*, into the "beginning of the World"; he becomes contemporary with the cosmogony. What is involved is, in short,

a return to original time, the therapeutic purpose of which is to begin life once again, a symbolic rebirth. (82)

For all its useful speculations, however, the problem with Eliade's analytical plotting of the sacred is that it presumes the sacred to be neatly plottable. Describing it as that which marks a radical "break" in the plane of the profane, he suggests that the sacred is not subject to the profane workings of representation itself. Indeed, he claims that the sacred is what stands over and against the illusory, the apparent, the imitative, the mimetic:

> [F]or primitives as for the man of all pre-modern societies, the sacred is equivalent to a *power*, and, in the last analysis, to *reality*. The *sacred* is saturated with being. Sacred power means reality and at the same time enduringness and efficacity. The polarity sacred-profane is often expressed as an opposition between real and unreal or pseudoreal. (12–13)

Striving to replot this "real" life, mimetic acts of myth telling and house building paradoxically simulate a way out of the fix of a virtual (pseudoreal) existence: "In short, through the reactualization of his myths, religious man attempts to approach the gods and to participate in *being*; the imitation of paradigmatic divine models expresses at once his desire for sanctity and his ontological nostalgia" (106).

Despite acknowledging that the sacred is invested with tremendous, superabundant power, Eliade's nostalgic equation of the sacred with the real betrays an idealism that neglects to take into account adequately Douglas' insistence on the difficulties inherent in any approach to the sacred. As the Latin root *sacer* reveals, what makes the sacred so tricky to figure is that it is something both consecrated and cursed, something both clean and dirty, something awe inspiring and appalling, something truly awful. The sacred is not simply a neat and tidy break with the profane. Instead, it is a difference on which it is difficult to get a fix. In the words of the postmodern theologian Mark C. Taylor: "The elusiveness of the sacred reflects its irreducible ambiguity. . . . Both holy and filthy, the sacred is simultaneously attractive and repulsive, alluring and forbidding. Such ambiguity and ambivalence render the sacred *fascinating*. The fascination exercised by the sacred cannot be explained rationally" (*Altarity* 136–37). In *Totem and Taboo*, Sigmund Freud describes how this fascination structures the relationship so-called primitive cultures have with objects, people, and spaces identified as taboo. Admitting his own difficulty in providing a rational explanation of such prohibitions—"the whole subject is highly obscure" (28)—he recounts archaic culture's ritual insistence that every attempt to seize on the taboo is bound to backfire. The schemer (or plotter) who makes unlawful contact with the forbidden in an effort to access its powerful charge gets branded unclean and contaminated, like the taboo itself. The community labels the violator infectious because the transgression, far from putting one directly in touch with a transcendent Real, serves only to promote destructive mimetic activity: "Anyone who has violated a taboo becomes taboo himself because he possesses the dangerous quality of tempting others to follow his example: why should *he* be allowed to do what is forbidden to others? Thus he is truly contagious in that every example encourages imitation, and for that reason he himself must be shunned" (42). The health of the archaic social unit thus depends on its ability to maintain a proximate distance in relation to this terrific Otherness. To plot otherwise is to risk a collective backfire.

The sacred, then, might be described as a form of waste resistant to appropriation by traditional technologies of speculative thought. As Taylor's term "altarity" suggests, it is a form of otherness or alterity that precipitates a philosophical crisis, in part because, like Jacques Derrida's notion of *différance*, the distinguishing 'a' cannot be spoken, and in part because the word 'altar' backfires when it comes to laying out the sacred properly:

> The semantic range of "altar" extends from high to low, sacred to sexual, eschatological to scatological: a toilet, the sex that modestly withdraws [the hymenal altar], a platform for offerings, or the communion table. So understood, the altar might mark and remark the site where one almost encounters the deity through the release of sacrifice, the sacrifice of a substitute victim—a ram, a daughter, a son, perhaps the word itself. (*Altarity*, xxviii)

Like virtual waste, the sacred is bound to confound expectations of enlightenment because it can be approached only as and through backfire. It is a creative and destructive fire smouldering beneath (or in back of) the ashes left by the scapegoat consigned to the flames at the sacrificial altar. It is a fire smouldering beneath (or in back of) the remains left by one who worships (vomits, expectorates, backfires) at the porcelain altar. In Deuteronomy, Moses reminds the Israelites that God did indeed show up for them, though only on the backside of their plot to figure the divine by firing up a golden calf (a mimetic scheme that backfires) and only as a nearly unfigurable Other withdrawn within a fire: "And you came near and stood at the foot of the mountain, while the mountain burned with fire to the heart of heaven, wrapped in darkness, cloud, and gloom. Then the Lord spoke to you out of the midst of fire; you heard the sound of words, but saw no form; there was only a voice" (Deuteronomy 4: 11–12).[2]

An infinitely unsettling loose end, the backfire of virtual waste thus challenges the authority of what the feminist theorist Luce Irigaray terms "phallocratism," patriarchy's social, onto-theological, and discursive determination to reduce all difference to the same in the name of logic, in the

name of Logos, in the name of the Father. According to Irigaray, patriarchy's logocentrism expresses itself as a commitment to a "mechanics of
solids" whose disciplinary imperative is to eliminate leaks, fluids, backfires
that jeopardize the realization of absolute knowledge or perfect *solid*arity:
"Thus if every psychic economy is organized around the phallus (or
Phallus) we may ask what this primacy owes to a teleology of reabsorption
of fluid in a solidified form" (110). In other words, phallocratism is founded on the expectation of achieving total fitness. Since discourse itself is dedicated to the end of producing solid meaning, virtual waste, which is linked
to compromising, unmanageable discharges and expectorations, appears
all but unspeakable. As Irigaray puts it: "[W]hat structuration of (the) language does not maintain *a complicity of long standing between rationality
and a mechanics of solids alone?*" (107). Nevertheless, she imagines a
"'mechanics' of fluids" whose aim, while inevitably implicated in phallo-
centricism's teleological thrust, is to entertain a fluid Other excluded from
consideration by a mechanics of solids. In her words, "This fluid is always
in a relation of excess or lack vis-à-vis unity" (117). Moreover, this fluid
bears traces of both the divine and the feminine: "There remain these/her
remains: God and woman, 'for example'" (111).

With such self-disruptive theoretical speculations as backdrop, *The
Waste Fix* argues that virtual waste places American consumer culture in
an anxiety-producing fix. The project also asserts that the nation has
rushed to get out of this fix by repeatedly promising to produce solidly
masculine bodies and texts. If, as Irigaray suggests, virtual waste always
leaves patriarchy haunted by theological and sexual anxiety, then one way
to see how the culture has systematically repressed the sacred is to examine its anxious, sustained determination to construct the masculine figure
as a waste-free ideal. As Calvin Thomas puts it in his book *Male Matters*:

> An abject masculine relationship to the maternal, to the feminine, to the
> nonidentical, also interprets—and is perhaps overdetermined by—an anx-
> ious masculine relationship to the male body, to the visibility of that body,
> the traverse of its boundaries, the representability of its products, the cor-
> poreal conditions of male subjectivity, and the unavoidable materiality of
> the signifying process itself. (15)

To historicize the idea that consumer culture's anxiety about the sacred is
bound up with anxiety about the male body and anxiety about the "materiality of the signifying process," I begin with a study of naturalist narrative. Using as a nexus the figure of Upton Sinclair, I demonstrate how the
aesthetics of naturalism and the principles of Progressive Era medicine
share an expectation of achieving salvation through purgation, an expectation made manifest in the pursuit of a masculinized, Anglo-Saxon ideal. I
place a study of Sinclair's famous muckraking novel *The Jungle* alongside

a study of his extensive nonliterary writings on the benefits of 'natural' diet and the strenuous life in order to show how naturalism's obsession with eliminating traces of the sentimental from the novel is linked to progressive culture's redemption-bound devotion to eliminating the feminine from the body. What makes Sinclair's case particularly compelling is that even as he participates in a campaign to put to shame anything that smacks of the sham or the virtual, his novelistic fascination with the slaughterhouse—the Chicago shambles—unsettles progressivism's purist intentions. The fact that the narrative progress of *The Jungle* falters or shambles when Sinclair insists on purging the abattoir from his text dramatizes how such a sanitary-minded plot to produce social solidarity and narrative closure is bound to backfire.

With Sinclair's meaty texts as further backdrop, I then address a series of postmodern novels that examine critically the expectation that waste can be reduced to something on which one can fully and virtuously capitalize, either by eradicating it (shed those extra pounds!) or by embracing it (shop 'til you drop!). At one level, the novels foreground male figures obsessed with wiping out unsettling remainders through repressive strategies of assimilation, utilization, exclusion, and disposal (e.g., Paul Auster's portrait of the hardboiled detective as anorexic figure dedicated to purging his case of loose ends; Don DeLillo's portrait of the contemporary professor as Hitler scholar dedicated to the final solution of eradicating his own fear of death; Mark Leyner's portrait of the celebrity author as hypermasculine bodybuilder dedicated to devouring his competition). At another level, the white male writers of these texts, while they work to distance themselves from the totalizing plots of their characters, resist making the equally totalizing assertion that their own plots express and/or embody a liberating excess. Instead of claiming to offer purely wasteful narratives, they adopt genres that have traditionally fetishized waste—surrealism, modernist minimalism, *noir* fiction, the domestic novel, the disaster novel—in order to deconstruct the logic of those narrative strategies from within. In this respect, they allow their own narratives to backfire.

The aim of these readings is thus twofold: first, to examine the unhealthy effects of twentieth-century America's drive to fetishize waste as an other whose thorough appropriation or expulsion releases the individual from the wasteland of modernity; second, to argue that certain postmodern texts represent alternative, nontotalizing responses to the hazards of modern life. I assert that Auster's private-eye investigations into "nothing," DeLillo's difficult faith in "white noise," and Leyner's effort to be what I call a "waste of time" constitute religiously inflected narratives in that the waste they process, with inevitable insufficiency, has much in common with the sacred.

Moreover, as the formal design of my work indicates, any expectation of capitalizing discursively on virtual waste is bound to backfire. Indeed, I

frame the study with three pieces labeled "backfires" which simultaneously spark and interrupt its forward thrust. For example, the latter two pieces
enable me to entertain virtually wasted male figures (Herman Melville's
Bartleby, the Scrivener; mobster boss Tony Soprano, the central character
in the recent HBO television series *The Sopranos*) who do not properly fit
within the scope of my analysis of twentieth-century literary texts. Taken
together, these three "backfires" illustrate how my own scholarly plot to
get a fix on the sacred necessarily amounts to something other than a neatly progressive, clean and proper, waste-free study.

CHAPTER ONE

Naturalism's Shambling Figure

1. JOINT ANXIETY

> The slaughterhouse is linked to religion insofar as the temples of by-gone eras (not to mention those of the Hindus in our own day) served two purposes: they were used both for prayer and for killing. . . . In our time, nevertheless, the slaughterhouse is cursed and quarantined like a plague-ridden ship. Now, the victims of this curse are neither butchers nor beasts, but those same good folk who countenance, by now, only their own unseemliness, an unseemliness commensurate with an unhealthy need of cleanliness, with irascible meanness, and boredom. The curse (terrifying only to those who utter it) leads them to vegetate as far as possible from the slaughterhouse, to exile themselves, out of propriety, to a flabby world in which nothing fearful remains and in which, subject to the ineradicable obsession of shame, they are reduced to eating cheese.
>
> Georges Bataille, "Slaughterhouse"

> Christ, Deckard, you look almost as bad as that skin job you left on the sidewalk. . . . Could learn from this guy, Gaff. He's a god-damn one man slaughterhouse. That's what he is.
>
> Captain Bryant, *Blade Runner*

To begin tracing how naturalist discourse turns its back on virtual waste, I would like first to speculate briefly on naturalism's legacy, a strategy that involves doubling back to a postmodern future where, due largely to a trouble with doubles, the time seems out of joint. The particular futuristic scene I have in mind, from the film *Blade Runner*, is a steam-choked, garbage-strewn Los Angeles sidewalk where police captain Bryant is addressing Deckard, the lead detective in charge of tracking down and killing (or "retiring") simulated humans (or "replicants"). As the epigraph cited above indicates, Bryant delivers the apparently throwaway remark that Deckard is a shambles. I say apparently because the significance of Bryant's words runs several layers of skin deep. After all, Deckard's haggard aspect is not simply due to the physical rigors of his job. If Deckard looks wasted, if he looks like a virtual replication of the replicant or "skin job" he has just wasted, it is due in large measure to the fact that his job of eliminating a serialized version of the human has transformed him, ironically, into a virtual serial killer (or a serial killer of the virtual). His work has converted him into "a god-damn one man slaughterhouse," a killing machine programed to cut out, with the aid of an assistant aptly named "Gaff," the dis-eased meat of bioengineered humans hiding within the social. In other words, the blade runner is a shambles to the extent that he stands for a near collapse of the humanist distinctions—human/machine, self/other, interior/exterior—he has been hired to preserve.

Just as the replicant is made to pass as an upstanding example of the human figure, Bryant's metaphor of the slaughterhouse is designed to pass, in the film, as an upstanding example of humanist figuration. Yet by making the trope of the slaughterhouse stand for the plight of the humanist in a posthuman world, the film participates in a retirement program analogous to the one carried out in the film against the replicants. At one level, the law in the film (Bryant) coerces Deckard out of retirement in order to erase those marks (the replicants) that threaten humanist ideology. At another level, the law (of the studio) coerces the signifier "slaughterhouse" to get a good make on Deckard's true identity by erasing the signifier's identity as graphic mark or skin job. To authorize the slaughter of replicants, Bryant necessarily disregards the machines' meatiness or humanity. To author the metaphor of the blade runner as slaughterhouse, the filmmakers necessarily disregard the metaphor's meatiness or materiality. Assuming the trope to be fully transparent and productive, the filmmakers overlook the fact that the figure of the slaughterhouse contributes to the very crisis supposedly made manageable through the metaphor's employment. For if the abattoir acts like a replicant in that it passes as a properly humanist figure, it also acts like a replicant (one of whom/which is named Roy Batty) in that it threatens to *abate*, or to bring down, what Tom Cohen, in his book *Anti-Mimesis from Plato to Hitchcock*, refers to as humanism's "regime of representational meaning" (262).[1] As instances of the mechanical reproduction of meat, both the abattoir and the replicant express humanism's mimetic impulse to re-create the other (the animal and the machine) in our own image, yet their skin jobs pose a hazard to mimesis by threatening to remain at large.[2]

Georges Bataille, in the short piece posted at the beginning of this essay, entertains the abattoir's radical heterogeneity through a description of the extent to which bourgeois humanism has anxiously tried to homogenize the shambles by figuring it as a toxic waste site "cursed and quarantined like a plague-ridden ship" ("Slaughterhouse" 14). According to Bataille, the slaughterhouse gets treated as a waste site not simply because there might be physical refuse—bloody membranes, squirming entrails, gristle, shit—spattering the walls and tainting the meat products but more so because the slaughterhouse bears traces of a remainder resistant to elimination no matter how thorough the inspection. A duplicitous site of production and destruction, the slaughterhouse resists philosophical recuperation as fit emblem of either the economic or the noneconomic. Instead, like "the temples of by-gone eras . . . used for both prayer and killing," it begins to shadow forth a more unsettling kind of noneconomic experience which bears resemblance to the unreservedly ruinous experience, at the altar, of the sacred. Such an uncanny joint produces anxiety by resisting a neat signifying fix. The shambles confounds the proprietary expectations of (representational) work, leading the proper bourgeois subject, driven by what Bataille terms "an unhealthy need of cleanliness," to expectorate it as disgusting.

Thus, if the figure of the shambles makes legible humanism's crisis, it does so, in part, by drawing attention to the limits of figuration. Bearing the trace of a staggering alterity, the trope is one whose progress as a bearer of meaning is invariably halting. The linguistic equivalent of a trick knee, it is a joint that never quite completely gives way. Indeed, the etymological connection between the noun 'shambles' and the verb 'to shamble' suggests that the slaughterhouse inevitably drags its feet or stumbles when called on to disclose what it stands for. A kind of *shambling figure*, it shuffles closer to representing what Tom Cohen refers to as a "prefigural moment," a semiotic instance in which the material sign—haunting the textual premises like a replicant haunting the premises of a futuristic Los Angeles—trips up the mimetic operation it carries out. The most striking convergence of Cohen's work with the slaughterhouse's encrypted links to shambling occurs when he cites the figure of legs as a crucial illustration of the prefigural. Undertaking a close reading of texts such as Shakespeare's *Othello*, Poe's "The Cask of Amontillado," and Conrad's "The Secret Sharer," he claims that repeated inscription of legs in these works does not simply signal a revolutionary privileging of the lower body and its symbolic attendants (unreason, waste) over the upper body and its symbolic attendants (reason, utility). Instead, the figure of legs deconstructs the binary logic governing these oppositions:

> The figure of legs . . . dismantles any bodily metaphor that permits a master-slave opposition between the Cartesian head (subject, meaning, cognition) and the legs (material conveyers), since it frequently happens in these texts that the legs usurp the position of the head, or become severed and independent agents of transvaluation. If legs may be understood as a corporeal analogue for the material base of language itself, that entails the

brute dependence of semantic relations on what precedes mimesis and figuration; on what, in the course of marking itself, gets woven into and
alters meaning-production; on what seeks and implements *a mimesis
without models*. . . . Legs is one term for a materiality that precedes figuration, that produces "figuration" as its evasion. (7–8)

Like the slaughterhouse—a place where legs literally become "severed
and independent agents"—the textualized legs Cohen admires constitute
an "anti-mimetic Other" (262), a figure slow to deliver meaning in any
*legi*timate fashion, even as a model of the truly illegitimate, the really low,
the utterly wasteful. Something other than the readily figurable antithesis
of figuration, the anti-mimetic dramatizes "alternate models of *mimesis*"(5)
whose virtue lies in the lameness of their effort to reflect that which
pre-cedes or pre-figures, like the veiled face of the sacred, any speculative
system. In this context, Bataille's statement—"The slaughterhouse is linked
to religion"—might be rewritten thus: the figure of the slaughterhouse is a
torn *liga*ture bound to(ward) the re*ligi*ous.[3]

Since the goal of this loopy preamble remains to approach an understanding of how naturalism posts the sacred, it's now worth stepping back
to note that while *Blade Runner* dramatizes a cultural effort to hide this
tear by transforming a shambling figure into an upstanding figure,[4] it does
so by mapping what Mark Seltzer refers to as a "cultural logistics" dating
back to the turn of the twentieth century. The film stages a drive to eliminate social and semiotic virtual waste against a backdrop of interrelated
practices and concerns—serial reproduction, serial violence, the humanist
preservation of a 'natural' self—which Seltzer shows to be centrally at
stake in naturalist discourse. In his book *Bodies and Machines*, he argues
that late-nineteenth and early-twentieth-century discourses are marked by
crises of subjectivity prompted principally by the nation's transformation
from a "market culture" to a "machine culture." These crises are defined
not so much by the disappearance of presumably humanizing structures
(the regional economy, the small community, the church) but rather by an
obfuscation of what constitutes the human. The intensified blurring of distinctions between the animate and the inanimate, the natural and artificial,
the body and the machine produces profound ontological anxiety. As
Seltzer puts it, the emergence of machine culture precipitates a radical "erosion of the boundaries that divide persons and things, labor and nature,
what counts as an agent and what doesn't . . ." (*Bodies* 21). Such erosion
generates particularly acute anxiety about what counts as self and what
counts as other, an anxiety recorded in what he calls "melodramas of
uncertain agency" (*Bodies* 21) played out across a variety of discourses.

In what follows, I argue that the discursive uncertainties displayed by an
emergent consumer culture need to be understood as expressing a kind of
joint anxiety insofar as they mark a juncture at which ontological anxiety

links up with religious anxiety about the nature of the sacred and with aesthetic anxiety about the nature of figuration. This joint anxiety is nowhere more in evidence than in the figure of Upton Sinclair, whose novel *The Jungle*, the most popular American novel during the first decade of the twentieth century, represents the crucial modern American attempt to address the figure of the shambles. I maintain that Sinclair acts out, in often spectacular fashion, a particularly complex resistance to virtual waste, a resistance whose dynamics can only be sorted out by joining a reading of *The Jungle* to a reading of his extensive writings in support of Progressive Era health reform. Emphasizing that this literary and nonliterary material share certain concerns, I trace the persistent appearance of a cultural prescription for alleviating joint anxiety that relies on the vision of a system (corporate, social, narrative, physiological) from which every trace of shambling has been removed. As the author who places charges of meat-packing atrocities within a socialist conversion narrative and as the author who places charges of improper biological consumption within a series of autobiographical dietary conversion narratives, Sinclair expresses progressive culture's rage to clean up every commercial, tropological, and anatomical joint. In other words, his calls for corporate and corporeal reform appear framed by a desire to realize what Bataille calls "a flabby world in which nothing fearful remains and in which, subject to the ineradicable obsession of shame, they [the bourgeoisie] are reduced to eating cheese." Yet what makes Sinclair's case particularly compelling is that even as he participates in naturalism's campaign to put both the sham and the shambles to "shame," he produces a literary slaughterhouse that haunts the joints of his famous novel (as the replicants haunt the joints where they were fabricated) in such a way as to unsettle his purist intentions.

2. SHIT FITS

All honor to Upton Sinclair! The physical culturists owe him a debt that they can never really pay. His splendid book, 'The Jungle,' dealt sledgehammer blows in favor of right-living. His writings on fasting are a beacon light that point the road toward perfect health, and you can rest assured that the medical profession from this time forward will do everything they can to discredit the man who heartily deserves the highest honor from this same profession.

Bernarr Macfadden, "The Editor's Viewpoint"

It is 1908, and Upton Sinclair is a shambles. Made world famous by his muckraking account of the Chicago stockyards published two years earlier, Sinclair nevertheless claims to suffer from an assortment of debilitating physical ailments—dyspepsia, constipation, headaches, hair loss, tooth decay, nervousness, insomnia—attributable perhaps to overwork and perhaps to the recent destruction by fire of Helicon Hall, his self-styled socialist community. In search of a remedy, the writer makes a recuperative stay at the "Macfadden health home," a sanatarium located in Battle Creek, Michigan, the mecca of progressivist health reform. Macfadden, a bodybuilder, food faddist, anti-vaccinationist, showman, writer, and successful publisher, appeals to the naturalist author for a number of reasons, not the least of which is his work as inventor and proselytizer of the physical culture program, an ascetic regimen designed to promote health through the following 'natural' activities: weight lifting, walking barefoot to insure being energized by the earth's magnetic currents; tugging the roots of one's hair to prevent hair loss; taking dry friction baths (accomplished by scrubbing with a towel) to revitalize the skin; eschewing white flour, tobacco, alcohol, prescription pills; "consuming" sunlight and pure air; and, last but not least, fasting. So apparently successful is this regimen in converting the figure in shambles to a perfectly fit figure that Sinclair provides Macfadden with a series of high-profile endorsements published over several years as articles in the latter's *Physical Culture* magazine.

Macfadden's *Physical Culture* editorial cited above—a combination book endorsement, evangelical exhortation, and professional barb—offers an initial illustration of how Sinclair's connection to progressive culture's popular health reform movement makes him an unusual nexus where a number of different discourses (literary, political, medical, religious) join, all of which have as their goal the achievement of "perfect health" through realization of a waste-free figure. Linking the virtues of narrative efficiency (*The Jungle's* "sledge-hammer blows") to the virtues of fasting and to the vices of a bloated medical establishment, the editorial shows how Sinclair's multifaceted career bears witness to a spirit of intense asceticism permeating every aspect of the culture, a spirit best defined as a belief in the virtue of eliminating waste from every *body*: the body of the text; the body of the patient; the body of the industrial laborer; the body of the corporate organization; the body of the community. Moreover, Macfadden's commentary directly correlates progressivism's mission of dismantling, or progressing beyond, the myth of progress (a dismantling exemplified by Sinclair's exposé of the meatpacking industry) to its mission of redeeming the modern individual through a prescription for "right-living."

One of the richest expressions of the religious rhetoric underpinning progressivism's war on waste is William James' description, in *The Varieties of Religious Experience*, of the "religion of healthy-mindedness." According to James, this system relies primarily on "a strange power of living in the moment and ignoring and forgetting . . ." (140). What the system ignores and forgets is an otherness that challenges its theological insistence on the unity, integrity, and whole-someness of God. The healthy-minded name this otherness evil:

> Whereas the monistic philosopher finds himself more or less bound to say,
> as Hegel said, that everything actual is rational, and that evil, as an ele-
> ment dialectically required, must be pinned in and kept and consecrated
> and have a function awarded to it in the final system of truth, healthy-
> mindedness refuses to say anything of the sort. Evil, it says, is emphatically
> irrational, and not to be pinned in, or preserved, or consecrated in any
> final system of truth. It is a pure abomination to the Lord, an alien unre-
> ality, a waste element, to be sloughed off and negated, and the very mem-
> ory of it, if possible, wiped out and forgotten. The ideal, so far from being
> co-extensive with the whole actual, is a mere *extract* from the actual,
> marked by its deliverance from all contact with this diseased, inferior, and
> excrementitious stuff. (132–33)

While the passage begins by suggesting that "healthy-mindedness" may
avoid the totalizing logic of Hegel's dialectic, the elaborate metaphoriza-
tion of evil as excrement reveals how this variety of religious experience
actually consecrates the Other as "a waste element," a form of negativity
dialectically subject to being negated ("wiped out and forgotten"). The
healthy-minded forgetter turns out to be no different from the type of individual James terms the "sick soul," a "morbid-minded" figure who claims
to embrace evil in all its wastefulness. In both cases, the adherent's apparent virtue leaves him lacking the courage to entertain evil as an alien unre-
ality, the metaphysical equivalent of a replicant. James himself struggles to
be so courageous, for though he dares to say that "it may be that there are
forms of evil so extreme as to enter into no good system whatsoever . . ."
(164–65), he is also prone to spells of forgetfulness. This amnesia is symp-
tomized by his determination to make the figure of the shambles fully illuminate the darkness obscured by the light of healthy-mindedness: "[T]he
slaughter-houses and indecencies without end on which our life is founded
are huddled out of sight and never mentioned" (90); "Our civilization is
founded on a shambles, and every individual existence goes out in a lonely spasm of helpless agony" (163).

The metaphorics of waste invoked in James' account deserve extended
examination insofar as they mark the joint at which spiritual anxiety over-
laps with ontological anxiety in progressive culture. Nowhere is this imbri-
cation more in evidence than in the discourse of public health reform, a
movement that draws heavily on waste rhetoric to rewrite machine culture's crisis of distinction between self and other as a physiological crisis.
Responding directly to the anxiety precipitated by a blurring of the boundary between body and machine, the reformers promise that, despite modernity's terrific stresses and dislocations, redemption is at hand for those able
to separate themselves from their "excrementitious stuff." In order to make
the healthy-minded message palatable to an increasingly secularized audi-
ence, they take James' scatological figures literally. Specifically, they popular-
ize the idea that humanity's fallen condition is the result of autointoxication,

a disease of self-pollution caused by the buildup of toxic sediments in the body. Like neurasthenia, the trendy modern complaint of enervation, paralysis, and jangled nerves, autointoxication gets etiologically traced to numerous phenomena seen as characterizing the treacherously "civilized" life of machine culture: gluttony (excessive consumption of food and excessive expenditure on material goods); over-refinement (of foods, manners, aesthetic sensibility); an accelerated lifestyle (exemplified by insufficient mastication of food as well as by the new forms of communication and transportation); congestion (of arteries, intestines, urban spaces); sedentary living (due to expanding bureaucratic administrations and corporate management structures, and resulting in improper absorption and evacuation of foods). The difference between neurasthenia and autointoxication is that while the former signals a general malaise, a vague feeling of personal disintegration, the latter suggests that the cause of this feeling is a specific internalized otherness, namely introjected junk. Neurasthenia describes a wasted body; autointoxication describes a body full of waste.

Many progressive health reformers, including Sinclair, attribute the presence of waste in an individual's system—the presence of an apparent evil within—to what they perceive to be a needless yet unpardonable sin: improper consumption. The modern American individual is a fallen individual for the simple reason that (s)he isn't eating right. Recasting in medical terms progressivism's agenda of curbing consumer culture's conspicuous consumption, reformers insist that poor health results most directly from filthy dietary habits. For Horace Fletcher, one of the most influential enthusiasts of the day and a figure James cites as an exemplar of healthy-mindedness, the leading examples of such corrupt forms of behavior are gluttony and the improper chewing of food, both of which invariably lead to the accumulation in the body of "inharmonious deposits." In a treatise against the perils of consumption titled *The New Glutton or Epicure*, published the same year *The Jungle* appears in book form, Fletcher describes how these deposits both implicate the offender as someone engaged in a wasteful (i.e. inefficient and excessive) activity and punish the offender by acting as toxic waste products which "burden and clog the lower intestines, form deposits in the bone, cartilege and kidneys, inflame the tissues, and otherwise create conditions favourable to the propagation of the microbes of disease" (153). Linking a healthy-minded religious sensibility with an anti-contagionist, mysophobic medical logic, such a diagnosis presupposes an otherwise fit figure whose spirit is reduced to a shambles when it allows material impurities to filter in from outside and make a shambles of its joints. The perverted eater, susceptible to internal putrefaction and the spread of ptomaines, is doomed to fall (Gk. *ptoma*: fall, fallen body, corpse). As Fletcher puts it: "Disease is nothing but dirt in the system and the result of dirt. It is our own dirt at that, having been introduced by our own carelessness or as the result of combined ignorance and greed" (178).

In their rage to distinguish the clean from the unclean, the intrinsic from the extrinsic, the self from the other, medical muckrakers express alarm not only about what passes from outside to inside but also about what passes from inside to outside. Demonstrating Mary Douglas' claim that in ritual activity "the power residing in the margins of the body is more often to be avoided" (118), Bernarr Macfadden adopts an almost Puritan rhetoric to describe his disgust at the body's discharges. The man known by the bizarrely excremental nickname "B. M." registers his horror at these emissions by paradoxically privileging the inorganic over the organic. He finds the material refuse of industrial life to be positively sanitary in comparison with the foul byproducts of corporeal activity: "Coal soot, dust, the ordinary dirt that we meet with in any thickly settled community does not materially harm the body. In fact, it might almost be called clean dirt, as compared with the dirt that emanates from our own bodies, which is the filthiest of all dirt ("Clean Dirt" 436). A shameful diet, of course, further compromises the ideal, natural constitution by introducing artificial or sham compounds whose presence signals the will's weakness and exacerbates the body's leakiness: "If you follow a dietetic regimen that includes heavy feeding on rich, indigestible combinations, you will need more frequent use of the soap and hot water bath in order to keep the body extremely clean" ("Clean Dirt" 436).

Macfadden's notion of "filthy dirt" both translates into material terms the healthy-minded concept of "excrementitious" evil and helps explain an intense cultural preoccupation with excrement. No one throws more fits over shit than John Harvey Kellogg, the developer of numerous breakfast cereals, the inventor of peanut butter, and a leading hygienic counselor of the age.[5] In a treatise aptly titled *Colon Hygiene*, Kellogg decries the damage done to the public health by constipation, a blockage representative of the extent to which the modern individual has abandoned the purity of natural rhythms for the impurity of a civilized routine: "Constipation is in most cases simply one of the unhappy results of the artificial conditions imposed upon us by modern civilized life" (202). This clogged state is particularly sinister because it virtually insures the development of autointoxication, or what he calls "alimentary toxemia":

> The prompt evacuation of the bowels in response to Nature's "call" is a sacred obligation which no person can neglect without serious injury. Ignorance of this fact is one of the chief causes of the prevalence of constipation, a condition in which the body becomes a storehouse of the most disgusting and offensive material, which saturates the tissues with its horrible effluvium and its virulent poisons and taints the very springs of life. . . . The brain and nerves show evidences of depression or irritation, according to the nature of the dominating poisons. Headaches, neuralgia, neuritis, paralysis, mental dullness, neurasthenia, even insanity, are the

results. Diseases of the liver, thyroid gland and spleen develop. Skin diseases of various kinds, and every sort of bodily derangement, are seen.
(123, 176)

To prevent the derangements resulting from an inability to defecate, one
must forsake all unnatural comestibles (among them meat, condiments,
tobacco, tea, and coffee) and unlearn all unnatural practices (including
insufficient mastication, sedentary living, skipped meals, incorrect breath-
ing, even hurried defecation): "The only escape from this terrible handicap
of all useful human activities is to be found in a rational return to Nature,
in the adoption, so far as is necessary to secure the physiological conditions, of natural and primitive habits, particularly in reference to diet,
sleep, exercise, and out-of-door life" (202). Ironically, this prescription is
itself marked by a certain derangement since the notion of a "rational
return to Nature" disturbs the oppositions rationalized/spontaneous and
calculated/instinctual used as tools in diagnosing overexposure to the hazards of civilization. Paradoxically, then, one is renewed by cultivating a
lack of cultivation. As Sinclair puts it in one of his articles for *Physical
Culture*: "[W]hen you want to know what is a proper diet for you to live
on, all you have to ask yourself is whether your tree-climbing ancestors
would have had it" ("The Raw Food Table" 137).

The inconsistency of this logic bears witness to what Seltzer calls "the
unnatural Nature of naturalism" (*Bodies* 14) and is reflected in the far-
flung, contradictory remedies Kellogg proposes as means of returning to a
natural state. On one hand, he advocates what he perceives to be unmediated, holistic, primitive methods of recovery: crouching, self-kneading, running
on all fours, correcting standing posture, and consuming 'pure' laxatives
such as bran, agar-agar, paraffin. On the other hand, he advocates a number of curative measures that require the individual to be connected to a
mechanical device. These literal couplings of body and machine include sitting in a vibrating chair, wearing a "wet girdle," working out in a "rowing
or surf bath," and the "application of a bi-polar electrode to the inner surface of the pelvic colon, which is the point of greatest delay in the majori-
ty of constipated persons" (68–69). Using electrical currents to control
excremental currents, Kellogg relocates progressivism's ascetic imperative
within a cybernetic framework. His contraptions are sometimes hilarious
models of a cyborg fantasy in which the self protects itself against a polluted other by becoming a veritable dynamo of elimination. In this scenario, food poses a threat to the body as smooth-running engine: "The
entrance of food into the rectum is like the closing of a switch which con-
trols the starting and stopping of a motor" (211).

The blurring of the inanimate and the animate informs Fletcher's famous
concept of "Economic Nutrition," praised in *The Jungle* as the "noble sci-

ence of clean eating" (406). A disciplined technique of food consumption, it promises to undo the damage of self-defilement by a method of auto-regulation so strict that nothing (neither flavor, nor nutriments, nor bodily energy) gets wasted and no waste enters the system. According to his pro-gram, the mouth becomes the site at which food undergoes a most vigor-ous inspection. Every morsel is subject to meticulous mastication—known variously as "Fletcherizing," "Buccal Thoroughness," and "Industrious Munching"—at the end of which process truly nutritional or good food passes into the digestive tract upon activation of the "Reflex of Deglutition." Whatever is left over in the mouth is indigestible stuff fit only to be expectorated. In this scenario, taste appears as the arbiter of value; it is a "natural guardian" which, if allowed to operate objectively by virtue of systematic chewing, discriminates between the pure and the impure, the useful and the useless: "If taste is the evidence of nutrition, and ceases to act upon dirt, WHAT SENSE is there in hurrying food past the sentry-box of Taste without giving the inspector time to select the nutrition and reject the dirt?" (196). Fletcherizing rationalizes the digestive process to the degree that each moment has to be accounted for (time spent chewing), each action has to be counted (number of chews, number of mouthfuls) and each byproduct has to be assessed (amount and type of excrement expelled).

By insisting on panoptic self-supervision of the most minute physiologi-cal movements—by isolating and analyzing every component of ingestion in an effort to extract maximum value from food—Fletcher effectively maps onto the body the principles of scientific management applied by Frederick Winslow Taylor to the modern workplace. The mouth becomes a quality-controlled environment; the digestive path becomes an assembly line putting every gram and gulp to profit. Fletcherism reduces the act of consumption to a series of repeated, routinized, finely calibrated motions performed by what might be called a *cyberconsumer*, an eating machine whose regularized behavior produces both dietary and spiritual whole-someness. Through adherence to a natural asceticism defined as automat-ed elimination of kinetic and alimentary excess, the practitioner achieves total fitness. Indeed, the devotee of "Dietetic Righteousness" ultimately finds that proper insalivation leads to nothing less than salvation: "In Economic Nutrition lies protection from sexual morbidity, alcoholic intem-perance, bodily disease, savage passions and all the brood of evil contami-nation and temptation. In Economic Nutrition lie possibilities of physical and mental energy and optimistic happiness such as the world has not been accustomed to in the memory of history" (263).

By posting in "the sentry-box of Taste" a legitimate, authoritative guard against degeneration, Fletcher promises that the individual who is physi-cally out of joint will be able to progress beyond, and put behind, the prob-lem of the posterior (the rear end; "the memory of history"). In fact,

Fletcherism posits a virtual negation of the posterior since evacuation is
to occur only once every six to ten days. Whatever does get posted by the
posterior can, like a clean and proper metaphor, be returned expressly to
sender. Fletcher holds out the possibility of a prompt return through his
example of a Fletcherizing writer who, after eight days without a
deposit, delivers virtually edible excrement: "The excreta were in the
form of nearly round balls, varying in size from a small marble to a
plum. . . . *There was no more odour to it than there is to a hot biscuit*"
(150). Talk about having your shit together! The cyberconsumer makes
sure that even waste doesn't go to waste. He embodies a self-enclosed
system which functions like an industrial-age Ouroboros. His shit fits.
In this physiological postal system, the mark of incomplete delivery—the
mark of the dead letter—is the frequent production of fecal matter
stamped with a foul smell, what Fletcher calls "tell-tale excreta" (142).
This is the shit that matters . . . shit whose mortal stink announces its
status as materiality, as artifact, as artifice, as shitty representation (of
the postmaster), as virtual waste. By contrast, the thoroughly naturalized postal carrier delivers immaculate *merde*: "The healthy faeces of
many wild animals is comparatively dry, odourless and cleanly . . ."
(143).

From Fletcherism's carefully calculated self-restrictions it is but a
short step to saying no to consumption altogether, a step about which
Upton Sinclair posts a significant autobiographical piece in a 1910 issue
of *Cosmopolitan* under the oxymoronic title "Starving for Health's
Sake." More than an early version of the celebrity health tip, the article
is a conversion narrative bearing witness to the author's deliverance
from the evil of what he calls "an abnormal appetite." The piece begins
with a confession about his former life as an errant eater whose "various ailments were symptoms of one great trouble, the presence in my
body of the poisons produced by superfluous and unassimilated food"
(742). Made physically and spiritually sick by his addiction to consumer
culture's artificial, imitative products—its patent medicines and mass-
produced foodstuffs—Sinclair finds himself unable even to imitate
Fletcher's model:

> I found that, so far as my case was concerned, my 'nature' was hope-
> lessly perverted. I invariably preferred unwholesome foods—apple-pie,
> and toast soaked in butter, and stewed fruit with quantities of cream
> and sugar. Nor did 'Nature' tell me when to stop, as she apparently
> does some other 'Fletcherites'; no matter how much I chewed, if I ate
> all I wanted I ate too much. (742)

The narrative goes on to document the writer's release from the bonds
of this addiction by means of the fast. Such extreme self-denial saves the

shambling writer by producing "a new state of being, a new potentiality of life; a sense of lightness and cleanness and joyfulness, such as I did not know could exist in the human body" (739). According to Sinclair, the fast is an effective agent of moral reform as well as a means of flushing noxious matter from the body; it functions as both prophylactic and purgative, prevention and cure. The physical symptoms accompanying the fast even function as a sort of penance, for during its course one literally tastes the foulness of one's sin: "The tongue becomes coated, the breath and perspiration offensive; and this continues until the diseased matter has been entirely cast out . . ." (744). With the aid of enemas, sitz baths, and "copious water drinking," it successfully exorcizes what Kellogg refers to as the "dyspeptic devil." As Sinclair puts it in his book-length treatment of the subject, knowledge of the fast restores one to a prelapsarian condition forfeited only if one consumes the apple of conventional medical knowledge: "The fast is to me the key to eternal youth, the secret of perfect and permanent health. I would not take anything in all the world for my knowledge of it" (*Fasting Cure* 25).

While Sinclair's quasi-revivalist health tracts share the other reformers' tacit presumption of a correspondence between the natural and the technological (he calls the fast "nature's safety valve"), what distinguishes his version of cyberconsumption is its explicit promise of reducing temporal waste. In a *Physical Culture* installment titled "Wheat—The King of Foods," Sinclair attacks the procedure of hulling or "purifying" grains by again first confessing to his own early indulgence in impure, artificial preparations:

> I look back with horror upon the tons of fresh bread and doughy biscuits, pancakes, pastry, 'doughnuts,' and 'angel cake' which have been gulped down my unfortunate anatomy. I have come through the test alive, but it was a very close shave. I propose for the rest of my life to do all in my power to open the eyes of others to the crime which they are committing against their stomachs. Scarcely a day passes that I do not encounter people with sallow complexions, pimply faces, toothaches, dyspepsia, rheumatism—troubles that I know are caused by this dietetic sin, of which Americans are more guilty than any other nation. (233)

His subsequent elaboration of the rewards to be gained by conquering "dietetic sin" presents a striking indication of the extent to which progressive investment in what might be called the *business of nature* is inextricably linked to its interest in the *nature of modern business*. Conversion to unrefined wheat promises relief not only because it acts as a natural laxative guaranteed to purge the clean and proper self of excre-

mentitious stuff—"I have tried every kind of food that has been recom-
mended for constipation, and the wheat is the best I know of" (234)—
but, more importantly, because it eliminates the problem of wasted time.
Framing in culinary terms Taylor's vision of a workplace in which all
superfluity, idleness, and discontinuity have been abolished, Sinclair
advertises unrefined wheat as part of a broader "raw foods" diet whose
greatest virtue consists in the speed and efficiency with which the meals
can be made and cleaned up: "This diet saves practically all the labor of
preparation. There is nothing to be done except to wash the fruit, and
perhaps to shell and grind the nuts, and to boil the wheat once or twice
a week. . . . We also use paper napkins, and save laundry" (238). A
streamlined practice of consumption, the "raw food table" is the
Progressive Era version of fast food. Like fasting, it idealizes those subjects of consumer culture who long to be consumption free, who strive
to be free from the subject of consumption as well as from the symptoms
of consumption (the "sallow complexions") associated with autointoxication. Sinclair's ideal consumer is one whose "natural" table conforms
to the exigencies of the modern timetable. Establishing a correspondence
among preserving health, saving time, and saving the soul, the naturalist writer seeks in all his dietary experiments a regimen that will turn
him into what Seltzer calls a "naturalist machine" (*Bodies* 25), a high-
performance writing engine that never breaks down. As Sinclair puts it:
"I want a diet which will permit me to overwork with impunity"
(*Fasting Cure* 82).

Thus, if Sinclair's prescriptions perform what Seltzer terms the "the
wild work of a techno-primitivism. . . . wild work that incorporates the
life process and the machine process such that the call of the wild represents not the antidote to machine culture but its realization" ("Serial
Killers [1]" 110), they do so by dramatizing naturalism's expectation
that cyberconsumption's mechanized practice of heeding nature's call
will provide an antidote to the problem of time. The cyberconsumer is a
figure fit for consumption both *within* and *by* consumer culture in that
it signifies streamlined progression to a time-out-of-time in which time
actually comes to a standstill. A mixture of the inorganic and the organic, cyberconsumption is a still-life practice, adoption of which yields a
life of perfect self-possession also attainable through acquisition and/or
contemplation of still-life paintings: "The uncertain relation between the
body and its representations is converted [through still-life painting]
into a reaffirmation of the body and its representations as possessions,
as the agents of the possessive individual whose agency is neither sepa-
rable from nor reducible to natural bodies and material possessions"
(*Bodies* 139).

Suggested here is the specific historical manifestation of a connection
between a soteriological anxiety about killing time and an aesthetic anx-

iety about stilling figure. To begin indicating how these stresses implicate each other, let me suggest that in Sinclair's longing for the still life
he is preoccupied with converting to proper use both the figure of the
shambles and the shambling figure. This double-edged desire is graphically expressed in a piece of his on, oddly enough, the virtues of the
slaughterhouse. In "The Use of Meat," a section of his book *The Fasting
Cure* where he recounts his successful experimentation with a diet
restricted to hot water and Salisbury steak (the prototype,not coincidentally, of the fast food burger), Sinclair actually praises the European
shambles as a waste-free scene of destruction, a model of efficient elimination. Like Captain Bryant, who stands behind the blade runner's
work as serial killer ("He's a god-damn one man slaughterhouse"),
Sinclair, despite his renowned chronicle of meatpacking abuses, stands
behind the serial killing of the rightly run abattoir:

> In Europe they have municipal slaughter-houses which are constructed
> upon scientific lines, and in which no filth is permitted to accumulate; also
> they have devised means for the killing of animals which are
> painless. . . . [T]hey fit over the head of the animal a leathern cap, which
> has in it a steel spike; a single tap upon the head of this spike is sufficient
> to drive it into the animal's brain, causing instant insensibility. (89)

What is at stake in this passage? 1. *So little is at stake*. In a narrative
"constructed upon scientific lines," all trace of the sacrificial stake disappears. A scene devoid of blood and ash, the alternative, European
slaughterhouse hides the shambling figure of altarity. 2. *So much is at
stake*. With proper posting of a stake into the animal's head, the well-
engineered slaughterhouse totally masters, at killing time, the other's
meat, just as the well-engineered consumer, with the posting of proper
food (such as the newly developed *Post* brands of cereal), kills time by
mastering his own meat. Moreover, this slaughterhouse inscribes, with
the aid of a "steel" stylus, a figure that doesn't buck, doesn't buckle,
doesn't waver, doesn't shamble off to die. An apparent model of
progress, the alternative shambles posts a trope of "instant insensibility," a figure brought to a complete standstill. It delivers a metaphor that
in no time at all goes blank, gets whited out with the serial punctuality
(L *punctus*: pricking, point) of "a single tap."

Nevertheless, questions still stand, however shakily. How does such a
white figure carry out its work of signification? How does such a drop
dead figure march forward in the name of progress?

3. Blank Posturing

> There was infantry and there was artillery in the procession. The
> infantry bore no arms, and was clad in shining white. The artillery was
> made up of carts, clean and freshly painted, each one covered with
> white canvas. The five hundred and fifty drivers sat up straight, each
> man on the right-hand side of his cart; and the fourteen hundred foot-
> soldiers marched in close-set ranks, shoulder to shoulder, keeping step
> to the music of the bands which led each battalion. The Stars and
> Stripes fluttered over the ranks, and the one sign borne in the proces-
> sion told the whole story: 420 MILES OF STREETS CLEANED
> DAILY.

> William W. Ellsworth, "Colonel Waring's 'White Angels'"

> Metaphysics—the white mythology which reassembles and reflects the
> culture of the West: the white man takes his own mythology, Indo-
> European mythology, his own *logos*, that is, the *mythos* of his idiom,
> for the universal form of that he must still wish to call Reason.

> Jacques Derrida, "White Mythology"

The photograph accompanying Ellsworth's 1896 magazine "sketch"
of the parade honoring New York City's Department of Street-Cleaning
reveals a squadron of mustachioed street sweepers, rubbish collectors,
and ash haulers standing at attention. (Figure 1) Arranged in orderly
units, dressed completely in white, these figures bear witness to a war on
waste orchestrated by former Civil War officer Colonel George E.
Waring, Jr., a leading sanitary engineer of the age and the department's
commissioner from 1895 to 1898. The parade's show of force is ostensibly designed to garner plaudits for the public health victories won in
the past year by the department: the consistent and thorough collection
of refuse; the timely removal of snow; the resulting decline in the city's
mortality rate. In this respect, the procession ceremonially reenacts the
allied occupation of New York thoroughfares once overrun by soot,
rags, paper, manure, broken glass, human excrement, rotting vegetables,
animal carcasses, and discarded furniture.[6]

WAITING FOR THE WORD TO MARCH

The Street-Cleaners' Parade in New York, May 26, 1896

Figure 1. Colonel Waring's "White Angels," from *The Outlook* 27 June 1896

However, the martial display functions as more than a celebration of municipal efficiency. By posting these sentries of sanitation, Waring dramatizes a progressive response to concerns about cultural degeneration and social unrest. On one hand, the street cleaners advance as literal muckrakers determined to clear the streets of trash. On the other hand, they represent a model for the way a population swelling with working class immigrants should move through a city's space. Recruited primarily from among the newly settled, unsettling lower orders, the disciplined corps both carries out and reflects a complex urban reclamation project in which unmanageable material and human elements are made valuable by being recycled, recovered, or clarified.[7] The commissioner seizes on his salvage men as saviors of a decaying civilization, "representative soldiers of cleanliness and health . . . self-respecting and life-saving" ("The Cleaning" 924). They represent an effort to rehabilitate a nation supposedly made subject to dis-ease by the unchecked absorption of foreign bodies.[8] Bearing the stars and stripes aloft, marching instead of shambling, these figures both protect the public and simulate an ideal public. Circulating through streets now virtually waste free, the garbage brigade makes up a virtual citizenry of the virtuous. As Ellsworth puts it: "[T]hey marched like honest, loyal citizens, proud of their glistening uniforms and proud of their organization and the man who led them" (1191).

In historical terms, Waring's simulated city on a hill turns out to imitate rather faithfully the simulated "White City" erected at the 1893 Columbian Exposition in Chicago to commemorate the four hundredth anniversary of the discovery of the new world. The Exposition's uniformly white buildings, like the parade's uniformly white bodies, conjure up an image of a city, and by extension a nation, unified and homogenous. As Alan Trachtenberg has noted, White City's virtual community is designed to forestall social disorder by replicating Enlightenment values of rationality, grace, and refinement. To that end, it re-creates a Chicago from which the slaughterhouse has been whited out:

> And culture served as the presiding genius, orchestrating design and style, coordinating effort. Illumination, clarity of design, a perfectly comprehensible ground plan dividing the Fair into distinct regions—all such signs of lucidity seemed to proclaim mystery overcome by an artfully composed reality: a reality composed, that is, in the mode of theatrical display, of *spectacle*. White City seemed to make everything clear, everything available. . . . Moreover, in choosing neoclassicism as it dominant style, White City made obvious allusion to European Baroque, to the monumental neoclassicism of capital cities in which radial avenues, open plazas, and façades of columns signified royal power, the authority of the state on display. (230–31)

Just as the exposition's neoclassical columns (or posts) reinforce the "authority of the state," the Colonel's mobile columns of men reinforce the obedience of the subject. Like White City's panoptic "lucidity," the white duck cloth worn by Waring's troops guards against the threat of national autointoxication by guaranteeing thorough inspection and "illumination" of a potentially toxic other: "A man in white duck is as incapable of concealing himself as an ostrich. A sweeper who comes out of a liquor-saloon becomes the cynosure of every eye in the block; and a section foreman, bicycling along an avenue, can tell at a glance down a side street whether his men are at their *posts* or not [italics added]" (Ellsworth 1192).

In broader terms, I wish to suggest that the posture adopted by Waring's "white wings" in the streets of New York dramatizes the imposition of what Derrida calls "white mythology," Western logocentrism's imperialist manipulation of Logos for the purpose of enlightening otherwise 'dark' cultures and its philosophic manipulation of *logos* for the purpose of whiting out metaphysical difference. What makes Waring's simulated war on waste a particularly intriguing reenactment of white mythology's repressive campaign is the fact that, according to Derrida, the mythology's protocols cannot be adequately understood apart from the problem of simulation, in as much as metaphor—the quintessential linguistic act of simulation—animates the language of philosophy itself. In the essay titled "White Mythology: Metaphor in the Text of Philosophy," he argues that in order for logocentric philosophy to substantiate the validity of its claim to the truth, it must deny, forget, or white out the metaphorical nature of its own language since metaphor always calls into question the possibility of positing truly transcendent significance. Metaphor forever jeopardizes the truth because, like the unsupervised street sweeper, it abandons its customary post, goes astray, shambles off, spends itself otherwise, gets wasted:

> [Metaphor] risks disrupting the semantic plenitude to which it should belong. Marking the moment of the turn or of the detour [*du tour ou du détour*] during which meaning might seem to venture forth alone, unloosed from the very thing it aims at however, from the truth which attunes it to its referent, metaphor also opens the wandering of the semantic. The sense of a noun, instead of designating the thing which the noun habitually must designate, carries itself elsewhere. (241)

According to Derrida, philosophy solves the problem of metaphor's errancy by insisting, paradoxically, on the *naturalness* of metaphor's artifice. Drawing on Aristotle's explanation of metaphor, he describes how belief in metaphor's naturalness stems from a belief that imitation (*mimēsis*) is the privileged, inherent, and natural means by which man is able to understand nature (*physis*):

> Physis is revealed in *mimēsis*. . . . [*Mimēsis*] belongs to physis, or, if you
> will, physis includes its own exteriority and its double. In this sense,
> *mimēsis* is therefore a 'natural' movement. This naturality is reduced and
> restricted to man's speech by Aristotle. But rather than a reduction, this
> constitutive gesture of metaphysics and of humanism is a teleological
> determination: naturality in general says itself, reassembles itself, knows
> itself, appears to itself, reflects itself, and 'mimics' itself par excellence and
> in truth in human nature. *Mimēsis* is proper to man. . . . The power of
> truth, as the unveiling of nature (*physis*) by *mimēsis*, congenitally belongs
> to the physics of man, to anthropophysics. (237)

Metaphor, conceived of as simply a refined form of mimesis, thus responds
to and expresses the call of nature: "Like *mimēsis*, metaphor *comes back
to physis*, to its truth and its presence. There, nature always finds its own,
proper analogy, its own resemblance to itself, takes increase only from
itself. Nature gives itself in metaphor" (244). As the culturally produced
instance of a return to *physis*, metaphor is the linguistic embodiment of
physical culture. Just as the all-natural physical culture diet animates an
otherwise neurasthenic physique, the all-naturalness of metaphor functions
as a vital force animating the otherwise neurasthenic body of *physis*:
"[M]etaphor sets before us, vivaciously, what the comparison more haltingly reconstitutes indirectly. To set before us, to make a picture, to exercise a lively action—these are so many virtues that Aristotle attributes to
the good metaphor, virtues that he regularly associates with the value of
energeia . . ." (239). Ironically, then, speculative philosophy's construction
of metaphor as the embodiment and animator of nature's true figure is
guided by an ascetic determination to deny (or white out) metaphor's *figu-
rativeness*—its status as an externality, a supplement, an open-ended figure,
a body. Western metaphysics seeks to rehabilitate metaphor as a dis-figured,
waste-free figure. In other words, metaphor becomes the model of total
semantic fitness: "Metaphor, therefore, is determined by philosophy as a
provisional loss of meaning, an economy of the proper without irreparable
damage, a certainly inevitable detour, but also a history with its sights set
on, and within the horizon of, the circular reappropriation of literal, proper meaning" (270).

I put into play an analogy that draws into relation logocentrism's insistence on the naturalness of metaphor and progressive culture's insistence
on the naturalness of the mechanized body in order to trace the intimate
correspondence between the naturalist conception of a proper text and the
progressivist conception of a proper body. Both conceptions adopt the logic
of white mythology in response to social and ontological anxieties related,
in complex ways, to an anxiety about *mimēsis*. To begin tracing this correspondence, I turn again to one of Upton Sinclair's articles in *Physical
Culture*, this time to a piece titled "The Raw Food Table" in which he
champions the benefits of giving up all cooked and processed foods.

Declaring that "I don't want my food chewed in a factory," he bemoans the dangerously derivative, inauthentic, adulterated composition of modern cuisine and, by extension, of the modern scene:

> Everything is done for us; and all we have to do is to let ourselves be transported here and there, and take our pleasures as they are brought to us. Even those of us who have to work are confined to one little routine task—we add up columns of figures all day, or we paste on labels in a canning-factory; and then we get into a trolley car and are carried home, and sit down and eat a meal which ten thousand other people have had a hand in getting ready; and when we want to be amused we ride out and watch some men who have been hired to play base-ball [*sic*] for us. (138)

While it is ostensibly concerned with the addictive properties of artificial foods, the article typifies Sinclair's more general concern about the addictive properties of the artifactual in the age of mechanical reproduction. From his perspective, a cultural phenomenon as apparently innocuous as professional baseball proves to be a form of toxic waste by virtue of its status as virtual play.

Moreover, his mention of being "confined to one little routine task" reveals how anxiety about the perils of autointoxication facing the modern eater masks a deeper anxiety about the perils of repetition facing the modern worker. As Seltzer has shown, the kind of labor Sinclair depicts—"add[ing] up columns of figures all day" or "past[ing] on labels in a canning-factory"—is an unsettling form of work because it is monotonous and because it calls into question what constitutes "real" work. A precursor to the postmodern labor of controlling and converting data, such employment entails the manipulation of bits of information (figures and labels). As such, it is labor representative of a shift from modes of direct production to modes of processing, a shift rendering uncertain the difference between the productive and the unproductive, the genuine and the imitative. Here is how Seltzer describes the challenge to these once seemingly stable dichotomies:

> The shift to processing as production pressures the basic assumptions of a social order premised on "real work"—that is, on the relays between work and nature, and correlatively, on the fundamental differences between "real work" and "mere" representation or mediation or processing. Hence it jeopardizes the axiomatic oppositions of body/mind, nature/culture, "real work"/simulation . . . ("Serial Killers (1)" 110)

In this context, Sinclair's simultaneous condemnation of processed foods *and* "processing as production" represents an attempt to recover the whole-someness of the real by denigrating every form of imitation as wasteful, noxious, unreal. His prescriptions provide assurance that all one has to do to avoid the loss of integrity or health precipitated by a breakdown of "axiomatic oppositions" is to choose the natural over the cultural, the literal over the figural, the raw over the cooked: "The staple articles of my diet are pine nuts, pecans, almonds, prunes, raisins, figs, bananas, oranges, and apples in winter, and peaches, pears, and berries in the summer. . . . I never drink anything but water, and I do not use bread or any other form of cooked food" ("Living" 37–38).

If these natural antidotes seem rather hard to swallow, it is not only because they are backed by rather dubious medical evidence but also because they carry unsavory ethical overtones. For instance, in his article "The Raw Food Table," Sinclair makes an unsettling distinction between, interestingly enough, those who do "real work" and those who don't: "[A]s a rule you will find that it is the lean people who live longest, and do most of the real work in the world" (140). The implicit stigmatization of fat as a mark of physical and moral degeneracy is a now familiar phenomenon, but it is particularly alarming here in light of the author's enthusiasm for America's newly formed eugenics movement, an interest made explicit in another one of his articles for *Physical Culture*:

> If there is any question more important than that of keeping ourselves free from disease, it is the question of so molding the race that it shall attain to its highest potentiality, and ultimately arrive at such a state that disease no longer need be considered at all. . . . [O]f course the state should intervene wherever possible, to prohibit the marriage of idiots, degenerates, and habitual criminals. . . . What avails it to teach the laws of hygiene, and to preach self-control to people, if we permit them—to say nothing of practically compelling them by law—to bring into the world children in whose bodies and souls are rooted the seeds of degeneracy and disease? ("Divorce" 316, 319)

But what is it specifically about obesity that makes Sinclair defile it as a mark of degeneracy? What causes the socialist author to abject an adipose other as the embodiment of shiftlessness, irresponsibility, waste? On one hand, the fat body haunts the modern bourgeois imagination as a residual reminder of what Peter Stallybrass and Allon White call the "grotesque body of carnival" (104). Fat calls to mind, often hysterically, carnival's transgressive challenge to a hegemonic subjectivity defined by its discretion and civility, a challenge displayed most graphically in the form of the bulging, gaping Rabelaisian body: "[Carnival] attacks the authority of the ego (by rituals of degradation and by the use of masks and costume) and flaunts the material body as a pleasurable grotesquerie—protuberant, fat, disproportionate, open at its orifices" (183). This fat body is grotesque because it celebrates the body's grottoes and leaks, particularly those of the

lower body, and thereby accentuates the permeability of the boundary sep-
arating self and other. Carnivalesque obesity, like the disobedient dustman,
signifies the return of an unruly lower realm repressed in the name of a
clean and proper identity.

On the other hand, Sinclair's claim that the condition of obesity pre-
cludes the performance of "real work" suggests that fat somehow spells the
disappearance of the real, a suggestion made explicit in Jean Baudrillard's
essay on obesity in contemporary America. According to Baudrillard,
today's fat people should be seen as "obscene" more from an epistemological standpoint than from a sociological or aesthetic standpoint. Obesity is
obscene because it is the somatic equivalent of information overload, a
physiological expression of the extent to which "processing as production"
has become all-consuming in the culture of simulation.[9] Specifically, the fat
person's cellular superfluity and epidermic distention mimic the effects of
simcult insofar as they begin to blur the boundary between inside and outside, private and public, body and world:

> A fetal obesity, primal and placental: as if they were pregnant with their
> own bodies but could not be delivered of them. The body grows and
> grows without being able to deliver itself. But also a secondary obesity, the
> obesity of simulation in the image of present systems, bloated with infor-
> mation they can never deliver, the obesity characteristic of operational
> modernity, in its frenzy to store and memorize everything, to pass, in the
> most total uselessness, to the very limits of the inventory of the world and
> of information, and in the process to set up a monstrous potentiality for
> which there is no representation . . . ("The Obese" 27–28)

In a culture marked by infinite reproducibility, the morphology of the obese
person reproduces the disappearance of natural production and thereby
produces the same anxiety metaphor does. One figure's excessiveness
threatens to make the 'real' body disappear, the other figure's excessiveness
threatens to make the body of the Real disappear. Because it appears to
undermine the natural (or real) work of representation—because it appears
unable to "deliver" the natural referent of the body—fat is, at bottom,
unnatural. As Sinclair posits it: "In a state of nature there are no fat animals, but in civilization there are not merely fat animals, but fat men to eat
the fat animals" (*Book of Life* 27). The figure carrying a series of fatty
folds seems to embody the culture of seriality, a culture defined by serialized production of artifacts and serialized codification of information. In
this regard, the shambles is a site with particularly "monstrous potentiality" since it serially packages fattened animals for consumption.[10]

Bearing traces of the carnival and the simulacrum, the fat figure thus
assumes, in the eyes of progressive culture, a doubly hazardous posture.
Progessivism's response is to promote the model of the fully naturalized

American im-poster, a figure who erases the burden of his past by converting from toxic consumption to cyberconsumption *and* who erases the burden of his posterior by converting flab into muscle. For if fat symbolizes the
transgression, even dissolution, of social, psychic, and epistemological
boundaries, naturalism's bulked up, hypermasculine figure—epitomized by
Waring's tight white corps of 'real' American men—symbolizes a body with
super-firm, impermeable boundaries. Not surprisingly, a number of
Sinclair's submissions to *Physical Culture* idealize the hardbody, including
one in which he makes traditional asceticism's desire to subdue the flesh
accord with the precepts of so-called muscular Christianity. Anticipating
Mark Leyner's contemporary novel about an author who achieves transcendent success in part through fashioning a ripped, hypertrophied
physique (see Chapter Four), the article promises deliverance from the evil
of constipation for those who whip themselves into shape by literally beat-
ing the shit out of themselves on a daily basis. Call it fit to shit:

> Constipation is perhaps the most wide-spread and fundamental disease of
> civilization. . . . No exercise or remedy which I have ever learned has
> proven so continuously efficacious as to give the abdomen a good pum-
> melling a couple of times a day. I do not mean by this that one should
> strike one's self so hard as to hurt, though by the exercises which I have
> here outlined one can quickly make the abdominal muscles so strong that
> it is impossible to hurt yourself with your own fists, and for that matter
> with anybody else's fists. ("Exercise" 285)[11]

The body with no soft spots and no loose joints represents the point at
which the naturalist logic of health reform and the logic of literary naturalism directly converge. The latter logic is made explicit in Frank Norris'
claim that the novel must no longer be "a sort of velvet-jacket affair, a studio hocus-pocus, a thing loved of women and aesthetes. . . . The muse of
American fiction is no chaste, delicate, super-refined mademoiselle of delicate poses and elegant attitudinizings . . ." ("Novelists" 1055). The poster
boy for such a masculinized p(r)ose might well be Sinclair, whose article
"Starving for Health's Sake" is accompanied by two photographs of the
writer which, according to the captions, bear witness to his transformation,
by virtue of the fast, from an enervated "spiritual" figure to a vigorous
"athletic" figure. (Figure 2) The 'before' photograph, set in a soft, oval-
shaped frame, shows him gazing dreamily into space to the side of the camera. He leans slightly forward, dressed in a pressed shirt and suit coat. The
background is indistinct, gauzy. The 'after' photograph, set in a rectangu-
lar frame, shows him looking boldly straight at the camera. He is dressed
in a bulky cardigan and is standing in a square-shouldered pose against the
backdrop of an enormous tree trunk. Through the self-denial of the fast, the
author has abandoned the effeminacy of the parlor for the ruggedness

MR. SINCLAIR'S EXPRESSION, AS SHOWN
IN THE LOWER PORTRAIT, USED TO
BE CALLED "SPIRITUAL." SYS-
TEMATIC FASTING HAS EVOLVED
THE ATHLETIC FIGURE
PICTURED ABOVE

Figure 2. Upton Sinclair starves for health's sake, from *Cosmopolitan* 48 (1909–10)

of the outdoors. The 'after' photo is a portrait of the artist as literary rough rider. Posting himself in Horace Fletcher's "sentry box of Taste," Sinclair stands (still) for a figure cleared of the sin of alimentary excess and for a text cleared of the sin of Victorian effeteness.[12]

Moreover, Sinclair's shamble-free posture illustrates the extent to which progressive culture's war on municipal, physiological, and aesthetic waste is carried out according to a multifaceted strategy of exclusion. In addition to displaying signs of a drive to white out feminine prose, the figure of the physical culture faster displays affinities with the figure of the post-World War I German Freikorps officer who, according to Klaus Theweleit, pursues the ideal of an "armored" male body. Like the progressive waste administrator, the protofascist soldier strives to fashion a self-enclosed, machine-like form as protection against what he perceives to be streams or floods compromising an otherwise proper identity, streams personified, in the Freikorps' imagination, by Bolshevist intrusions into Germany after the war. In Theweleit's words: "Nothing is to be permitted to flow, least of all 'Red floods.' If anything is to move, it should be the movement (i.e., one-self)—but as one man; in formation; on command as a line, a column, a block; as a wedge, a tight unit. Death to all that flows" (*Male Fantasies 1* 230).

The connection between the naturalist hardbody and the totalitarian hardbody is made clear in Bernarr Macfadden's embrace of Italian fascism. Attracted to Mussolini's strong man magnetism and to his espousal of race nationalism, Macfadden visits Il Duce in 1930 as a member of President Hoover's committee on Child Health and Welfare. According to a report published by Macfadden himself, his admiration for the Premier's politics only deepens after the visit:

> He saw that here was a nation completely awakened to the importance of building a new generation and building it right, namely, by insisting that growing children and youth be taught to acquire sound physical bodies. Such a nation was bound to reap a harvest in individual happiness and national glory. (Morgan 17)

As a result of this visit, Mussolini handpicks forty cadets from the Fascist Academy in Rome to undergo physical culture training with Macfadden in New York. In a glowing account of the cadets' experience provided by Thomas Dixon, the white supremacist writer made infamous by his pro-Ku Klux Klan novel *The Clansman* (1905), he describes them as having become completely waste free by virtue of their submission to the physical culture regimen: "When the final physical examinations were made and photographed by Dr. Clinton the improvement was astounding. Every ounce of surplus fat had disappeared, and each man stood sun and wind tanned and ready for the severest battle of life" (53). While Dixon

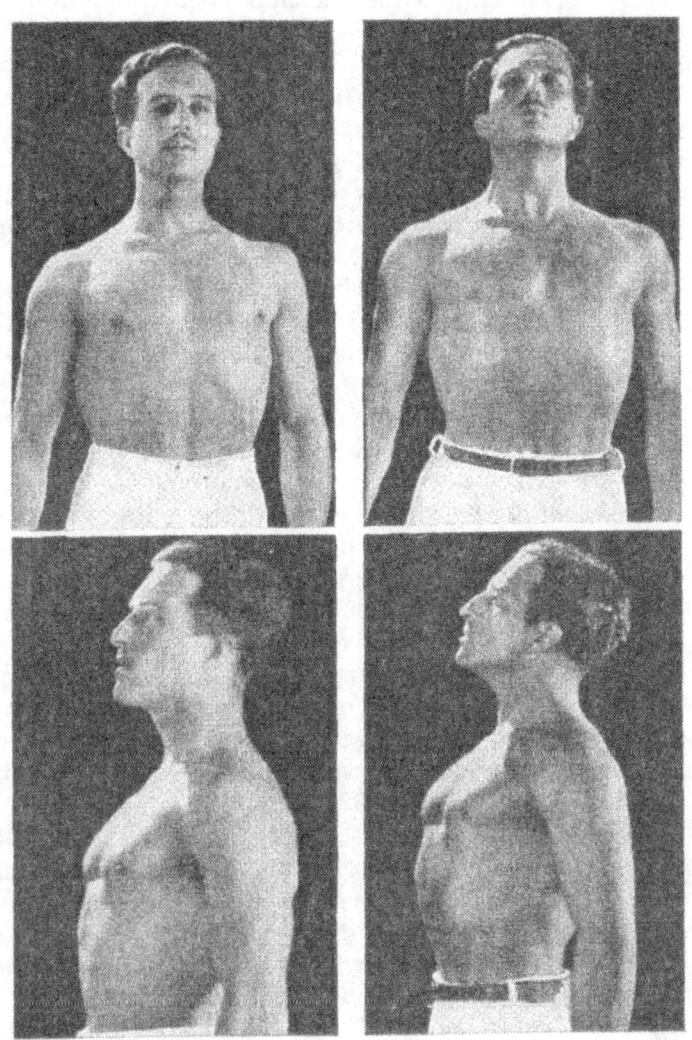

On Arrival — On Departure

Speranza, Giuseppe. Very enthusiastic about everything pertaining to physical culture and sports. Good at swimming. Supreme in the art of fencing.

Figure 3. An Italian fascist cadet before and after the physical culture regimen, from Thomas B. Morgan, *Italian Physical Culture Demonstration: A Report of the Visit Training and Accomplishments of the Forty Italian Students Who Were Guests of Bernarr Macfadden during a Stay of Six Months in the United States Studying His Methods of Physical Culture*. New York: Macfadden Book Company, Inc., 1932

frames the visitors' success in terms of a natural deliverance from the "fat" of serial culture, the photographs he describes, reproduced in a book by Thomas B. Morgan titled *Italian Physical Culture Demonstration: A Report of the Visit, Training and Accomplishments of the Forty Italian Students Who Were Guests of Bernarr Macfadden during a Stay of Six Months in the United States Studying His Methods of Physical Culture,* constitute an homage to the virtues of serialization. The before-and-after sequences of photos are proof of each individual's transformation from a shambling posture to an upstanding, still-life posture. (Figure 3)

Like Waring's training of the white wings, Macfadden's training of Mussolini's nationalist cadets betrays American fears of impending race suicide, Anglo-Saxon culture's xenophobic conviction that the United States is suffering from a case of national autointoxication due to unchecked incorporation or consumption of foreign bodies. Macfadden himself expresses this anxiety in an editorial for *Physical Culture*: "With a birth-rate among foreigners twice as great as among native-born Americans it is only a question of time when the real American race will be extinct" ("Editor's [1910]" 415). Not surprisingly, the most famous physical culture disciple expresses such racist anxiety about national deterioration in a novel ostensibly sympathetic to immigration when he describes figures brought in to break a workers' strike against the slaughterhouse: "[A]ll night long gangs of strike-breakers kept arriving. As very few of the better class of working men could be got for such work, these specimens of the new American hero contained an assortment of the criminals and thugs of the city, besides negroes and lowest foreigners—Greeks, Roumanians, Sicilians, and Slovaks" (*The Jungle* 321–22).

Equally suggestive of a link between naturalism and fascism is Theweleit's description of how members of the Freikorps reinforce the masculinist model of national health by repeatedly recruiting into their writings the trope of whiteness in order to spread what he calls "the white terror." On one hand, the soldiers and officers use white to conjure up the image of a de-feminized woman, a virginal, still-life figure from which all streams (of sexual passion, menstrual blood, etc.) have been whited out. On the other hand, they use white to conjure up the image of "empty space," a public scene from which revolutionary streams have been whited out (with white bursts of gunfire):

> *White* is the anti-hybrid, brilliant cold, the shroud of devivification. It is the marble body of the white countess nurse, the womb from which no teeth-gnashing monsters threaten. Whitewash: the *shot* that banishes disorder. (*Male Fantasies* 2 283)

White represents an experience purged of red masses—placental as well as proletarian—that threaten to engulf a subject bent on upholding the law of the Father(land).

If naturalism's totalizing drive to secure a waste-free body bears the dangerous trace of a totalitarian imperative to stop all incarnations of a red flood, what does it mean for Sinclair to muckrake the slaughterhouse, a site where blood flows freely? Insofar as it seeks to sanitize the shambles, does *The Jungle* deserve to be written off as a literary sham blind to its own impulse to absolutize? Or is it possible to revisit *The Jungle* as a text with something stuck in its narrative passage, something which cannot easily be expectorated? Perhaps what makes *The Jungle* a novel worth going back to is the degree to which, despite its longing for social and semantic purity, the narrative is vitally corrupted by a figure it aims to white out. Perhaps the figuration of the shambles actually signals the first halting steps of a nearly useless inquiry into a form of waste all but left out of consideration by progressivist thought, a waste so radically Other that naturalism's white mythology can do nothing but render it all but inconspicuous. Perhaps this virtually illegible remainder within Sinclair's literary text has something in common with Herman Melville's Bartleby, the scrivener, a barely stirring figure to whom I will turn in the next chapter. Like Bartleby, this remainder may only appear hidden behind a folding screen set up on a lawful premises. Moreover, like Bartleby, who "mechanically" performs the serial task of knocking off copies, this remainder may bear a resemblance to the slaughterhouse.

4. SHAM(BLE) FICTION

The Jungle has long been considered Upton Sinclair's most lasting gift to posterity, a critical assessment due in large part to the conviction that the novel renders slaughterhouse waste altogether legible.[13] The novel is most famous for its graphic accounts of the way the turn-of-the-century Chicago shambles treats its workers, animals, and meat products. Dramatizing Bataille's contention that in our time "the slaughterhouse is cursed and quarantined like a plague-ship," Sinclair indicts the abattoir on the grounds that, as the epitome of a dehumanizing, profit-driven economy, it poisons both the life of the wage laborer subject to its oppressive conditions and the life of the consumer exposed to its contaminated products. Ironically, the slaughterhouse, as Sinclair figures it, wastes body and soul by refusing to let anything go to waste, whether it be scraps of time or scraps of offal. With its dedication to maximum speed and relentless productivity—with its dedication to serial killing—the slaughterhouse, like the blade runner, dramatizes the humanist fear of a collapsed distinction between body and machine: "All year round they [the workers] had been serving as cogs in the great packing machine; and now was the time for the renovating of it and the replacing of damaged parts" (96). Moreover, Sinclair takes pains to insist that the beef trusts' directive to capitalize on even the most seemingly unusable refuse is really a charge to transform the genuine (animal parts) into the artificial (consumer products):

> No tiniest particle of organic matter was wasted in Durham's. Out of the horns of the cattle they made combs, buttons, hairpins, and imitation ivory; out of the shin bones and other big bones they cut knife and toothbrush handles, and mouthpieces for pipes; out of the hoofs they cut hairpins and buttons, before they made the rest into glue. From such things as feet, knuckles, hide clippings, and sinews came such strange and unlikely products as gelatin, isinglass, and phosphorous, bone black, shoe blacking, and bone oil. (50)

Sharing cyberconsumption's need to re-form or convert every body's joints into something "strange and unlikely" through mechanized efficiency, the meatpacking industry nonetheless generates nothing better than a simulation of authenticity ("imitation ivory") and therefore offers only a sham version of a conversion narrative.

What immediately complicates matters here is that if the unregulated slaughterhouse has a narrative analog it is conversion narrative. According to a "canonical reading" of the phenomenon described by Geoffrey Galt Harpham in his book *The Ascetic Imperative in Culture and Criticism*, conversion entails nothing less than the bestowal of transcendent significance on a life otherwise in shambles. At the moment of conversion, the heretofore duplicitous, errant subject suddenly "stands in total univocity, single-minded before God, his will one with that of his maker" (93). Furthermore, one permanently secures a perfect joining with God only when one succeeds in providing a masterful, unified account of one's entire life. The self becomes fully intelligible to itself only when it fashions a narrative in which seemingly scattered, expendable, wasteful experiences are re-collected and made meaningful by being joined together in a plot organized around the conversion. As Mark Taylor puts it: "In order to achieve this coherence, it is necessary to relate the multiple experiences the self has undergone in such a way that they constitute a comprehensive and comprehensible totality" (*Erring* 44). In one respect, then, conversion narrative mirrors the shambles by turning shambling figures to proper use. Not coincidentally, *The Jungle* is itself a conversion narrative, a story about a Lithuanian immigrant named Jurgis Rudkus whose familial and bodily joints are ravaged by the degradations of the abattoir but who ultimately finds deliverance from the capitalist pit when, while attending a sermon on socialism, he experiences a conversion fit: "He could not think at all, he was stunned; yet he knew that in the mighty upheaval that had taken place in his soul a new man had been born. He had been torn out of the jaws of destruction, he had been delivered from the thraldom of despair; the whole world had been changed for him—he was free, he was free!" (368).

Conversion narrative also mirrors the slaughterhouse in that it shares the latter's goal of maximum profit through serial reproduction. According to Harpham, the traditional Christian ascetic's belief in conversion's ability to relieve joint anxiety expresses itself as a belief in the need to join a long series of hagiographical models. The once self-divided subject comes to see, most often in a sudden fit, that his life fits into a meaningful narrative framework first put in place by Christ and then repeated in the lives and texts of martyrs. In an "assent to imitation," the converted subject submits his life to the logic of the Logos—his words to the author-ity of the Word—by getting hooked on hagiography. As Harpham illustrates through a discussion of Augustine's *Confessions*, the ascetic self tries to eliminate joint anxiety through an act of duplication. He dedicates himself to fashioning an imitable autobiographical text based on previous conversion narratives:

> The significance of the imitative element in conversion is that Augustine understands himself, awakens to himself, possesses himself, only as a repetition of other selves. Augustine converts when he joins a community—or, rather when he recognizes that he has always been joined to the community—organized around a few texts that are finally grounded in the mediating figure of Christ, whose radiant "Follow me" stands at the origin of imitation. This origin is itself an imitation, translating divine power into knowledge through what might be called primary repetition, originary imitation. . . . In converting, Augustine is situating himself in the chain of imitation that extends back to and even includes the origin. (96)

Augustine copies in pursuit of a redemptive origin-ality. Reading and writing his life in terms of models, he even builds into his autobiography other tales of "assent to imitation"—other versions of conversion—in a systematic, serialized "stacking of models." The ascetic who crafts a conversion narrative is thus a saintly version of a serial killer. Like the cyberconsumer, he believes serialized incorporation will kill off a wasteful, errant self.

Given that conversion narrative shares with the Chicago stockyards a drive to process or conserve waste through serialized activity, it is not surprising to find Sinclair's ostensibly proletarian conversion narrative labeled a conservative text. Standard assessments of *The Jungle* tend to gloss Sinclair's figuration of the shambles as a good, upstanding representation of capitalist dehumanization while fretting about the nature of its narrative progress. In her book *Taylored Lives*, Martha Banta pursues this line of argument, contending that the novel winds up reflecting the values of what she calls "the culture of management" (5), a culture in which narratives ostensibly critical of the scientific management of bodies, tasks, and schedules are actually shaped by the strategies they critique:

Once managers are invited to make pronouncements for "the others," their visions are apt to slide into prophecy, a move that does strange things to acts of narrating. Gérard Genette observes that true "narrating can only be subsequent to what it tells." In contrast, "predictive narrative" lays down the ways things will be; by nature, it becomes complicitous with the managerial style it is meant to interrogate. (15)

For Banta, *The Jungle* exemplifies such a prophetic narrative. The novel's declarations about the salvational nature of the socialist movement reduce it to the fictional equivalent of a foreman bent on eliminating all superfluous movement: "As narrative, Sinclair's amelioration process merges its methods with those used by managers who try to eradicate obstacles to perfection" (333 n.42).

In the novel, the authorial fantasy of administering a waste-free plot emerges most conspicuously at the point where Sinclair all but kills off the deeply embodied, brutish, rude character of Rudkus. Sinclair replaces his shambling protagonist with a series of model socialists, among them the authorial model of Jack London: "And then there was a young author, who came from California, and had been a salmon-fisher, an oyster pirate, a longshoreman, a sailor; who had tramped the country and been sent to gaol, had lived in the White-Chapel slums, and been to the Klondike in search of gold" (388). Last in the series is a fictional character named Dr. Nicholas Schliemann, a former philosophy professor who gives up his post after coming to believe that "he was selling his character as well as his time" (395). As Sinclair's socialist mouthpiece, he is designed to be the aesthetic embodiment of the cyberconsumer's stilled life. Appearing as the narrative action slows to a series of political pronouncements and contributing to the serial killing off of Sinclair's shambling protagonist, Schliemann is dedicated to whiting out his own figure through a combination of Fletcherism and celibacy: "He studied the composition of foodstuffs, and knew exactly how many proteins and carbohydrates his body needed; and by scientific chewing he said that he tripled the value of all he ate, so that it cost him eleven cents a day. . . . [H]e would never marry, for no sane man would allow himself to fall in love until after the revolution" (395–96). Moreover, his utopian vision of an "Industrial Republic" emerges out of a diatribe against what he terms "the negative wastes of competition" (406) fueling the emergent consumer culture:

Consider the energies wasted in the seeking of markets, the sterile trades, such as drummer, solicitor, bill-poster, advertising agent. Consider the wastes incidental to the crowding into cities, made necessary by competition and by monopoly railroad rates; consider the slums, the bad air, the disease, and the waste of vital energies. Consider the office-buildings, the waste of time and material in the piling of storey upon storey [sic], and the burrowing underground! Then take the whole business of insurance, the enormous mass of administrative and clerical labour it involves, and all utter waste—. (404)

Sinclair piles story upon story of dirty joints and story upon story of socialist saints in an effort to make his narrative function like an efficient slaughterhouse dealing out what Bernarr Macfadden, in his previously cited praise of the novel, refers to as "sledge-hammer blows."

In his well-known study of early twentieth-century leftist American fiction, Walter B. Rideout argues that such systematic blows actually turn the text into something other than literature:

> Jurgis's conversion is probable enough, the Socialist explanation might well flash upon him with the blinding illumination of a religious experience; but practically from that point onward to the conclusion of his novel Sinclair turns from fiction to another kind of statement. Where the capitalist damnation, the destruction of the immigrants, has been proved almost upon the reader's pulses, the Socialist salvation, after its initial impact, is intellectualized. The reader cannot exist imaginatively in Jurgis's converted state even if willing, for Jurgis hardly exists himself. What it means to be a Socialist is given, not through the rich disorder of felt experience, but in such arbitrarily codified forms as political speeches, an essay on Party personalities, or the long conversation in monologues about the Coöperative Commonwealth which comprises most of the book's final chapter. *The Jungle* begins and lives as fiction; it ends as a political miscellany. (35–36)

The novel succeeds insofar as it delivers its message in some organic fashion ("proved almost upon the reader's pulses") but fails insofar as it resorts to an artificial, inorganic structure ("arbitrarily codified forms"). Though he finds virtue in Sinclair's desire to imitate the authenticating experience of conversion, Rideout insists such imitation winds up converting *The Jungle* from real fiction ("the rich disorder of felt experience") into sham(bling) fiction ("political miscellany").

Such a reading of the novel not only treats Sinclair's figuration of the shambles in the first half of the novel as an unproblematic representation of the real (a misreading to which I will return in a moment) but also overlooks the novel's built-in anxiety about the act of representation. For even as the conversion narrative offers up for imitation the model of Dr. Schliemann, the ascetic hero himself recites the cyberconsumer's mantra that the most toxic threat to a healthy national and individual constitution is mimetic activity: "'Of course, imitation and adulteration are the essence of competition. . . . A government official has stated that the nation suffers a loss of a billion and a quarter dollars a year through adulterated foods, which means, of course, not only materials wasted that might have been useful outside of the human stomach, but doctors and nurses for people who would otherwise have been well . . . '" (403). Through this character, Sinclair re-creates what Harpham refers to as the "flamboyant ambivalence" of the early Christian ascetic, an internal conflict in which the desire to negate corporeal desire is offset by a desire to be reborn as a part of a serialized corpus. The problem in both ascetic types is that while conversion is defined as transcendence of materiality, imitation requires the use of linguistic material that shares with the demonic qualities of ambiguity, deception, errancy. As Harpham puts it: "Oddly enough, the act of conversion, requiring as it does an assent to imitation, contains a resistance to conversion, so that the term designates not only a principle of radical change in life, but also a principle of recalcitrance and unchangeability. As a turn to 'authenticity,' conversion remains earthbound, containing its own 'error'" (100). In other words, mimesis turns out to be doubly deadly. It works to mortify the instinctual and deaden the personal, *and* it risks the self-defeating possibility that the copy will be mistaken for the original: "[T]he illusion that one had reached an ideal or perfect identification with Christ the Word was the most notorious and insidious of temptations, slamming the door closed at the very moment when one had proven oneself worthy of entering. Hence, asceticism, the discipline of the essential self, is always defined as a quest for a goal that cannot and must not be reached, a quest with a sharp caveat: 'seek but do not find'" (Harpham 43). Caught in a double bind, the true ascetic knows the presumption of absolute authenticity to be the most shameful kind of sham. He may imitate self-emptying in the name of perfect virtue, yet he recognizes that such imitation necessarily leaves him short of the bliss of being totally wasted . . . leaves him, in short, virtually wasted.

This anxiety about mimesis actually informs Sinclair's conversion to socialism, and thus his eventual authorship of *The Jungle*, in that the conversion is literally bound up with a case of literary shamming. In 1902, he publishes a novel titled *The Journal of Arthur Stirling*, the story of a romantic poet who, failing to meet with any commercial success, drowns himself in the Hudson River. The deception Sinclair perpetrates involves the appearance of Stirling's obituary in *The New York Times* on June 9, 1902, an event that leads the press to treat the book as the diary of a real-life figure until the hoax is exposed several months later. The following year Sinclair tries to account for the sham in an article titled "My Cause," a literary manifesto in which he revisits the fictional death of his poet-aesthete in light of his rebirth as socialist artist: "My one desire was to raise a sensation: first, to sell the book, of course, and, second, to give me a standing ground from which to begin the agitation of My Cause" (304). While "My Cause" exploits conversion rhetoric to convey the author's apparent discovery of a sincere, natural voice—"I could not count the times in the last few days that I have raised my hands to the sky and cried out that I need no more think of 'What the Public Wants!'" (309)—the explanation of the hoax implements a dubious notion of sincerity described by the critic

Christopher Wilson in an piece titled "American Naturalism and the Problem of Sincerity." Wilson illustrates how naturalist authors such as London, Norris, and Sinclair repeatedly invoke the term sincerity to legitimize a "merger of Romance and Realism" (517), an aesthetic strategy according to which the act of documenting gritty reality is achieved by capitalizing on those masculinized business skills romanticized by both the modern editor and the modern executive: bluntness and forcefulness of tone ("My one desire"); hard-sell aggressiveness ("to sell the book"); cultivation of personality ("to raise a sensation"; "My Cause"). Given Sinclair's blending of a desire for commercial success with a commitment to personal conviction, it is no wonder he should open "My Cause" with a self-identification suggestive of romanticist/realist double dealing: "I, Upton Sinclair, would-be singer and penniless rat . . ." (302).

My goal in shambling through Sinclair's relationship to the issue of the sham is not to gain critical currency by exposing him as some kind of literary imposter. Far from wanting simply to rat on him, I'm interested in trying to figure out how Sinclair's anxiety about shamming is joined to his anxiety about the shambles, a joint anxiety usefully explored by examining the penniless rat's investment in the figure of the rat itself, a creature that haunts the premises of the slaughterhouse:

> There would be meat that had tumbled out on the floor, in the dirt and sawdust, where the workers had tramped and spit uncounted billions of consumption germs. There would be meat stored in great piles in rooms; and the water from leaky roofs would drip over it, and thousands of rats would race about on it. It was too dark in these storage places to see well, but a man could run his hand over these piles of meat and sweep off handfuls of the dried dung of rats. These rats were nuisances, and the packers would put poisoned bread out for them; they would die, and then rats, bread, and meat would go into the hoppers together. This is no fairy story and no joke; the meat would be shovelled into carts, and the man who did the shovelling would not trouble to lift out a rat even when he saw one—there were things that went into the sausage in comparison with which a poisoned rat was a tidbit. (163)

An expression of fascinated disgust, this narrative tidbit brings to mind the case of Freud's rat man. Like the rats in the patient's "great obsessive fear"—first diagnosed by Freud a year after book publication of *The Jungle*—Sinclair's slaughterhouse rats are charged with traces of excremental currents that mark the creatures as a special kind of currency. Indeed, Freud begins to join excremental and monetary currents when analyzing the associative material generated by the patient in "the story of the rat punishment" (*Standard* 215):

What the rat punishment stirred up more than anything else was his *anal erotism*, which had played an important part in his childhood. . . . In this way rats came to have the meaning of money. The patient gave an indication of this connection by reacting to the *'Ratten'* ['rats'] with the association *'Raten'* ['instalments']. In his obsessional deliria he had coined himself a regular rat currency. When, for instance, in reply to a question, I told him the amount of my fee for an hour's treatment, he said to himself (as I learned six months later): 'So many florins, so many rats.' (*Standard* 213)

Since in *The Jungle* the figure of the rat infests a literary scene stamped with an authorial seal of authenticity—"This is no fairy story and no joke"—the penniless rat's rat currency would seem to constitute tropological gold. In the rat we trust. Yet while the rat scurrying across workers' consumptive expectorations is expected to be consumed by readers as a reliable representation of the shambles' wastefulness, its dreadful powers of contamination (its feces is everywhere; it gets poisoned and then gets into everything) lend it the destabilizing charge of a taboo. The religious implications of such abhorrence are addressed by Christopher Herbert in his analysis of rat aversion in Henry Mayhew's sociological study *London Labor and the London Poor*. As Herbert puts it:

Mayhew claims to discuss rats, like every other topic, in strictly factual terms, but the evil glamor that they take on in his pages identifies them as playing a very specific cultural and imaginative role: that of the taboo animal *par excellence*, the superlative modern-day referent, at least for city dwellers, of the many biblical injunctions against contact with unclean "creeping" things that it is forbidden to touch or, most especially, to eat . . . . [T]he whole modern system of uncleanness thinking that constructs the image of the rat to begin with—has the specific structure of a primitive religion. (14, 20)

Sinclair's seemingly casual assertion that the rat is eventually eaten by unsuspecting consumers does more than provide a gruesome example of autointoxication; it recalls primitive sacrificial acts in which meat labeled infected and infectious is ingested for the sacred power it is believed to possess. In Herbert's words: "Sacredness is conveyed in totemic sacrifice through the eating of the sacred/unclean flesh, as in various Old Testament references to secret cults in which the most abhorred taboo animals receive superstitious worship and are treated as sources of blessing. Isaiah, for example, proclaims the Lord's anathema upon those 'that sanctify themselves, and purify themselves in the gardens . . . eating swine's flesh, and the abomination, and the mouse' (66.17; see also Isa. 65.4, Ezek. 8.10)" (19–20).

Sinclair's rat spectacle thus situates the slaughterhouse on speculative philosophy's fault line. This virtually abysmal site is again brought out of total obscurity by Freud's rat man, a figure who first hears the awful story of anus-burrowing rodents while sitting "between two officers" during a break (fault, crack) in military maneuvers. Not coincidentally, it is the site at which he loses his spectacles: "During a halt I lost my pince-nez, and, although I could easily have found them, I did not want to delay our start, so I gave them up" (*Standard* 165–66). Anxious to avoid making his unit appear to be a shambling lot, anxious to avoid having his unit *bring up the rear*, the rat man shambles away from the site/sight of the rats with faulty vision. Not coincidentally, Sinclair's immigrants, who are approaching Chicago by train, have their first sight of the city literally obscured by emissions from the abattoir. In *The Jungle*, the slaughterhouse is introduced as that which not only clouds the passengers' vision but also generates an anxiously fascinated olfactory response reminiscent of the rat man's ambivalent response to the story he has heard:

> And along with the thickening smoke they began to notice another circumstance, a strange, pungent odour. They were not sure that it was unpleasant, this odour. . . . They were divided in their opinions about it. It was an elemental odour, raw and crude; it was rich, almost rancid, sensual and strong. There were some who drank it in as if it were an intoxicant; there were others who put their handkerchiefs to their faces. The new emigrants were still tasting it, lost in wonder, when suddenly the car came to a halt, and the door was flung open, and a voice shouted—'Stockyards!' (32)

If the novel seeks to expose the slaughterhouse as a house of sham(e), it also turns out to host the slaughterhouse as a kind of para-site, a nearly invisible Other hiding out on the inside and threatening to paralyze the text's progress(ivism). Designed to be the narrative equivalent of the cyber-consumer's body, the novel's body nevertheless gets eaten up from within, as if by a burrowing rat. As Michel Serres says in his book *The Parasite*, "[T]he battle against rats is already lost; there is no house, ship, or palace that does not have its share. There is no system without parasites" (12).

Something more than an emblem of capitalism's parasitic drive to prey on its labor force and its livestock, Sinclair's figure of the shambles serves as a reminder of Serres' emphasis that in French the word *parasite*, in addition to meaning a biological organism and a social leech, means static, interference, white noise. In the process of articulating principles of communications theory, Serres describes how information is transmitted only with the help of that which also disrupts the signal:

> A wire does not have to be heated very much for noise to increase. This
> excitement stops the message from passing. But sometimes it allows a mes-
> sage to pass, a message that cannot cross an unexcited channel. . . . White
> noise is the condition for passing (for meaning, sound, and even noise),
> and the noise is its prohibitor or its interception. Noise, or again, the par-
> asite, is at the three points of the triangle: sending, reception, transmission.
> Heat a little, I hear, I send, I pass; heat a little more everything collapses.
> The smallest increase, in one direction or another, can transform the entire
> communications system from top to bottom. (194)

Like a good muckraker, Sinclair heats up his text with the sensational in the
expectation of passing (off) the figure of the shambles as an appalling signal of absolute waste (or noise). Nevertheless, in the heat of the narrative
the slaughterhouse defies expectations and behaves more like white noise,
thus anticipating Don DeLillo's contemporary effort to figure the sacred
(see Chapter Three). Sinclair's abattoir is a staticky, virtually wasted, pre-
figural "condition for passing"—or condition for figuring—which stalls
the transmission of naturalism's white mythology even as it facilitates the
naturalist author's determination to post a salvational agenda. In Serres'
words: "The parasite hides behind the noise and to-do of the devout"
(218). Shrouded in a pall of smoke, the figure of the shambles is a different shade of pale, or rather a different shade of the appalling. Like the most
unsettling kind of social parasite (of which the replicants in *Blade Runner*
are a good example), it is an imposter that challenges distinctions between
legitimate and illegitimate, insider and outsider, authentic and sham. Even
after Sinclair appears to have cooled his text—returned it to a homeostat-
ic state—by purging it of this parasitical figure, white noise remains in the
air, emitted in the heat of the steel works where Jurgis goes after losing his
post in the stockyards:

> Jurgis stood where the balcony of the theatre would have been, and oppo-
> site, by the stage, he saw three giant cauldrons, big enough for all the dev-
> ils of hell to brew their broth in, full of something white and blinding,
> bubbling and splashing, roaring as if volcanoes were blowing through it.
> . . . Jurgis shrank back *appalled* . . . there fell a pillar of white flame, daz-
> zling as the sun, swishing like a huge tree falling in the forest. A torrent of
> sparks swept all the way across the building, overwhelming everything,
> hiding it from sight; and then Jurgis looked through the fingers of his
> hands, and saw pouring out of the cauldron a cascade of living, leaping
> fire, white with a whiteness not of earth, scorching the eyeballs.
> Incandescent rainbows shone above it; blue, red, and golden lights played
> about it; but the stream itself was white, ineffable. Out of the regions of
> wonder it streamed, the very river of life; and the soul leaped up at the
> sight of it, fled back upon it, swift and resistless, back into far-off lands,
> where beauty and terror dwell [italics added]. (247)

In the absence of the shambles, the nearly blinding spectacle of the forge works as a literary replacement joint with which to shamble after a virtually blank, "ineffable" alterity. After all, the god of the forge is a joiner slowed by a disfigured leg. The passage suggests that despite Sinclair's determination to narrativize a shamble-free state, his text is repeatedly hamstrung by a shrouded impulse to hobble after the shambling figure of the sacred: "Like Hephaistos. Those who limp are the discoverers; inclination is the beginning of the world" (Serres 32).

In the context of such halting gaits, the lameness of the novel's narrative progress should not simply be written off as a case of sham literature. While the latter part of *The Jungle* drags so severely that the socialist periodical *Appeal to Reason* actually ceases serial publication of the text, its shorter second leg nevertheless stands as a legacy of the author's struggle to repress a posthumanist inclination to stage that which remains virtually beyond all appeal to reason. In fact, the novel's gradual thinning—Sinclair even offers that "the incidents in the second half of my book move too swiftly and . . . its characters are insufficiently realized" (qtd. in Folsom: 249)—anticipates abstract modernism's goal of eliminating shambling figures by bolting from figuration altogether.[14] In the search for socialist figures as good as gold, he ends up producing a prose whose flatness conforms to what Walter Benn Michaels refers to as the *"trompe l'oeil economy"* structuring the logic of naturalism. According to Michaels, the popularity of *trompe l'oeil* painting at the turn of the century reflects an intense cultural preoccupation with finding a natural form of figuration that effectively hides (or whites out) its status as an imitation. He suggests that this preoccupation also informs the claim made by supporters of the gold standard that gold ought to be considered the only legitimate form of money since it is intrinsically or naturally worth the value ascribed to it: "Focusing on objects so flat that they are physically similar to the support on which they will be represented, the *trompe l'oeil* painter repeats the goldbug demand for a material equivalence between the representation and the objects represented, an equivalence that guarantees the representation's authority by minimizing the degree to which it is a representation" (162). Naturalism's hard-money distrust of fiat currency repeats naturalism's hardbody distrust of fat. For the hard-money advocate, the system based on precious metals is not susceptible to the poisonous effects of inflation (bloating) and counterfeiting (shamming). Like the cyberconsumer, the system spits out whatever is not the thing itself: "Defending gold or silver, the money writers end up articulating an economic theory that, in its most outlandish and fetishized claims on behalf of 'real' or 'primary' money, actually stages for itself . . . the escape from a money economy" (148). The goldbug's determination to realize an economy from which the promissory note has been expectorated is similar to Sinclair's determination to realize a literary narrative from which even the character with socialist promise is expectorated or, better yet, is left cleaning up after the literal expectorations of other socialists while struggling to expel his autointoxicating doubts: "[T]o keep Hinds's hotel a thing of beauty was his joy in life. . . . Jurgis scrubbed the spittoons and polished the banisters all the more vehemently because at the same time he was wrestling inwardly with an imaginary recalcitrant" (384–85).

As *The Jungle* staggers to a close, Sinclair attempts to stage an escape from sham(bling) figures not only by making his characters disappear but also by making himself disappear. At the end of the novel, he has an anonymous socialist orator post a pronouncement designed to secure, once and for all, the authenticity of the author's signature: "'We shall have the sham reformers self-stultified and self-convicted . . .'" (412). Read one way, the statement functions as an act of self-exoneration. Anticipating accusations of sham representation, it is a ventriloquized defense of a Sin-clair voice. Read another way, the statement represents an authorial attempt to self-exempt from the very project of representation. According to this fantasy, the muckraking text doesn't represent or figure the corrupt elements; they figure out (self-convict) themselves somewhere else. In other words, the muckraking artist strikes the pose of an im-poster who strikes all sham(bling) figures from his literary post, thereby saving himself and his work from the wasteland—or the jungle—of figuration. Whitewashing his truly radical efforts to inscribe a pre-figural joint, he uses the platform of socialist reform to try to craft a blank fiction.[15]

As a kind of postscript, I would like to suggest that Sinclair's entire authorial career is bound up with the problem of how to leave the sham(bling) behind. Indeed, a photograph of the novelist as a stooped, elderly man illustrates this anxiety about imposture by reframing it as an anxiety about posterity. Taken not long before his death, the print shows him standing next to his gift to posterity: a single, enormous stack of books comprising all of his writings piled one on top of the other. At first glance, what strikes the viewer is the height of the textual column, a monument to the naturalist's nearly lifelong commitment to writing like a machine. Yet the picture's composition is also striking in that the aging author, as he gestures toward his accomplishment, appears to be vanishing into his oeuvre. The camera, which makes his extended forearm and hand look as though they have disappeared into the texts, repeats, in visual terms, the desire expressed by early Christian ascetics to leave behind the vagaries of identity by converting self into script. As Harpham indicates, these ascetics, while ever aware of the unstable, contingent nature of language, frequently commit themselves to paper through the writing of hagiographies. Such exercises constitute rites of purification by functioning as panoptic instruments of self-discipline. The written record enables the self-reflective subject to dispel the demonic by bringing all dark, errant, shameful impulses to light: "[T]he ascetic text erases the distinction between inner and outer by serving simultaneously as an external record of inner thoughts and as an internalized eye of social judgment" (14). In other words, the faithful transcription of life into letters acts as a form of metaphysical Fletcherizing. It is a systematic effort to expose internal corruption and curb appetite through a process of careful rumination. Harpham actually borrows metaphors from the ascetics' own writing to make clear this connection between a self-purifying method of composition and a self-purifying method of consumption: "Life is the 'cry of nature,' while textuality is the lions' teeth, grinding the meaningless into the meaningful, the useless into the productive" (15).

In the photograph, Sinclair's textual post(erity) strikes the pose of a body converted from the unsignifying "nature" of the world to the signifying anti-nature of words. His post made of script—his postscript—is a virtual embodiment of naturalism's waste-free body. It stands as a fat-free, phallic model, the kind of figure the shambling author is dying to disappear behind or die into.[16] As Sinclair himself suggests in a *Physical Culture* article titled "Returning to Nature," the true nature lover is a monastic composer who retreats to the country and into the desert of textuality:

> I have always been accustomed to live a hermit's existence while I am writing my books, and accordingly I am a specialist in the art of eliminating house-work. One year, before I knew anything at all about physical culture or the raw-food regimen, I solved the problem by making up my mind to eat nothing wet and nothing hot, and to eat all my food from paper. (626)

Food from paper and paper as food. Consumed with writing, virtually replacing consumption with writing, Sinclair attempts to avoid the halts and tears of material life by embodying what he imagines to be the seamless materiality of his own corpus.

To die into letters would be to realize the humanist dream, pursued with a vengeance by the hypermasculine, barbell-lifting naturalist, of eliminating the most stubborn bar to real Being . . . the bar barely legible in the syllabic foot "ble" that drags behind the sham . . . the bar (a joint of sorts!) whose noise can be faintly heard in the *ble*at of the sacrificial beast . . . the bar encrypted in the pale, pre-natural(ist) figure of Bart*leby*, the figure formerly posted in a Dead Letter office . . . the bar that leaves me a virtual sham B. L.

Backfire II

Melville's (Un)flinching Faith

Strangely huddled at the base of the wall, his knees drawn up, and lying on his side, his head touching the cold stones, I saw the wasted Bartleby.

Herman Melville, "Bartleby, the Scrivener: A Story of Wall-Street"

Before beginning to trace a literary historical line of progress from naturalism's shambling narratives to postmodern fictional narratives, I feel compelled to turn aside—to shamble off as it were—in order to consider a literary figure who unsettles the very premise of such a progress report, a figure who, pictured lying on his side at the end of the story, is not quite a stand-up guy. After all, Melville's pallid scrivener is a figure with an obscure background who appears out of nowhere seeking a job as copyist in the narrator's Wall Street law firm. What's more, Bartleby's story, presented as the narrator's hindsight on his experience of his mysterious employee, is marked by backfire. When the scrivener is first hired he copies relentlessly, religiously. Far from being a shambling employee prone to wasting time, he seems dedicated to the virtues of creating virtual documents. However, the narrator's decision to hire him backfires when Bartleby stops copying. The scrivener suddenly backs off any kind of work, though, even more strangely, he also refuses to leave the law firm, to back out of his place of employment. To complicate matters further, the narrator recognizes that even though Bartleby turns out to be someone who refuses to do his work as copyist, he is not a figure who lacks virtue. He cannot be labeled a total sham or mere imposter. As the narrator insists: "It was not to be thought of for a moment that Bartleby was an immoral person" (27). Indeed, the narrator imagines that this marginal, working class figure will, like a progressive streetsweeper, eventually hop to and fall in line: "I tried to fancy that in the course of the morning, at such time as might prove agreeable to him, Bartleby, of his own free accord, would emerge from his hermitage, and take up some decided line of march in the direction of the door" (36). But this assumption backfires, for while Colonel Waring's bleached drill team of dustmen models assumption of a proper post, the scrivener "blankly declined" even to take "letters to the post-office" (32). And yet . . . it's not like he's completely out of line; it's not like he's a total slouch; it's not like he's gone AWOL. In fact, though he won't even run an errand to the post office, he, in a strange way, mans a post in the office: "He was a perpetual sentry in the corner" (23).

Given that he generates so many backfires, Bartleby turns out to be particularly (un)fit for my purpose. Though he is, as the narrator puts it, "more a man of preferences than assumptions" (34), he does assume a "wasted" position "at the base of the wall" near Wall Street when he is thrown in prison by the end of the story for the various outbreaks he precipitates. In one respect, the location of this posture illustrates that any serious consideration of the makeup of the modern marketplace must take his kind of refuse into consideration. In another respect, this posture illustrates that while he appears on the American scene before the emergence of naturalist narrative, it is appropriate for me to situate an examination of his story at the beginning (or base) of a set of readings of contemporary texts that dramatize the premises of American consumer culture while refusing its premise that art must somehow always work, whether it be by enriching our time, killing our time, or wasting our time. According to Maurice Blanchot, in his essay "Literature and the Original Experience," the notion of literature being something other than either a good use of time or a waste of time is foreign to traditional humanist thought, which insists on making two instrumental claims on art. On one hand, it asserts a utilitarian claim that art should serve a political or moral purpose. On the other hand, it asserts a romantic claim that art should serve as a refuge from the utilitarian, that art's value lies in its autonomy and purposelessness. Whether it counts or doesn't count, works or doesn't work, art is thus calculated to be valuable. Blanchot articulates the either/or appropriation this way:

> At this stage, art is what we call humanistic. It oscillates between the modesty of its useful manifestations (literature tends increasingly toward effective, interesting prose), and useless pride in being pure essence. This pride is most often expressed by the triumph of subjective states: art becomes a condition of the soul, it is "criticism of life," it is useless passion. ("Literature" 218)

The problem with these assumptions is that in either case the work of art becomes reified or commodified. Art circulates inside a productive, limited economy, even if it is cast as an embodiment of the unproductive or the noneconomic. Within this framework, the best art can do is to simulate radical inutility or waste since even its negativity turns out to be a redeeming positivity.

For Blanchot, art loses its power to the extent that it both enlightens and is brought to light: "[W]hat ruins it is that it *seems* true. For from this semblance of truth is drawn an active truth and an inactive illusion which is called the beautiful" (229). Swept up by modern history's teleological "commitment to a realized goal" (230), the work of art gets wrenched from the obscurity of its semantic and historical folds and processed as either an object of knowledge or an object of pure reflection, much as the police physically wrench Bartleby from the obscurity of his office divider or folding screen and process him, on his way to prison, in "silent procession . . . through all the noise, and heat, and joy of the roaring thoroughfares at noon" (42). The result is that, like the imprisoned Bartleby, there is *nothing stirring* about this work—nothing vital, nothing subversive, nothing astonishing—because it has been fixed, objectified, walled in, walled up, made lawful. Art is thus caught up in an essentially ascetical culture bent on redeeming itself by bringing to light, and thereby rooting out, the dark, scandalous elements that compromise the system's integrity. By deadening the self, the ascetic seeks to escape the mischievous materiality of the body. By objectifying art, humanism seeks to escape the mischievous materiality of the text. As Blanchot puts it:

> For in the usual [art] object (this much we know), matter itself is of no particular interest; and the more the matter that made it made it right for its use—the more the material is appropriate—the more it nears nothingness. And eventually all objects become immaterial, a volatile force in the swift circuit of exchange, the evaporated support of action which is itself pure becoming. ("Literature" 223)

Of course, nowhere is the work of literature more quickly put into self-obliterating "action" (frequently, nowadays, by being turned into a live action feature) than in American consumer culture. Nowhere does the "swift current of exchange" run more swiftly, making the issue of marshaling aesthetic resistance to its reductive, repressive force all the more pressing. To begin imagining such resistance—a counterforce that must be something other than outright refusal—allow me to turn back to Bartleby.

Readers of Melville's story have tried to seize on the scrivener by processing his wasted condition. For instance, the scrivener's "wasted" position "at the base of the wall" off Wall Street has been read as an unflinching critique of an emergent marketplace whose design includes the construction of numerous walls which, if anything, have become more impenetrable in a full-blown consumer culture: walls dividing social classes, walls shutting out aesthetic difference, walls producing personal isolation.[1] In this account, Bartleby is no longer what the narrator terms an "unaccountable scrivener." Instead, he is assumed to be a totally wasted figure. Wasted by the impersonalized cash nexus, he is alienated labor. Wasted by the homogenizing effects of the culture industry, he is paralyzed artist. Wasted by the anonymous urban crowd, he is lost soul. The unreasonable law copyist is ultimately made subject to the law of reason. He is brought into line or placed in chancery: "**in chancery: 1** : in litigation in a court of chancery; *also* : under the superintendence of the lord chancellor <a ward in chancery> **2** : caught in a chancery hold in boxing or wrestling" (*Webster's*). It is just such a hold the narrator—a Master in Chancery at the time—periodically imagines he has established over (or on) Bartleby. While Jacob's wrestling match against a virtually unfigurable "man" makes him a shambler, the narrator imagines that, with the help of the arm of Biblical law, he can pin down his rather incalculable copyist and emerge unscathed: "I grappled him and threw him. How? Why, simply by recalling the divine injunction: 'A new commandment give I unto you, that ye love one another.' Yes, this it was that saved me" (36).

However, something remains untreated in this apparently masterful, redemptive treatment of Bartleby. His wasted state cannot be grappled with so easily, for it is precisely his being in chancery, or more specifically, his being lodged in the Chancery's chambers, that makes him so wasteful. After all, what confounds the narrator to no end—what places *him*, ironically enough, in chancery: "**in chancery 3** : in an inextricable predicament" (*Webster's*)—is Bartleby's refusal to quit the Master of Chancery's premises. The narrator comes to understand that if the scrivener were asked to leave, even just to dispatch a letter, he "would refuse point-blank" (25). What then is Bartleby's point? Blankness? Total void? Utter waste? The problem with these assumptions, aside from the fact that the scrivener is "more a man of preferences than assumptions," is that Bartleby is never totally wasted. Though frequently given to staring at stony walls in "dead-wall reveries" (29), he can't be written off as completely stoned. Indeed, his stoniness, far from leaving the narrator stone cold, continually astonishes: "But there was something about Bartleby that not only strangely disarmed me, but in a wonderful manner touched and disconcerted me" (21). Refusing to be dispatched regardless of how patiently he is considered, Bartleby is not only nearly inconsiderate; he is nearly inconsiderable, or, rather, he is consideration's refuse. No amount of speculation can recuperate or re-fuse him. Neither an insider nor an outsider on Wall Street, Bartleby is one who challenges the fundamental oppositions inside/outside, valuable/worthless, work/idleness structuring any speculative economy. In this unemployed capacity, the scrivener traces a persistently unmanageable form of inutility which resists being made philosophically useful, even as an emblem of the utterly useless. Not exactly a true vagrant ("It is because he will *not* be a vagrant, then, that you seek to count him *as* a vagrant"[38]), not quite the same as sheer rubbish, not really a total waste, Melville's copyist stands, falteringly, for virtual waste.

How then is one to take into consideration a literary figure who, because he "slid[es] aside" when called on to perform certain legal work, calls into question what it means to have faith in the work of literature? The lawyer or reader who endeavors to put Melville's story to work certainly cannot be said to display no faith in the narrator's slippery employee, yet neither can the reader be said to display unflinching faith. Is there such a thing as unflinching faith in Melville? What, if anything, does Melville have to say on the subject of flinching and faith?

These questions strike me as rather monstrous, and so my initial preference is to begin trying to respond to them by copying out, like a dutiful scrivener, the definition of "flinch": "flinch *vi* **1 a** : to withdraw or shrink (as from an enterprise or responsibility) usu. because of danger, difficulties, or distress involved or foreseen **b** : to shrink from or as if from physical pain : WINCE, START **2** *obs* : to slink off or away ~ *vt, archaic* : to draw back or hold back from (as some indulgence)" (*Webster's*). To flinch would seem to be to demonstrate irresponsibility, to avoid duty, to back out. However, if I am to look unflinchingly at the matter of flinching, I must also copy out the fact that slinking around in back of the word "flinch" is the word "flense," as *Webster's* definition of the latter word makes clear: "**flense** *or* **flinch** [D *flensen* or Dan & Norw *flense*; akin to MGF *vlans* large mouth, mouth of an animal, Norw *flans* horse's pizzle, Icel *flanni* penis] : to strip (as a whale or seal) of blubber or skin." Paradoxically, then, to flinch also means to try, in a rather aggressive, penetrative, unflinching manner, to cut to the bone.

Not coincidentally, Melville calls attention to the duplicitous nature of flinching when, in *Moby-Dick*, he describes what he calls "the tumultuous business of cutting-in and attending to a whale . . ." (319). In one regard, the flenser or flincher behaves tenaciously, attaching himself to the whale like a kind of parasite: "[I]n very many cases, circumstances require that the harpooner shall remain on the whale till the whole flensing or stripping operation is concluded" (319). Ironically, however, the flensing procedure is so "tumultuous" that it cannot be performed unflinchingly. This is because it is impossible to get a good physical fix on the whale, which remains "almost entirely submerged, excepting the immediate parts operated upon" (319). Never showing anything more than a bit of its back, the whale is itself a kind of para-site (and keeping in mind Serres' notion of parasite as white noise, Melville's white whale is a particularly disturbing parasite) which forces the mariners alternately to draw back and dig in, to engage in flinching of both kinds: "[T]here is much running backwards and forwards among the crew. Now hands are wanted here, and then again hands are wanted there. There is no staying in any one place . . ." (319).

Bartleby, it turns out, is an unsettling parasite in his own right (he lodges himself within the chambers of his employer/host yet doesn't seem to derive any nourishment from the attachment) and produces a similar tumult amongst the crew in the law office. Despite, or perhaps because of, the scrivener's apparent thinness—"His face was leanly composed" (20)—it is impossible for anyone to trim the excess from him, to cut him down to size: "Turn the man out by an actual thrusting I could not." Every effort to look Bartleby in the eye and flense him is bound to backfire because, as his repeated statement "I prefer not to" suggests, Bartleby is always already withdrawing or flinching. There is no possibility of having a showdown with him; there is no opportunity to make him flinch. Unlike a 'real man,' Bartleby won't take it outside and have it out, a dilemma that challenges the very premise of the narrator's phallocentric law: "It was his wonderful mildness chiefly, which not only disarmed me, but unmanned me, as it were" (27). Instead of drawing Bartleby's fire, the narrator elicits only a "wonderful mildness" that, as Ann Smock eloquently notes, tends to ignite the rage of others:

> It all gets everyone else quite hot under the collar, not to say red in the face. The narrator, upon occasion, fairly burns to flare up at Bartleby. The coolness of the "unaccountable scrivener" goads even this peaceable gentleman in to goading him: "to elicit some angry spark in him answerable to my own. But indeed I might as well have essayed to strike fire with my knuckles against a bit of Windsor soap." Incombustible, inert, Bartleby is practically insupportable. (73)

However, even the assumption that Bartleby is perfectly cool is not quite an unflinching account of his case because, as we learn at the back end of the story, there is, in Bartleby's background, a trace of fire. After recounting the scrivener's death, the narrator tacks on a supplemental text which opens with the promise of finally laying Bartleby to rest: "There would seem little need for proceeding further in this history" (45). Yet the cool, collected premise of this postscript immediately backfires as the narrator proceeds to struggle, somewhat feverishly, with the issue of whether to confide something else about the singular copyist: "Yet here I hardly know whether I should divulge one little item of rumor, which came to my ear a few months after the scrivener's death. . . . The report was this: that Bartleby had been a subordinate clerk in the Dead Letter Office at Washington" (45). He wonders aloud whether the scrivener, in his former post, was in the habit of "continually handling these dead letters, and assorting them for the flames? For by the cart-load they are annually burned" (45). Within this narrative backfire, then, the dead Bartleby comes back to life as the ghostly survivor of a holocaust. He is the dead letter of a difference that sets ablaze those systems—informational, legal, ethical—dedicated to burning off all waste through postal pyrotechnics. In Smock's words:

[T]he sheer responsiveness of this creature whom no word, no gesture seems to reach—makes the narrator feel responsible and then detached, warm then cool, hot then cold, "human," and then "inhuman." For it enlists yet idles, calls upon yet unemploys his word. It quickens in him a sympathetic pain which it deadens; it ignites and extinguishes his responsibility; it sets a dead fire to burning in him. (75–76)

Remarkably, the narrator himself suggests that impossible attendance to this "dead fire" is linked to the question of faith: "It is not seldom the case that when a man is browbeaten in some unprecedented and violently unreasonable way, he begins to stagger in his own plainest faith. He begins, as it were, vaguely to surmise that, wonderful as it may be, all the justice and all the reason is on the other side" (22). But what does this other side look like? Can it be neatly copied out? Is it, like a spent scrivener, something exhausted, something wasted by too much copying? The problem of faith in the other side is made literal when the narrator stops by the office on Sunday on his way to hear "a celebrated preacher," only to find access to his own chambers barred by Bartleby, who, unexpectedly, is on the other side of the door. Turned aside, the narrator soon returns to find that though he is able to admit himself and dig into the "recesses" of his employee's drawer (Bartleby now being temporarily absent), the strange experience of this never fully present "other" side leaves him backing away from his former spiritual path. Bartleby's virtually inconspicuous figure has made him flinch at the idea of spectacular ("celebrated") faith: "I did not accomplish the purpose of going to Trinity Church that morning. Somehow, the things I had seen disqualified me for the time from church-going" (29).

The narrator flinches at the thought of church because he is confronted by a perpetually flinching figure who occupies a scene defined by unflinching commitment to converting the useless to the useful as quickly as possible. In the "snug retreat" of his workplace, the narrator anticipates the principles of scientific management in that he is an ascetic figure obsessed with not wasting time. For example, Bartleby first refuses to copy after being summoned to work with what the narrator calls "my haste and natural expectancy of instant compliance" (20). Though this refusal lays waste to his expectations, the narrator temporarily gets around the fix he is in by insisting that he simply can't afford to waste time on such a wasteful figure: "What had one best do? But my business hurried me" (21). In effect, the narrator tries to white out this blot by assuming his business' primary responsibility, which is to reproduce blot-free texts that are fully active in the eyes of the law. His scriveners and their copies should work so well in recreating the original that their own materiality actually evaporates or becomes nothing. The texts should be so identical or so uniform as to white themselves out, much as the scrivener's sensuous life gets whited out by having to perform his unvarying, uniform task in the shadow of the chamber's "white wall."

It is tempting, in this context, to read Bartleby as the embodiment of a romantic aesthetic. He seems to be a figure whose virtue resides in his rejection of a utilitarian economy. However, as I have been suggesting, if the Melvillean copyist is an original, he is so only by virtue of the fact that he refuses to be reclaimed even as absolute refuse. Exemplifying what Blanchot terms "the superabundance of refusal" ("Literature" 228), Bartleby refuses both the utilitarian and the romantic. He assumes (without making any assumptions) an impossible neither/nor position that might be described as asceticism with a difference. At first glance, he looks and acts like a real ascetic. He adopts, at least initially, his employer's utilitarian ethic, performing, without the smallest break or the least waste of time, a long stint of copying: "He ran a day and night line, copying by sun-light and by candle-light" (19). Not coincidentally, the scrivener's apparent devotion to copying recalls the early Christian ascetic's practice of seeking redemption by imitating the 'original' hagiographical texts produced by previous saints: "To a great extent ascetic discipline is a science of imitation made possible by the mimetic imitations of texts such as *The Life of Anthony*" (Harpham 13). Indeed, Bartleby continues to copy the copy-minded traditional ascetic even when he appears all copied out, for at that point he begins to starve himself. Trading imitation for inanition, he exchanges the trial of fashioning a dematerialized text for the trial of fashioning a dematerialized body, an exchange that represents a return to the roots of capitalism's "worldly asceticism" exposed by Weber in *The Protestant Ethic and the Spirit of Capitalism*: "That powerful tendency toward uniformity of life, which to-day so immensely aids the capitalistic interest in the standardization of production, had its ideal foundation in the repudiation of all idolatry of the flesh" (169).

In refusing to be turned out, Bartleby turns out to be a different kind of ascetic. His ascetic activity, whether it be writing or fasting, shows him conforming to the evaporative pursuit of transcendental significance, yet such activity simultaneously undermines the pursuit. While Bartleby practices austerity, he holds something in reserve from austerity's conservative economy. He embodies what the narrator calls an "austere reserve" (28). Instead of being completely whited out, Melville's scrivener haunts the premise(s) of asceticism with his "white attenuated mouth" (30). He signifies an attenuated or absent presence which, like Melville's white whale, staggers a system operating according to the principles of total domination and full revelation. In this irreducibly ambiguous role, Bartleby begins to perform what Blanchot considers art's responsibility to a kind of impossible work: "Art is originally linked to this fund of impotence where everything falls back when the possible is attenuated" ("Literature" 243).

Moreover, Bartleby's dizzying inscrutability—his muted withdrawal from asceticism's utilitarian withdrawal—works as art because, as Blanchot points out, the aesthetic production only really becomes a work of art, only expresses art's need to work as something other than a useful work, when it labors, without complete success, to summon the Otherness of the sacred: "The work bespeaks the divine, but only inasmuch as the divine is unspeakable" ("Literature" 231). Given that the sacred is what cannot be brought into plain view—what cannot be reduced to the instrumental, the useless, or the true—an imaginative effort to entertain the sacred, despite its inevitable failure, marks the beginning of art's resistance to the "swift circuit of exchange." In Blanchot's words:

> It [the work of art] is hidden and preserved by the presence of the god, manifest and apparent through the obscurity of the divine, and again kept safe in reserve by this obscurity and this distance which constitutes its space and to which it gives rise as though thus to come into the light. It is this remove that permits the work to address the world and at the same time to reserve comment, to be the ever reserved beginning of every story. ("Literature" 233)

To begin is to begin making meaning, to begin doing something productive, to begin practicing asceticism. Literature approaches the sacred only insofar as, in a rather shambling fashion, it begins without beginning, it begins by holding something in reserve, it begins by holding back, it begins by backfiring. Having backed away from my progress report in order to approach the figure of Bartleby, I have not properly begun an analysis of contemporary American literary efforts to entertain the sacred. Instead, I have tried to provide an indication of the extent to which the scrivener's infinitely reserved burning backs this project. Through Bartleby's "austere reserve," Melville creates a story characterized by "reserved beginning." The text is grounded in an awareness of an unreadable origin(al) reproduced as a terrifically blotted copy. For Melville, this lost origin is the sacred, a prodigious waste glimpsed only through a veil of virtual waste. As the narrator says of his scrivener: "[L]ike the last column of some ruined temple, he remained standing mute and solitary in the middle of an otherwise deserted room" (33). In this ruinous condition, Bartleby is not simply one in whom nothing stirs (though he doesn't budge!) but rather one in whom the sacred stirs in back of the improper name of "nothing." Indeed, if there is anything Bartleby prefers, it is to speak unflinchingly about an impossible "not," though such a desire always makes him flinch. Standing before the prison wall, he almost says as much to the narrator, though he doesn't look him in the eye, though he keeps his back turned: "'I know you,' he said, without looking round, —'and I want nothing to say to you'" (43).

CHAPTER TWO

Nothing to Go On:
Paul Auster's Cracked Case

1. CATCHING A BREAK

> Nothing happens. And still, it is not nothing.
>
> Paul Auster, "White Spaces"

In *Ghosts* the middle volume of Paul Auster's critically acclaimed *New York Trilogy*, a detective named Blue, who has been hired by a man named White, finds himself with next to nothing to do. Per White's instructions, Blue is staking out a mark named Black, but the marks Black makes—both the impressions he makes on Blue and the words he writes on sheets of white paper—lead to nothing conclusive. Indeed, the subject of Blue's surveillance appears all but black to him. Like a good scrivener, the detective copies out the mark's movements in the form of reports written up and posted to White, but even here Blue seems to be virtually wasting his time. It's almost as though he is drawing a blank: "[T]his is what he gets: a case with nothing to do. For to watch someone read and write is in effect to do nothing. The only way for Blue to have a sense of what is happening is to be inside Black's mind, to see what he is thinking, and that of course is impossible" (166).[1] So, as a break from this ambiguous, stuttering work, Blue turns to a popular pulp magazine of the time (the story is set in 1947) devoted to real-life crime stories: "He is a devoted reader of True Detective and tries never to miss a month. Now, with time on his hands, he reads the new issue thoroughly . . ." (168).

Using this allusive scrap of information as a starting point for scholarly investigation of Auster's work, I begin with two queries: What, if anything, might a reader of *The New York Trilogy* pick up from this clue? What, if anything, does this clue have to do with the problem of "nothing" in Auster's trilogy? In one regard, the installments in *True Detective Mysteries* are, unlike the volumes of the trilogy, highlighted by tales of solved crimes. In another regard, the installments are, unlike Blue's later reports, inspired by a belief that proper posting of information leads to effective elimination of criminal waste:

> [I]n 1931, True Detective Mysteries inaugurated the "Line-Up," which publicized the identifying physical characteristics of felons and murderers wanted by the police. . . . [It] started a pictorial feature, "Crime Does Not Pay," and a department devoted to the problems of scientific crime detection. . . . It printed a series on parole as practiced in the United States, and it offered $1000 rewards for information leading to the solution of unsolved mystery cases. (Ernst 84)

Given the magazine's dedication to disciplining the fugitive through strategies such as serial depiction of criminal postures, it may come as no surprise that *True Detective Mysteries* is founded in 1924 by Bernarr Macfadden, the fitness guru and fascist sympathizer who not only equates physical bearing with moral development—the motto emblazoned on his magazine *Physical Culture* reads "Weakness is a Crime"—but who also posts numerous photographs of himself locked in bodybuilding poses.[2] Blue consumes stories published by the hardbodied progressive reformer in an effort to re-form his shambling case in the image of the classic hardboiled private eye. In other words, Blue seeks to justify his position as Black's tail by, ironically, taking a break from his post in order to consult the work of a figure dedicated to eliminating the problem of physiological and investigative letdown. For Macfadden, both the physical culturist and the private dick keep it up 'til the end.

However, the reader who consults Paul Auster catches a different kind of break. Macfadden's still-life poses depict a life in which, ideally, nothing happens once and for all and Macfadden's *True Detective Mysteries* offer narratives in which something will always happen, but *The New York Trilogy* consists of narratives in which nothing happens again and again. To say "nothing happens" in the three stories is not to say they are plotless but rather to indicate that the plots are continually foiled by a singularly elusive otherness resistant to apprehension by the standard procedures of systematic interrogation, empirical analysis, and deductive logic. In these stories, the detective—who is also a writer—records evidence, plots strategy, and traces marks, but his calculations and sketches lead to no final illumination, no climactic discovery: "He had nothing, he knew nothing, he knew that he knew nothing" (*City* 124); "He has learned a thousand facts, but the only thing they have taught him is that he knows nothing" (*Ghosts* 202–03); "What I had done so far amounted to a mere fraction of nothing at all" (*Locked* 245). While the goal of detection is to uncover the whole story, in Auster's work nothing, especially not *nothing*, is grasped in its "all." No case is closed, though this lack of closure does not mean that the case comes to naught. Remaining open, Auster's cases point toward a remainder necessarily overlooked by the teleologically oriented detective determined to achieve "a desired end." Each tale entails a tail job, like Blue's, spoiled by repeated bewilderment, perpetual crossing (out) and retracing, interminable wandering.

This refrain of nothing in Auster's writing marks a revision of the existentialist belief that experience is arbitrary, accidental, and meaningless. An example of the latter actually appears in *The Locked Room*, where the narrator declares: "In the end, each life is no more than the sum of contingent facts, a chronicle of chance intersections, of flukes, of random events that divulge nothing but their own lack of purpose" (256). Such an assessment occurs repeatedly in Auster's work. It is heard again, for instance, in his novel *In the Country of Last Things*, a bleak vision of late twentieth-century life transposed onto an unnamed, entropic urban setting: "Our lives are no more than the sum of manifold contingencies, and no matter how diverse they might be in their details, they all share an essential randomness in their design: this then that, and because of that, this" (143–44). Examined one way, these textual clues, suggesting that nothing coheres and that nothing adds up, might lead a reader of Auster's fiction to suspect the novelist of embracing a kind of nihilistic despair. However, I wish to argue that this refrain of nothing turns out, paradoxically, to undermine confidence in such a dead end and instead signals an investigation into the effects of projects that assert the presence of any kind of comprehensive end. Put another way, it places under scrutiny a series of narrative patterns—including the naturalist narrative of the divine hardbody and the modernist narrative of the divining hardboiled detective—embraced with evangelical fervor by the American cultural imagination, each of which makes the soterial promise of delivering the good(s) in the end.

Let me be quick to point out that this clue to Auster's mysteries ought not to be misconstrued as a sign that the trilogy ends up making for a perfectly endless story. Trading heavily on the mass cultural tradition of texts like *True Detective Mysteries*, Auster acknowledges the naiveté inherent in imagining a narrative form from which the powerful seductions of the end might be completely whited out. As I explain in greater detail in the third section of this essay, the first installment in the trilogy, *City of Glass*, is a particularly striking example of the novelist's determination to expose the repressive logic at work in certain twentieth-century practices through simulation of end-game strategies employed by the private eye, the modernist minimalist, and the anorexic. A slender book crafted in a spare style, the novel depicts two ascetic investigators who undertake rituals of purgation and starvation in pursuit of nothing but the truth. The auster(e) detective writer and the auster(e) detective who writes both seem to be puritanical operatives undertaking a redemption-bound quest to uncover transcendent significance. One seeks to eliminate waste from the body of the text; the other seeks to eliminate waste from the text of the body. *City of Glass* dramatizes how the culture's efforts to make fast what Eliade describes as a "break-through" of the sacred into the plane of profane experience have taken the form of investment in shows characterized by *fast breaks*: the detective's sudden break in the case; the minimalist artist's radical break with figuration; the progressive as well as postmodern subject's break with consumption through fasting.

In what follows, I aim to show that Auster exposes, or catches out, the culture's fast break mentality by tailing a fugitive so singularly elusive that it neither totally vanishes nor fully shows up. As in Blue's case, this nearly untraceable nothing marks a virtually dead link to a darkness that refrains from coming to light even as total Blackness. Moreover, as I elaborate in the next section, one catches in this refrain the strain of a religious sensibility indebted in part to the work of the poet/postmodern theologian Edmond Jabès, a figure whose importance to Auster the latter registers in a letter to Mark Taylor in 1992: "'Yes, Edmond and Arlette [Jabès' wife] have been friends of mine for over 20 years—almost like spiritual grandparents—and even though Edmond is now dead, he is still with me. He taught me lessons I will keep for the rest of my life'" (*Hiding* 68). In an essay translated by Auster (with Rosmarie Waldrop), Blanchot describes Jabès as a figure whose "double vocation" as Jew and poet manifests itself in the ethically charged practice of imagining what lies in the margins of a system committed to achieving a final solution. For Jabès, this practice results in the creation of disjointed, nearly uncategorizable texts which enact two impossible binds or catches: 1. The catch of how to speak of Jewish identity in the wake of unspeakable displacement and persecution, described by Blanchot as a "rupture suffered in history, where catastrophe still speaks, and where the infinite violence of pain is always near: the rupture of violent power that has tried to make and mark an entire era" ("Interruptions" 48); 2. The catch of how to survive and bear witness to such violence by holding fast to a covenant which, according to classic Jewish theology, is made fast, paradoxically, through withdrawal, refrain, absence, breaking off of the Word. As Blanchot puts it: "Then, the other, the original rupture, which is anterior to history, and which is not suffered, but required, and which, expressing distance in regard to every power, delimits the interval where Judaism introduces its own affirmation: the rupture that reveals [in Jabès' words] 'the wound . . . invisible at its beginning . . .'" ("Interruptions" 48).

The narrative that wrestles with such ontological, theological, and linguistic rupturing is bound to be a bit of a shambles, like Jacob with his ruptured hip. With nothing to go on, such a narrative initially moves forward, like Bartleby, by mimicking the procedures of patriarchal, humanist law. Both Auster and Jabès appear to offer legal aid to readers of their postmodern texts by bringing into the investigation figures traditionally portrayed as exegetical experts. So, for instance, in the first of his seven volume *Book of Questions*—a series in which, according to Auster, "The question is the Jewish Holocaust, but it is also the question of literature" ("Interview" 3)—Jabès introduces fictional rabbinical scholars who comment on the work in progress. Likewise, in *City of Glass* the writer-turned-detective named Quinn assumes the author-itative name "Paul Auster" and tracks down another writer of the same name in an effort to bring the case to a close. However, such legal work is characterized by ceaseless interruptions which draw attention to what remains hidden in the cracks (or wounds) of the case humanism makes for onto-theological purity and presence. Like Bartleby, Auster and Jabès end up refraining (from) the work of the humanist in order to work diligently at doing nothing .

2. NOTHING DOING

> In the beginning was Nothing, which has no beginning.
>
> Edmond Jabès, *The Book of Margins*

> Nothing is definite in this place. Considering the possibilities, you should be glad of that.
>
> Paul Auster, *In the Country of Last Things*

In Donald Barthelme's short story "Nothing: A Preliminary Account," the author sets out to make a list of all the things that nothing is not, hoping, by a process of elimination, to arrive at what nothing is. At the same time, he realizes that any such assessment, no matter how conservative or thorough, is unable fully to calculate, or to profit from, nothing. Nothing, in this respect, is that which can neither be counted on nor counted up: "Nothing must be characterized in terms of its non-appearances, no-shows, incorrigible tardiness. . . . Nothing is not a nail" (248). Bartheleme's nothing cannot be nailed down. Any account of it is preliminary because it is the always improper name for that which, in philosophical terms, resists being thought through to the end. Posing at the limit of absolute knowledge, it is wholly Other, a radical heterogeneity, an irreducible difference, an unreclaimable residue. Neither presence nor absence, neither being nor nonbeing, Barthelme's nothing is (yet *is* not) utter (yet unutterable) waste. Refusing to be re-fused into the productive economy of the known, this different kind of nothing is what I am inscribing as nothing , a virtually illegible trace residing at the margins of any field of representation. As Barthelme's ever-failing list illustrates, nothing gives structure fits because it fits nowhere. Nothing ties any system up in (k)nots.

Jabès' work reveals an equally scandalous investment in nothing. In an interview with Auster, he rewrites Barthelme's speculation in theological terms by suggesting that, particularly in the wake of the Holocaust, to speak of God is a trial, one which proceeds only by means of preliminary accounts of the divine as a kind of virtual waste:

> What I mean by God in my work is something we come up against, an abyss, a void, something against which we are powerless. It is a distance. . . . the distance that is always between things. . . . We get to where we are going, and then there is still this distance to cover. . . . And the extraordinary thing is that in the Jewish tradition God is invisible, and as a way of underscoring this invisibility, he has an unpronounceable name. What I find truly fantastic is that when you call something "invisible," you are naming something, which means that you are almost giving a representation of the invisible. In other words, when you say "invisible," you are pointing to the boundary between the visible and the invisible; there are words for that. But when you can't say the word, you are standing before nothing. (19)

Such a project leaves Jabès, according to one of his recurrent images, wandering or erring in the wastes of the desert, on the verge of being totally wasted. In other words, for the writer whose line of questioning demands the assumption of a vertiginous stance "before nothing," it is difficult to have confidence in the idea of making a book that will put God's case to rest. For the writer who wrestles with the task of assuming nothing, no words (not "invisible," not "Word") can be expected to bear full witness. No matter how hard the writer tries to make them obey mimetic law ("Do you swear to tell the whole truth and *nothing* but the truth?"), words invariably sputter, clam up, digress, or turn up dead somewhere. As Jabès puts it, in his typically broken off, gagged style: "Word: overload of nothing" (*Margins* 166). To write responsibly about God's anti-mimetic altarity is to recognize that the job of trying to make God's mark is bound to involve an act of betrayal, an act of violence, a crime: "To obey the word means going from murder to murder" (*Resemblances*, Vol. 2 26). For Jabès, it is not that God is dead but that the book designed to bring God fully to life is dead. Moreover, on close examination, such a textual corpse reveals nothing less than a divine wound . . . God's holey blow to the grave, to the absolute seriousness of such a textual engraving: "All that finally remains of the completed book is a gaping hole, the same dark hole that is covered by a sleeper's lids. The silenced word is a killer" (*Margins* 65).

Taking up Jabès' impossible investigation of nothing, Auster turns to a literary genre whose form and content have been marked by a determination to silence nothing. As he indicates in *City of Glass*, the traditional detective novel is governed by a totalizing imperative; it presumes a structure and a case in which nothing goes to waste since everything is reducible to an original, author-itative cause:

> What he liked about these books was their sense of plenitude and econo-my. In the good mystery there is nothing wasted, no sentence, no word that is not significant. . . . Nothing must be overlooked. Everything becomes essence . . . (9)

Bound by the teleological formula of a clear beginning, middle, and end, the "good" book is a secular construct that nevertheless offers the reader the salvational promise of "plenitude" by appearing to be a utilitarian, waste-free work in which nothing must be overlooked. Like the Christian plot of history, the good mystery is designed to be a masterful narrative in which both author and investigator are able to reassure us we are not wandering in a wilderness of ambiguous signs. In this case, writer and detective set out to achieve what Taylor refers to as "the closure of the book" (*Erring* 73). They aim to shut the book on a case by breaking off the synchronic and diachronic play of difference that makes signification possible. Thus, it makes sense that in *City of Glass* the writer-turned-detective Daniel Quinn binges on these closed books while otherwise manifesting a penchant for literal and figurative acts of purgation: "When he was in the right mood, he had little trouble reading ten or twelve of them in a row. It was a kind of hunger that took hold of him, a craving for a special food, and he would not stop until he had eaten his fill" (9).

In contrast to this "special food," Auster's postmodern potboilers are harder to digest because nothing works out in the end, or, rather, nothing works out through the loose ends of the texts' fabric. Deviating from the straight-and-narrow form of the closed book, *The New York Trilogy*—despite having a design that recalls the tripartite structure of Christian history—constitutes what Taylor calls "erring scripture" (*Erring* 170). Auster's texts are errant versions of the traditional detective novel's redemptive-bound script; they stress that subjects and signs are never single, straightforward, or self-evident but rather are always duplicitous, always (at least) double and deceptive. In *City of Glass* there are *two* operatives (or three if one counts the author)—Quinn and the theologian Peter Stillman—both of whom err by roaming the streets of New York on religious quests to establish the univocal presence of the paternal Word. Quinn seeks to "save Peter Stillman" (110) by establishing the identity and intention of Stillman's true father, also named Peter Stillman. Stillman, Sr. seeks to save the world by recovering the unerring intentionality of "God's language" (59).

Each quest in the trilogy is defined by the *err*oneous, the ab*err*ant, and the *err*atic, in part because Auster's postmodern version of the private eye, like *Blade Runner*'s posthuman version of the private eye, is not a perfectly composed private "I." Auster's investigators are neither unique nor self-possessed. Never sure of themselves, they are double-crossed from the beginning. Quinn writes under the pen name William Wilson (the eponymous character from Edgar Allan Poe's tale of doubling) and then loses himself in the role of detective "Paul Auster." The narrator/writer in *The Locked Room* becomes obsessed with tracking down a man named Fanshawe (the eponymous character from Nathaniel Hawthorne's first novel), his "closest friend" from childhood, a "blood brother" and "twin" about whom the narrator says: "[W]ithout him I would hardly know who I am" (235). Fanshawe has disappeared, leaving the narrator to assume his life—to marry his wife, to publish his writing, to write his biography—but the narrator still fails to organize a proper reunion with this other; Fanshawe appears at the end only as an absent presence, speaking through the crack of locked "double doors." Always self-divided and dis-integrated, always exiled from the ground of self-identical Being, always, in one sense, a missing person, Auster's private eye/I inevitably comes off, like the detective in *Ghosts*, Black and Blue. As the narrator in *The Locked Room* puts it:

> In general, lives seem to veer abruptly from one thing to another, to jostle and bump, to squirm. A person heads in one direction, turns sharply in mid-course, stalls, drifts, starts up again. Nothing is ever known, and inevitably we come to a place quite different from the one we set out for. (297)

Nothing is ever known in Auster's writing because he works through the resistance to nothing which marks (a) traditional detective work in order to draw attention to the blindness that always accompanies the insight of a private eye/I.

But these narratives with nothing to them are also errant because the signs the sleuths stumble upon refuse to yield an *a priori* logic, "a coherence, an order, a source of motivation" (*City* 80). Governed by the fantasy of matching signifier to signified, or clue to crime, the stereotypical gumshoe is confident that signs conform to a humanist economy of representation. In his view, language, far from being marked by errancy, is characterized by a glassy stillness:

> His method is to stick to outward facts, describing events as though each word tallied exactly with the thing described, and to question the matter no further. Words are transparent for him, great windows that stand between him and the world. . . . Oh, there are moments when the glass gets a trifle smudged and Blue has to polish it in one spot or another, but once he finds the right word, everything clears up. (*Ghosts* 174)

However, the reader of *The New York Trilogy* cannot stick to the outward facts of the case because Auster continually calls attention to the cracks in the panes of language. Like the other two texts in the trilogy, *City of Glass* is a glassy text in an altered sense of the term. In this novel words, like identities, are unstable, fragile, chancy, *glissant*: "Slippery; (fig.) ticklish, delicate, hazardous" (*Cassell's*). *City of Glass* refracts language as a shifty, aleatory medium, a place of displacement in which the profits of (a) work are forever deferred. While the work of the detective and the work of detective fiction are defined by the goal of leaving nothing to chance, Auster's nearly useless work is marked by what he calls the music of chance, an example being a character's shambling gloss on the name of his writer-detective: "'I see many possibilities for this word, this Quinn, this . . . quintessence . . . of quiddity. Quick, for example. And quill. And quack. . . . I like your name enormously, Mr. Quinn. It flies off in so many little directions at once'" (*City* 90). This quintessence of quiddity: the essence of the essential (a tautology) or the essence of a trifle (a paradox). The series of associative glissades never cuts to the quick; it denies transparent access to a transcendental signified or, in Quinn's case, to a private I. In Auster's revision of the *noir*, the clue-seeking reader sees through a (magnifying) glass darkly.

The music of chance scored in(to) Auster's sheets of glass answers Norman O. Brown's plea to "get the nothingness back into words. The aim is words with nothing to them; words that point beyond themselves rather than to themselves. . . . Empty words, corresponding to the void in things" (259). Borrowing from M. M. Bakhtin, Mark Taylor argues that language with nothing to it is analogous to the grotesque body of the carnival participant. Marked by levity instead of gravity, it freely admits its own incompletion, open-endedness, and wastefulness.[3] Like the bulging, gaping body of the Rabelaisian reveller, the language of   is irreducibly meaty. As word made fleshy, it subverts the conception of language as pure reflection, as a medium thin to the point of transparency. Instead of conforming to the sober logic of monovalence, it violates the rules of propriety governing the discrete subject and delights in the transgressive discharge of repressed meanings: "The body of the incarnate word marks the negation of the transcendence that is characteristic of God, self, and history" (*Erring* 168). Auster magnifies this scene of theological, ontological, and linguistic carnage by building cases which leave the reader-detective with   to do. *The New York Trilogy* thus simulates what Jabès describes as "[v]ision of a strange world behind the glass, which escapes the eye, but can be glimpsed—a surprised, transparent reality—in the test and silence of bold thinking as it is engulfed by the sovereign intolerance of the unthought" (*Margins* 199). In the official police report, the record of such a glimpse is hard to make out. For the private eye anxious to leave unexamined "the unthought," such a dizzying glimpse is bound to make his stomach turn.

3. ABSENT-MINDED HUNGER

First of all, there was the question of food.

City of Glass

Food, like language, is originally vested in the other, and traces of that
otherness remain in every mouthful that one speaks—or chews. From the
beginning, one eats for the other, from the other, with the other: and for
this reason eating comes to represent the prototype of all transactions with
the other, and food the prototype of every object of exchange.

Maud Ellmann, *The Hunger Artists*

Not "In the beginning was the Word," but rather "First of all," or,
"From the beginning," was the question of food. As the glassy prose of *The
New York Trilogy* illustrates, language is never redeemed by the full presence of an Author-God but rather is always already fallen, haunted by
"empty spaces." Likewise, food, beginning with the forbidden fruit, calls
attention, physiologically and symbolically, to the subject's empty spaces.
Drawing on eating as a crucial instance of "transactions with the other,"
Auster invokes images of self-starvation in several of his writings to critique the dangerous absent-mindedness of schemes designed to realize a
subjectivity purged of self-absence. The subject of nothing—and the nothingness of the subject—cannot be ventured without addressing the question
of food, since consumption, as the ritual indulgences of carnival demonstrate, always bears "traces of that otherness" defiling the proper subject.

In Auster's work, writing and the refusal to eat are inextricably linked in
ways deserving extended explanation. In an early essay titled "The Art of
Hunger," he valorizes the nameless and nomadic protagonist of Knut
Hamsun's novel *Hunger*, an aspiring writer who is, in Auster's words,
"willing to risk everything for nothing." He prefers to starve himself rather
than to rely on any sustenance—alimentary, financial, social, spiritual—
from existing economies or institutions. Refusing the physiological obliga-
tion to eat, "Hamsun's character systematically unburdens himself of every
belief in every system, and in the end, by means of the hunger he has inflict-
ed upon himself, he arrives at nothing" (20). To arrive at nothing—which
is not to arrive in the sense of reaching a terminus—is to have rejected any
promise of *parousia*, any guarantee of total satisfaction. Vagrant and vacuous, his pockets stuffed with unfinished manuscripts, the errant writer
turns away from every course that promises to be (ful)filling. *Hunger*
enacts a disgust with the concept of a finished book, with the notion of a
proper subjectivity, and, ultimately, with the belief in God as transcendent
presence. As Auster puts it: "In the end, the art of hunger can be described
as an existential art. It is a way of looking death in the face, and by death

I mean death as we live it today: without God, without hope of salvation. Death as the abrupt and absurd end of life" (20). To practice what Auster calls "the aesthetics of hunger" is to confront mindfully the fact that language, like life, is perpetually wanting.

In her study titled *The Hunger Artists: Starving, Writing, and Imprisonment*, Maud Ellmann describes the nature of this want in psychoanalytic terms by arguing that the desire for food, while indicative of the self's drive to establish a stable identity by digesting the world around it, is also indicative of the self's forever expropriated, unwhole-some state, its inevitable dependence on, and penetration by, otherness:

> It is by ingesting the external world that the subject establishes his body as his own, distinguishing its inside from its outside. If the subject is founded in gustation, though, this also means that his identity is constantly in jeopardy, because his need to incorporate the outside world exposes his fundamental incompleteness. . . . The catch is that the very need to eat reveals the 'nothing' at the core of subjectivity. (30)

As the tempting yet toxic agent of dissolution and disorder, hunger is the catch that undermines the fast break to perfect self-presence. To give in to one's own cravings is to admit that identity, like language, is always haunted by difference. In Ellmann's words: "Our bodies are composed of what we eat, and what we eat is always foreign to ourselves. Eating, then, confounds the limits between self and other . . ." (56).

The refusal to eat is thus a rage to establish boundaries between self and other by taking to the extreme the cultural *"logic of distribution"* defined by Julia Kristeva in her book *Powers of Horror: An Essay on Abjection.*[4] Self-starvation is a ritual in which everything has become taboo. The subject strives to eliminate "the 'nothing' at the core of subjectivity" by allowing nothing to enter. The decision not to eat represents an attempt to eradicate hunger. Self-emptying turns out to be nothing less than a strategy for achieving absolute self-fulfillment. Ellmann terms this profit-driven scheme of self-negation "an economy of sacrifice" and finds it governing both modernist aesthetics, where authors such as Yeats and Kafka depict the artist's search for "an implacable aesthetic that demands the decreation of the flesh" (59), and modern eating disorders, wherein the attempt to push a *fast* break to the end expresses a desire to transcend flesh and culture altogether: "There is something more *eschatological* at stake in self-starvation than the fashionable taste for slenderness or the equally fashionable ideology of 'self-control'" (16).

A good description of the degree to which modernist literary aesthetics is riddled by eschatological anxiety about hunger is Mark Anderson's article "Anorexia and Modernism, or How I Learned to Diet in All Directions." Anderson makes the compelling argument that certain modernist writers respond to the fragmentation, ephemerality, and contingency characterizing modern life by constructing texts that portray a radically ascetic denial of the world. Experiencing a sense of spiritual decay, semiotic confusion, and personal alienation, these writers dramatize rejection of a world that appears inane, a world that seems devoid of sense and sustenance: "When the self can no longer ingest and digest the world as food, can no longer turn the raw matter of sensation into abstract concepts, judgments, and generalizations, the subject is thrown back on itself for nourishment, becoming both brute matter and pure spirit" (31). Particular modernist authors—Anderson cites the writings of Kafka and Beckett as prime examples—enact this austere strategy of introversion and autophagy by crafting minimalist texts that struggle to embody a discarnate form. Such a self-consuming work strives to become an "anti-body" purged of the world's contaminating corporeality, its phenomenal fat.

Anderson's identification of what he terms "textual anorexia" hinges on the idea that modernist minimalism—like the nonrepresentational painting of abstract expressionism and the dis-figured buildings of International Style architecture—articulates a disgust with conventional language. The hunger artists who practice this craft of aversion inscribe on their textual bodies a conviction that the signs of traditional discourse are corrupt, exhausted, and opaque, unable to operate as clear, redeeming forms of mediation between self and world. In order to fulfill Ezra Pound's famous command to "Make It New," these writers try to spit out the old language as nutritionless and fattening, the discursive equivalent of empty calories. Adopting a revolutionary aesthetic diet, they strive to fashion a perfectly attenuated text. The goal is to produce what Anderson calls a "language-body" that, by virtue of a restrictive and relentless regimen, gets rid of semantic flab: "Having rejected the notion of art as mediation of the world, the minimalist constitutes his own body as a second and alien self, as a 'world' that he can control, discipline, mold into an ideal" (36). The skeletal text is similar to the anorexic woman in that it undertakes the torturous task of shaping a bodiless body or of saying something without speaking. Just as the anorexic verges on physical collapse even as she approaches what she imagines to be an ideal figure, the emaciated narrative wastes away in the process of eliminating waste. It is frequently on the verge of breaking off, shutting down, or collapsing, a good example being the exhausted opening of Beckett's *Endgame*: "Finished, it's finished, nearly finished, it must be nearly finished."[5] In this radically pared-down play, characters with food-related names (Hamm and Clov) are stuck in a scene reduced to a "bare interior," a painfully contracted space devoid of any organic, linguistic, or spiritual pabulum.

Like the anorexic body, these hollowed-out bodies and books also threaten to produce in the reader a kind of interpretive collapse through their display of what Anderson terms a "cipher text," an unsettling, spectacularly silent corpus resistant to easy diagnosis or decipherment. Texts such as Melville's "Bartleby, the Scrivener" and Kafka's *The Metamorphosis*—stories stuffed with images of inappetence and antipathy toward food in which the protagonists eventually starve to death—create what Anderson refers to as a "hermeneutical blockage," an explanatory impasse that makes it difficult for readers inside (Bartleby's lawyer, Gregor's family) and outside to digest or make sense of them: "The text's literal nature refuses to be transformed by a transcendent, allegorical spirit, remains stuck in the throat, unassimilable, 'beyond interpretation'" (31). Aiming to refuse both alimentary and communicative exchange, these body-texts try to act out an abstention from the familial, financial, social, semiotic, and political exchanges defining modern bourgeois culture. But in becoming inane, they also admit a certain powerlessness in the face of these economies. Anorexia ravages the woman's frame; Bartleby expires in prison; Kafka's hunger artist dies alone in his cage.[6]

Thus, while self-starvation can be read as a form of resistance to specific historical forces, according to Anderson it should principally be understood as expressing a desire to resist all comprehension, a desire to make the story and the subject so thin that they avoid the defiling effects of criticism and of time. Put another way, the obsession with purging the fleshy wor(l)d signifies an absent-minded longing to remember a prelapsarian state of plenitude:

> Anorexia and modernism both provide a countermyth to the story of Creation, a subversively private and individual strategy for sneaking back into the garden of childhood. Ultimately they can be seen as particular forms of narcissism and masochism—strategies of self-denial *and* self-negation that seek to establish a primal unity uncontaminated by the 'filth' of the other: sexual differentiation, social hierarchy and power relations, temporality and 'history.' (37)

Anticipated in Upton Sinclair's naturalist embrace of the fast, minimalist modernism's hunger for emptiness carries with it the expectation of a waste-free Being purged of the contaminated meat of representational language.

Auster's novels contain several examples of physiological and aesthetic rituals of asceticism undertaken in the hope of eliminating "the 'filth' of the other." In *Moon Palace*, Marco Stanley Fogg, an orphan with a name steeped in allusion to European exploration and colonization of the dark other, begins his story by recounting how he nearly starves himself to death while a student at Columbia University in the late 1960s. Haunted by genealogical gaps, familial losses, and the political upheavals of the time, the self-styled M. S. Fogg (foggy manuscript) decides to turn himself into a perfectly blank text by secluding himself in his apartment, by devouring then selling (or purging) the books his uncle has bequeathed him, and, finally, by watching his money and food run out. Once evicted from his apartment, he makes a self-destructive attempt to sneak back into the garden of childhood by taking refuge in Central Park. Like Macfadden with his assurances about the healing powers of walking barefoot and wielding Indian clubs, Fogg taps into the fantasy of returning to a pristine state of grace by going native:

> I suddenly began to dream of Indians. It was 350 years ago, and I saw myself following a group of half-naked men through the forest of Manhattan.... A soft wind poured through the foliage, muffling the footsteps of the men, and I went on following them in silence, moving as nimbly as they did, with each stop feeling that I was closer to understanding the spirit of the forest. (70)

In one respect, Fogg's severities of self-consumption constitute a hunger strike, an act of individual withdrawal made in symbolic protest against America's refusal to withdraw from Vietnam and its refusal to curtail investment in the space race: "I was an instrument of sabotage, I told myself, a loose part in the national machine, a misfit whose job was to gum up the works. . . . I was living proof that the system had failed, that the smug, overfed land of plenty was finally cracking apart" (61). However, in another respect his fast functions as a personal corollary to the public events swirling around him; he nearly cracks apart attempting to subdue difference in the name of a united state. Separated from the presence of a founding father, Fogg tries to overcome feelings of incompletion, ambiguity, and ache by subjugating the absences inscribed in his flesh: "I was trying to separate myself from my body, taking the long road around my dilemma by pretending it did not exist" (29).

In his novel *In the Country of Last Things*, Auster pokes dark fun at the trendy rites of self-renunciation whose internal demands promise to release one from the problems of social decay, cultural barrenness, and spiritual torpor. In a disintegrating domain where "food is a complicated business"—food shortages, food theft, and black market corruption being the rule—some people attempt to overcome the need to scavenge in the streets by fasting: "It is also possible to become so good at not eating that eventually you can eat nothing at all" (3). Belief in the salvational work of self-denial reaches its apotheosis in "the Runners," a sect whose members commit suicide by racing through the streets until they collapse from exhaustion. Similar to an anorexic, a Runner self-destructs in the effort to be liberated from the limitations of the body. The goal is to catch a permanent break from the ravages of hunger and history by sprinting (fast breaking!) to a life-in-death. As Auster's female narrator indicates:

I suppose it's a kind of religion. . . . Once you have been accepted, you
must submit to the code of the group. This involves six to twelve months
of communal living, a strict regimen of exercise and training, and a gradually reduced intake of food. By the time a member is ready to make his
death run, he has simultaneously reached a point of ultimate strength and
ultimate weakness. He can theoretically run forever, and at the same time
his body has used up all its resources. This combination produces the
desired result. (12)

The aesthetic equivalent of this ecstatic self-erasure is the work done by
a character named Ferdinand, a radically diminished version of the imperialist Spanish king who confines himself to a room where he creates
exquisite, ever-smaller renderings of the ship-in-a-bottle. A mumbling,
marginalized, powerless old man disgusted by the fact that the country of
last things turns out to be something other than a utopia—he claims that
"'It's all death out there'" (52)—he has become obsessed with a hermetic
medium to the point where he imagines assembling a figure so miniature as
to be totally dis-figured, completely invisible: "'The smaller the better,' he
said to me one night, bragging about his accomplishments as an artist.
'Some day I'll make a ship so small that no one can see it'" (55). In this
minimalist fantasy, the desire to place nothing under glass is a desire to
negate the glassy nothingness infecting representation. To model such a
spare text would be to rediscover a new world paradise.
    Auster's political conviction that the minimalist aesthetic constitutes an
inverted application of the imperialist economy of domination is most
clearly spelled out in his novel *The Music of Chance*. In this book, two
American millionaires, Stone and Flower, imprison on their grounds two
visitors, Nashe and Pozzi, whom they have cleaned out at poker. The
"guests" are forced to pay off their gambling debt by rebuilding, in a meadow, the imported stone ruins of a fifteenth-century Irish castle. The stones
are to be reassembled into the shape of a single, linear wall, an abstract artwork envisioned by Flower as "rising up like some enormous barrier
against time" (86). While the wall's monumental blankness dis-figures the
castle's old world structure and context, the work of construction, overseen
by an increasingly sinister foreman with the puritanical name of Calvin
Murks, walls off Nashe and Pozzi from the outside world. Equally ominous is Stone's model construction of "the City of the World," an elaborate, miniaturized depiction of a utopian future. Unlike *City of Glass*, the
City of the World offers a social vision of absolute unity where, as Flower
gushingly narrates, "'the past and future come together, where good finally triumphs over evil'" (79). What makes this exercise in minimalist mega-
lomania frightening is that the rage for total harmony yields "a model of
some bizarre, totalitarian world" (87). As the miniature scene of a prison-
er being executed suggests, the dream of wholeness demands the extermi-
nation of difference: "[T]he overriding mood was one of terror, of dark

dreams sauntering down the avenues in broad daylight" (96). In this context, it makes sense that the millionaires, trying to sneak back into the garden, should eat like children, serving, before the game of poker, "a kiddie banquet . . . hamburger patties on white, untoasted buns, bottles of Coke with plastic straws sticking out of them, corn on the cob, and a ketchup dispenser in the shape of a tomato" (88).

White, untoasted buns. Like the beasts knocked out in Sinclair's scientific slaughterhouse and the texts knocked off by minimalist modernism, these fast food items bear traces of a desire to make a fast break from nothing. They smack of white mythology's determination to deliver meat in a blank fashion. Unscorched by the nearly all-white fire of an ever-fading altarity, their refined blankness promises to fill you up for good. As Flower puts it, "At times I feel that we've become immortal" (75).

4. FIRING BLANKS

One writes before or after God.

God is the blank present.

Edmond Jabès, *The Book of Questions: Volume V*

Whiteness, and then more whiteness. How can you draw something if you don't know it's there?

Paul Auster, *Moon Palace*

City of Glass looks like an incarnation of minimalist modernism. It is, on the surface, an austere text, a novel stripped of any stylistic ornamentation or excess, a bare bones book. Like the glass curtain of the modernist skyscraper to which the title alludes, Auster's slim volume would appear to embody, in its immateriality and abstraction, a desire to realize a formless Form, a pure language shed of the dumpy, disfiguring folds of figuration.[7] However, whereas the disciples and descendants of the Bauhaus idealized their distilled, disembodied buildings as re-presentations of the Absolute and the Real, Auster adopts an ascetic modernist form in order to scramble the logocentric values assumed by such dis-figuring designs. Fashioning an emaciated text crammed with images of askesis, Auster models a spectacularly self-obliterating script that still manages to entertain a play of difference and to bear witness to the repressiveness inherent in the notion of a fat-free system of signs.

Simulating a case of textual anorexia, *City of Glass* re-creates the modernist drive to construct a perfectly decontextualized text. The novel's body language models Ellmann's claim that the refusal to eat is invariably bound up with a determination to negate, or make a break from, materiality and history: "*Self-inflicted* hunger is a struggle to release the body from all contexts, even from the context of embodiment itself. It de-historicizes, de-socializes, and even de-genders the body" (14). Though Auster's story does have a specific geographical and historical setting (New York City in the early 1980s), to the reader and to the detective the location frequently transforms into a kind of anti-*topos* or place of absence. The result of this narrative and environmental emptying out is that *City of Glass* repeatedly refuses hermeneutical and topographical orientation. The story seems to yield nothing. For instance, when Auster's detective, like a 'good' reader, goes back, after his failure to wrap up the case, to the scene where his assignment began, he finds it "stripped bare . . . the rooms now held nothing. Each one was identical to every other: a wooden floor and four white walls" (151). Likewise, the final image of the city is one in which the landscape threatens to white out or be reduced to a blank: "The city was entirely white now, and the snow kept falling, as though it would never end" (158). Offering an inane domain or a starved space, *City of Glass* appears to throw up a hermeneutical block that frustrates the reader's expectations just as it haunts the detective's dreams: "In his dream, which he later forgot, he found himself alone in a room, firing a pistol into a bare white wall" (10).

Even more than the glass curtain, this fired-on blank wall would seem to be the most appropriate architectural attire in which to dress up *City of Glass* as a model of modernist minimalism. For as Mark Wigley suggests in his book *White Walls, Designer Dresses*, the history of modernist architecture is a history of obsession with white surfaces. Expressed most canonically in Le Courbusier's embrace of "Purism," this obsession consists of a complicated desire to clothe structures in a material that, like the skin of the anorexic, is meant to display a form purged of the marks of time and desire:

> Le Courbusier does not identify it [white] with nature, the source of psychological associations. Its only affinity is with the sun, that part of the natural world that makes nature visible. In the three-way tryst between light, surface, and psyche that produces the architectural experience, the white surface leans away from the psyche and the body to bond with the light. The unique artificiality of white even takes it out of the realm of time and space. The white surface is meant to be pre-bodily, pre-psychological, pre-temporal, and pre-spatial. (276)

With its paradoxical blend of "the natural" and "artificiality," the white wall recalls the mechanized naturalism of the progressive cyberconsumer. Just as John Harvey Kellogg's and Horace Fletcher's all-white uniforms signal reform of an autointoxicated body, the modernist white wall signals reform of an architectural tradition autointoxicated by its incorporation of ideas drawn from the world of fashion. According to Wigley, the modernist believes any alliance architecture might have with fashion is corrupt because fashion privileges surface over depth and cultivates a hunger for the transitory, the changeable, the time-bound:

> To produce a modern architecture is not to strip ornament off a building, but to preserve the building from the fast-moving time of the fashion world that would render it ornamental. . . . To be a modern architect is to act in a way that does not accelerate architecture's inevitable participation in evolution of fashions. (174)

Like Bernarr Macfadden's near-nude bodybuilding poses, the bare white surface aims to hold a still-life posture immune to the consumption-mad world of style: "All the elaborate attempts to isolate the white wall from fashion, locating it within a millennial tradition passing from ancient Egypt through the Mediterranean vernacular, may, in the end, be insufficient to block the obvious thought that it is just a look. But not just any look: It is the look of a resistance to fashion, the antifashion look" (*White Walls* 121–22). Architecture not devoted to the solarized white wall can produce nothing better, nothing grander, than a moon palace.

The white look promoted by modernist architecture has much in common with the muscular look promoted by the progressive cyberconsumer because buried within the former's blank expression of anxiety about the fashionable is an anxiety, shared by the private dick and the physical culturist, about the feminine. As Wigley puts it: "If modern architecture is a form of dress, it has to be controlled by heroic figures, architects, and historians whose masculinity and heterosexuality is established by their very ability to control the surface. . . . The public image of masculine control is produced by the private mastery of the stereotypically feminine art of the surface" (361). The white wall is designed to be a "disciplined surface" purged of the gauzy, damask excesses of Victorian design. In other words, it is meant to function as the architectural equivalent of physical culture's hypermasculinized body: "The white wall is the sports outfit of architecture, a thin coat over the newly pumped-up body of the building, an exercise outfit like those that can be found in so many images of modern architecture that show its occupants working out. . . . The body that needs to be tamed, disciplined by the emerging and regular rhythms of anonymous production, was understood to be feminine" (119).

Moreover, if the modernist architect employs white as a cloth of concealment, it also employs white as an agent of revelation. Like the white, masculine, hardboiled detective, the white, masculine, hardboiled wall brings to the surface the dark, the stained, the errant. Indeed, according to Wigley, who cites Le Courbusier's seminal 1925 work *L'art decoratif d'au-*

jourd'hui, modernist investment in white is made with the goal of erecting a well-trained (private) eye:

> Whitewash liberates visuality. It is a form of architectural hygiene to be carried out in the name of visible truth. "His *home* is made clean. There are no more dirty, dark corners. *Everything is shown as it is.*" The true status of the object is exposed. Cleansed of its representational masks, it is simply present in its pure state, transparent to the viewer: "Law of Ripolin, Coat of Whitewash: elimination of the equivocal. Concentration of intention on its proper object." . . . More than just the appropriate setting for the look (a "neutral background, like a gallery wall"), and even more than the active removal of distractions from the eye, the whitewash is itself an eye: "Put on it anything dishonest or in bad taste—it hits you in the eye. It is rather like an X-ray of beauty. It is the court of assize in permanent session. It is the eye of truth." It is not simply the look of cleanliness but a cleaning of the look, a focusing of the eye. (3, 8)

White's double virtue as agent of total exposure and agent of total efface-ment promises to close the book on fashion's effeminate desire for the new and different.

No wonder, then, that in *City of Glass* white imagery glosses a narrative in which the private eye, Daniel Quinn, is a hunger artist of sorts. Haunted by the death of his wife and son, Quinn, a mystery writer by trade, has adopted a strategy of ascetic withdrawal and self-negation; he cuts himself off from the world in the effort to white out his losses. On one hand, he starves himself of all social and professional interaction, severing personal contact with friends, agent, and publisher, walling himself up behind his Poe pseudonym, William Wilson. On the other hand, he tries to (a)void himself—to evacuate his own subjectivity or to attain "a salutary emptiness within" (4)—by turning himself over to the subject of his own writing, the narrator-hero Max Work:

> If he lived now in the world at all, it was only at one remove, through the imaginary person of Max Work. His detective necessarily had to be real. The nature of the books demanded it. If Quinn had allowed himself to vanish, to withdraw into the confines of a strange and hermetic life, Work continued to live in the world of others, and the more Quinn seemed to vanish, the more persistent Work's presence in that world became. (10)

Quinn's quest to blank himself out is fired by a longing to realize a real, waste-free self experienced virtually through a detective who always lives up to his name. Though Max Work does "live in the world of others," he remains a tough egg, a hardboiled dick, a tight-lipped loner whose maxi-mum dedication to his work always enables him to put the pieces back together again, to solve the crime, to make sure nothing is left hanging.

Quinn is thus a hunger artist in that his narrative drive to catch a fast break turns out to be a lot like fasting. In fact, by investing so heavily in the figure of Max Work, Quinn is taking to the max what Harpham identifies as the ascetic work of all intensely figural discourse:

> Tropes operate in the mode of negation: they admit the world of discourse, but deny it as their own. Literary language is ascetic in that it tends to repress the world, inclining toward what Roland Barthes calls "Utopia of language," a self-sufficient universe of discourse. An ascetic artist such as Flaubert can even dream of a novel so utopian that it would be "about nothing," drawing its being not from any referent but entirely from the resources of language itself. (71)

As I indicated when examining Upton Sinclair's utopia-minded conversion rhetoric in *The Jungle*, one type of story that tries to be purely "about nothing" (and therefore tries to be a story purged of nothing) is the early Christian ascetic's conversion narrative. Just as Quinn seeks to repress the world by dying into a textualized life of Work, the hagiographical writer seeks to repress the world by mimicking, in writing, the textualized work of previous ascetic heroes:

> For the effect of mimesis is to displace and so stabilize the wandering subject, to humble human pretensions to autonomy by submitting life to the rules of grammar, rhetoric, and generic convention, including the constant interpolation of citations from Scripture. Textuality constitutes an ascesis, a deadening, a purging of materiality and mutability that anticipates the release of the soul from the body at death. Hence for the early Christians textuality was closely linked with martyrdom, which lent a purpose and even ideality to the randomness of existence, as well as "repeating" the death of Christ. . . . The unrelenting ambition of these people was precisely to eliminate the "*hors-texte*" from their existence, to become their own texts. (Harpham 14–15)

To "stabilize the wandering subject" is to put an end to errancy. Auster's ascetic repeats a redeeming death by encrypting himself in the idealized Work of an other.

In the plot of *City of Glass*, this rigorous pursuit of a life and a book stripped of nothing is apparent from the novel's opening, at which point Quinn refuses to respond to a mysterious other whose words reach him, in the beginning, through a knot of cables and who speaks only through an intricate "not": "It was a wrong number that started it, the telephone ringing three times in the dead of night, and the voice on the other end asking for someone he was not" (3). Placed from "the other end"—or the Other's end—the wrong number, or errant call, appears by chance and arrives at the protagonist's place only to dis-place him, only to mistake him for an other, "someone he was not."[8] Not surprisingly, Quinn responds to this first k(not)ty transmission by saying he will have nothing to do with the Other: "'There's nothing I can do for you'" (8). Not coincidentally, he does not respond at all to the second call because he is "in the act of expelling a turd" when the phone rings. Splicing together electronic and excremental currents (or technological and biological calls), Auster playfully suggests that the phone, like feces, is a reminder of the self's hole-y status.[9] Interrupted while emptying himself, Quinn is temporarily forced to confront the impossibility of eliminating all exchange and circulation, the impossibility of not accepting the charges and discharges which show identity to be irreparably incomplete.

By introducing this virtually unanswerable call in the beginning, Auster sets up a sustained conviction that the self, the book, and the divine are knotted together by virtue of their connection to shambling, a conviction emphasized by the fact that when Quinn really tries, the third time around, to answer the call in good faith, he does so only by shamming. Specifically, he responds to the caller's request for the Auster Detective Agency by pretending to be a subject who runs (and embodies) a proper agency: "'This is Auster speaking'" (12). Blanking himself out by taking the call in the name of the (novel's) father, Quinn earnestly simulates the presence of a transcendent paternal Authority. Shamming the role of a detective, he posts himself as a shamble-free, upstanding figure.

To accomplish the dissembling resurrection, he abandons his (max) work as fiction writer for a sleuth's seemingly even more self-deadening work as disembodied observer and mimetic transcriber of facts. This new, supposedly objective writing seems to offer a better way of realizing perfect purgation, of "discarding the slack and embellishing the gist" (*Ghosts* 174). To purify his case, Quinn begins the task of making notes by cleaning off his desk and stripping off his clothes.[10] In other words, he tries to replicate the nude, unadorned look of the white wall:

> He cleared the debris from the surface—dead matches, cigarette butts, eddies of ash, spent ink cartridges, a few coins, ticket stubs, doodles, a dirty handkerchief—and put the red notebook in the center. Then he drew the shades in the room, took off all his clothes, and sat down at the desk. He had never done this before, but it somehow seemed appropriate to be naked at this moment. He sat there for twenty or thirty seconds, trying not to move, trying not to do anything but breathe. (46–47)

This purification rite aims to exorcize nothing by sweeping away the waste that huddles, like Bartleby, at the base of every lawful wall: the useless residues (dead matches, spent cartridges) that resist proper employment; the loose change (a few coins) that remains uninvested in a proper economy; the signs of leakage (dirty handkerchief) that compromise the proper subject; the idle marginalia (doodles) that deform the frame of the good book. Whereas Melville's copyist is characterized by vagrant stillness, Auster's copyist tries "not to move" in a proper (anti)fashion.

Since this blank detective shoots to make a case for immobility, it makes sense that a man named Peter Stillman hires him to tail his father. But since the father figure winds up wandering around the city without leading to anything definite—"He could be followed to the end of time, and still nothing would happen" (78)—Quinn eventually decides that the only way to protect his client and save his case—the only way to get rid of nothing once and for all—is to conduct a stakeout in which he neither moves nor eats. He sets up an around-the-clock watch on the younger Stillman's residence, an exercise in staying put that requires him to try to eliminate the distraction of food since any kind of break, even just for fast food, results in an absence from his post:

> His ambition was to eat as little as possible, and in this way to stave off his hunger. In the best of all worlds, he might have been able to approach absolute zero, but he did not want to be overly ambitious in his present circumstances. Rather, he kept the total fast in mind as an ideal, a state of perfection he could aspire to but never achieve. He did not want to starve himself to death—he reminded himself of this every day—he simply wanted to leave himself free to think of the things that truly concerned him. (136)

The total fast—the fast for totality—leaves nothing to (the music of) chance.

If the destructive psychosomatic effects of this absent-minded strategy are most evident in the fact that Quinn is all but doubled over as a result of his abstention, the destructive theological and political implications of such a strategy are most evident in the actions of Peter Stillman, Sr., a figure who appears to have his own double (Quinn is unsure, from the beginning, whether he is tailing the right mark). Like Quinn, Stillman is dedicated to eliminating waste by arresting marks, though the task he sets for himself is a more explicitly religious one. In a book where he glosses the work of one Henry Dark—"an ardent Puritan, a student of theology" (55)—Stillman argues that the dark glassiness of words is evidence of humanity's fallen condition:

> Adam's one task in the Garden had been to invent language, to give each creature and thing its name. In that state of innocence, his tongue had gone straight to the quick of the world. His words had not been merely appended to the things he saw, they had revealed their essences, had literally brought them to life. A thing and its name were interchangeable. After

the fall, this was no longer true. Names became detached from things; words devolved into a collection of arbitrary signs; language had been severed from God. The story of the Garden, therefore, records not only the fall of man, but the fall of language. (52)

As opposed to Jabès' ethically suspended faith in a blank presence that never fully shows up within the dark cracks of words, Stillman espouses Dark's ostensibly ethical solution that by making words fit things exactly humanity will recover a prelapsarian state of total fitness:

If the fall of man also entailed a fall of language, was it not logical to assume that it would be possible to undo the fall, to reverse its effects by undoing the fall of language, by striving to recreate the language that was spoken in Eden? If man could learn to speak this original language of innocence, did it not follow that he would recover a state of innocence within himself? (57)

This prescription for salvation recalls those written up by progressive health reformers as a cure for what I have called joint anxiety. For Stillman, anxiety about the corrupt, shambling nature of the sign is joined with an anxious conviction that society is in a shambles. According to his evangelistic vision of a reform program, the contemporary American landscape, epitomized by New York, is characterized not only by what he calls the "serious error" of linguistic errancy but also by environmental degradation, cultural decay, and spiritual anomie. The city appears to be the kind of wasteland that T. S. Eliot, in the poem "Gerontion," calls "a wilderness of mirrors" (23), a city of glass:

The brokenness is everywhere, the disarray is universal. You have only to open your eyes to see it. The broken people, the broken things, the broken thoughts. The whole city is a junk heap. It suits my purposes admirably. I find the streets an endless source of material, an inexhaustible storehouse of shattered things. (94)

The world, as well as the language used to apprehend it, is shivered, riven, dis-integrated; it is the semiotic equivalent of Humpty Dumpty. To overcome modernity's cracked condition, to, in his words, "'put the egg back together again'" (98), Stillman acts as a deranged recycler, hoping to rid language of its difference while ridding the streets of detritus. Both poet and litter patrol, both scrivener and scavenger, he picks up "valueless" items and restores their "original" value by assigning them proper names in a red notebook:

> Each day I go out with my bag and collect objects that seem worthy of investigation. My samples now number in the hundreds—from the chipped to the smashed, from the dented to the squashed, from the pulverized to the putrid. . . . I invent new words that will correspond to the things. (94)

Trying to live up to his name, Stillman collects rubbish in a linguistic and theological quest to re-collect the still point of a fixed, transcendent origin. One of the king's men, he conducts a muckraking campaign designed to "Make It New" by re-membering a uniform Form, a perfectly hardboiled egg.

What reinforces my contention that *City of Glass* is something other than an irresponsibly hermetic postmodern novel about nothing is that this purist project has a dark side. Like Quinn on his stakeout, Stillman undertakes an experiment in askesis, but he does so by locking up his son in a room for nine years with the hope that, removed from circulation, he will learn to speak the "original language of innocence." Substantiating Ellmann's claim that "writing and starvation are implicated in imprisonment" (95), he starves his son of contact with the outside world, depriving him of the fashion-bound (d)rifts of words in an effort to get him to fire linguistic blanks. The father takes literally logcentrism's claim that the glassiness of language is negated by the constant presence of a paternal figure, a speaking subject who acts as what Derrida calls "the *father* of his speech." Stillman strives to repress the waywardness of writing by embodying an authority who prevents his *logos* from going astray. As Derrida puts it: "*Logos* is a son, then, a son that would be destroyed in his very *presence* without the present *attendance* of the father. . . . Without his father, he would be nothing but, in fact, writing" ("Plato's Pharmacy" 77). Nothing but the nothingness of writing, Peter Stillman the younger is buried alive at the paternal address in what amounts to an act of self-starvation since fasting can be understood, in psychoanalytic terms, as the subject's symbolic attempt to shut the "trap" on an other who has been enclosed in the crypt of the self through a cannibalistic fantasy of incorporation. As Ellmann puts it: "Starving also keeps the other in and fortifies the stronghold of the ego, lest the ghosts within the self should break out of their tomb" (95). The son is only expelled from the father's all-consuming system when, according to the son's wife, the father realizes how much his project is backfiring and decides to start a fire: "'I think he [the father] reached some point of final disgust with himself that night and decided to burn his papers. But the fire got out of control, and much of the apartment burned. Luckily, Peter's room was at the end of a long hall, and the firemen got to him in time'" (32).

As the survivor of his father's holocaust, Peter Stillman, Jr. is a spectral figure worth tailing for a bit because, like the "mildly cadaverous"

Bartleby, he incarnates a nearly dead link to the sacred. As the son himself says, when filling Quinn in on his post-traumatic condition: "'In the dark I speak God's language and no one can hear me'" (25). He is a shambling character—"he tottered as he went, listing first to the right, then to the left, his legs by turns buckling and locking" (28)—who speaks, in stuttering fashion, a language of terrific interruption: "'Every time Peter said a word, his father would boom him. At last Peter learned to say nothing. Ya ya ya. Thank you'" (24). Put another way, he has acquired the tongue of nothing. Indeed, he seems to personify the pallid, blue-tinged font that signals an inoperable internet link:

> Everything about Peter Stillman was white. White shirt, open at the neck; white pants, white shoes, white socks. Against the pallor of his skin, the flaxen thinness of his hair, the effect was almost transparent, as though one could see through to the blue veins behind the skin of his face. This blue was almost the same as the blue of his eyes: a milky blue that seemed to dissolve into a mixture of sky and clouds. (18)

Given that he hires Quinn to track down his father, this theologically fired blank figure would seem to point the reader/detective in the direction of a transcendent signified; however, he functions less like a modernist icon of redeeming dis-figurement and more like an anti-mimetic sign hovering at the limit of the figurable: "As their eyes met, Quinn suddenly felt that Stillman had become invisible. He could see him sitting in the chair across from him, but at the same time it felt as though he was not there" (18). In this regard, he might be said to resemble Wallace Stevens' snow man, who incarnates "The nothing that is not there and the nothing that is"(10). If he resembles anyone else it is Mr. White in *Ghosts*, the man who hires Blue to tail Black but appears to be a somewhat shady character himself: "And then there is the skin, which seems inordinately white, as though covered in powder. Blue is no amateur in the art of disguise, and it's not difficult for him to see through this one" (162). In Blue's case, it gets to the point where if White communicates with the detective at all it is only to fire off a letter rebuking Blue for leaving his post in an attempt to track White down at the post office: "No more funny business, it says, and though it's not much of a word, for all that Blue is glad to have received it, happy to have cracked White's wall of silence" (199). What are we to read in this White crack? Is it a wise crack? On the surface, it is a dead serious letter. "No more funny business" is White's way of saying, point blank, that Blue is not being tough enough (or man enough) in his work. In other words, White is saying that Blue is not being true blue to the case. According to this reading, the crack in "White's wall of silence" restates modernism's insistence on whiting out and walling off the personal, the contingent, the chancy, the whimsical, the fashionable. Read another way, though, the crack is a virtually wasted letter, "not much of a word" or not much of the Word. "No more funny business" might then stand as a cracked reminder of Blue's (and Quinn's) unbridgeable distance from an infinitely reserved *tout autre* described in equally faulty terms by Jabès: "*God is pronounced in the deafening violence of a white voice. In whiteness, as in the face of eternity, no saying holds up. Except the silence where all is said. Whiteness has swallowed the book*" (*Resemblances, Vol. 3* 43). God is a blank, whose Word is fired off only around back of modernist architecture's blank designs. As Jabès puts it: "What if white were only the mental distance we maintain between white and white, the insensible passage from accepted absence to unimaginable absence?" (*Resemblances, Vol. 3* 47).

In the end, Quinn avoids a disastrous final solution to his renunciatory practice of pursuing an "accepted absence" only by beginning to entertain "unimaginable absence." When he returns to his apartment after his unsuccessful stakeout, he encounters a new occupant, a woman "wearing a white nurse's uniform," who, shocked by his disheveled appearance, drops her grocery bag, from which "milk gurgle[s] in a white path toward the edge of the rug" (148). This milky way bears the trace of a forever inaccessible origin of plenitude (the primal nurse; the maternal breast) and sends Quinn staggering back to the apparent origin of his detective case, Peter Stillman, Jr.'s now evacuated residence. In this blank space, he once again removes all his clothes. This time, however, the act signifies a dawning awareness that his rage to close the book on the case has backfired. Like the author of *City of Glass*, Quinn occupies a minimalist premises in order to begin revising the plot of a self-consuming austerity: "In his heart, he realized that Max Work was dead" (153).

Perhaps, then, it is not quite by pure chance that, in the course of shedding this skin, he receives a gift of food which shows up from out of nowhere: "There was a tray of food beside him on the floor, the dishes steaming with what looked like a roast beef dinner. Quinn accepted this fact without protest. . . . There was a white linen napkin, and the silverware was of the finest quality" (153–54). By breaking his hardboiled fast, he becomes parasite to an absent host whose offering, framed by white linen, so exceeds expectations it can be only partially digested: "Quinn ate the food—or half of it, which was as much as he could manage" (154). On a site with nothing to it, he ruminates incompletely on an Other whose action at a distance—whose revelation through the refrain of   — also flares up back at the point where Quinn is recording the elder Stillman's peregrinations in the city. While faithfully performing the parasitical work of sticking to his mark, Quinn copies out this figure's errant routes on paper and thinks the resultant traces may add up to the phrase THE TOWER OF BABEL. After ruminating on this possibility, he is nearly convinced the marks add up to nothing—"It was all an accident, a hoax he had perpetuated on himself" (86)—until, on the edge of sleep, virtually wasted, he seems to catch a glimpse of virtual waste:

His last thought before he went to sleep was that he probably had two more days, since Stillman had not yet completed his message. The last two letters remained—the "E" and the "L." Quinn's mind dispersed. He arrived in a neverland of fragments, a place of wordless things and thingless words. Then, struggling through his torpor one last time, he told himself that El was the ancient Hebrew for God.

In his dream, which he later forgot, he found himself in the town dump of his childhood, sifting through a mountain of rubbish. (87)

CHAPTER THREE

(Mis)spelling Disaster:
Faith in *White Noise*

1. DIS-ASTROLOGIC

> disaster: 1. An unfavourable aspect of a star or planet; 'an obnoxious planet.' *Obs.* 2. Anything that befalls of ruinous or distressing nature; a sudden or great misfortune, mishap, or misadventure; a calamity. Usually with *a* and *pl.*, but also without a, as 'a record of disaster.' 2b. A bodily affliction or disorder. *Obs. rare.*
>
> *Oxford English Dictionary*

> The disaster: break with the star, break with every form of totality, never denying, however, the dialectical necessity of a fulfillment. . . . The disaster, touch of the powerless infinite: it does not come to pass under a sidereal sky, but here—a here in excess of all presence.
>
> Maurice Blanchot, *The Writing of the Disaster*

At one point in Don DeLillo's *White Noise*, the narrator, Jack Gladney, a professor of Hitler Studies at a sleepy midwestern college, believes he may have met with disaster. Fearing he has accidentally ingested some of the "toxic agents" released into the atmosphere over the town in which he lives, he reports his potential absorption of hazardous waste to authorities at the evacuation center to which his family has fled. A technician for SIMUVAC, an organization specializing in simulated evacuations, enters this information into a system and then describes the unsettling stellar simulation of his condition that appears on the screen: "'I tapped into your history. I'm getting bracketed numbers with pulsing stars'" (140). Yet the predictions based on this hi-tech constellation are inconclusive; the astrological report does not prove disaster has struck. Instead, the technician's blackly humorous assessment that "'we definitely have a situation'" actually serves as DeLillo's indirect diagnosis of a more indefinite disaster, a nebulous affliction that cannot simply be attributed to any case of waste consumption. The "pulsing stars" begin to spell out this more haunting disorder by reminding Gladney that death remains absolutely beyond his control despite his academic efforts to master it through study of a figure, Hitler, dedicated to total elimination of an other he considered waste. Put another way, death looms as a hazardous cloud of metaphysical waste resisting the most concerted efforts to absorb or disperse it. Like numerous other plots in this novel of middle class American domestic life, the computer's luminous pattern is designed to domesticate death by bringing it to light, by rendering it a "strictly professional matter" (74); however, the astral readout produces in Gladney the feeling that he cannot be at home with death: "It makes you feel like a stranger in your own dying" (142).

Marked by several fallouts, this scene suggests the possibility that in *White Noise* DeLillo is most concerned with trying to document a different kind of hazardous waste, a form of refuse whose composition can be provisionally analyzed by drawing on Blanchot's notion of "the disaster" of death. In a radically fragmented set of philosophical meditations titled *The Writing of the Disaster*, he struggles to inscribe death as a darkness on the edge of knowledge whose irreducible alterity challenges logocentric ideals of full illumination, total appropriation, pure presence: "The throes of death are thefts from unity, lost multitudes" (46). Death obeys a dis-astrous logic because it exceeds every systematic attempt to chart it, because it cannot be explained by reference to an unfavourable star or obnoxious planet, because it is approachable only *"as withdrawal outside the sidereal abode"* (133). Death cannot even be spelled out as a disastrous end to everything since the very statement "end to everything" reflects a desire to recuperate death as sheer loss or complete disaster. As Blanchot puts it: "There is, however, practically nothing disastrous in this disaster: this is surely what we must learn to think, without, perhaps, ever knowing it" (60). Death reduces philosophy to a shambles because it can be approached, insufficiently, only as what Blanchot calls "lost loss" or "expired meaning" (41). Ruining binary logic's devout wish to make of it a consummation, death is waste that cannot be properly treated as either the scene of total waste or as the scene of virtuous recovery. Death lays waste to every representation, simulation, or virtualization of its reality. It is disastrous because it "takes care of everything" (3). It wipes out totalizing thought's presumption that everything is assimilable. Death, in other words, is virtual waste. Put another way, death is a kind of white noise, a "percussive stillness" (49) haunting the houses of language and consciousness as "the repeated, motionless step of the speechless unknown, there at our door, on the threshold" (39).

In this context, I wish to read *White Noise* as a meditation on the importance of entertaining death's "absent meaning" (*Writing* 41) at a time when, according to Gladney, "The world is full of abandoned meanings" (184).[1] Like most of DeLillo's fiction, the novel addresses the fact that modern history is marked by disastrous schemes to colonize and/or purge otherness in the name of a waste-free state. This conviction partly informs a statement Gladney makes, not coincidentally, during one of his lectures on Nazi Germany: "'All plots tend to move deathward. This is the nature of plots'" (26). The aphorism suggests that all plots—political, psychological, religious, literary—court disaster insofar as they are spellbound by the final solution of achieving perfect unity and absolute closure. *White Noise* shows American consumer culture to be engaged in just this kind of plotting. The novel dramatizes the complex rites of eating and buying that define consumer culture in order to spell out how such rituals are governed by a misguided progressivist faith in the ability to achieve a transcendent, perfectly possessed, waste-free state of self-realization. DeLillo's characters are either stuffing themselves or starving themselves, stocking up or cutting back, all in an attempt to make death, as he puts it, "'less strange and unreferenced'" (229). Living in the desert of American excess, they alternately devour and purge what the culture has conveniently labeled waste in a soteriological effort to eliminate the virtual wastefulness of death's absent meaning. One of the remarkable moves the novel makes is to suggest that this evangelical strategy reenacts, in the relative safety of American prosperity, the horrific agenda of totalitarian plots to eliminate difference in the name of social fitness.

Since the narrative impulse is in part structured by a teleological drive to construct unified, masterful, clean and proper meaning, it may be true that "all plots tend to move deathward." However, some plots move deathward with a difference. *White Noise* dramatizes such an alternative movement. Plotwise, it fits the generic classification of a disaster novel only in part (section II, titled "The Airborne Toxic Event"), though even this subplot differs from a formulaic disaster novel because, as Gladney's encounter with SIMUVAC's star system indicates, the victims involved are "ambiguously death-sentenced" (146). For DeLillo, such ambiguity is due not only to the dubious effects of the toxic spill but also, more broadly, to the dubious nature of being. His novel illustrates that, despite scheming to do away with death in the name of self-presence, the self is always already put to death by the difference death makes. As Gladney puts it: "If the self is death, how can it also be stronger than death?" (268). Trying to write without the disaster genre's built-in expectation of disaster relief (relief from disaster and relief brought by the arrival of disaster), DeLillo nevertheless acknowledges what Blanchot refers to in the opening epigraph as "the dialectical necessity of fulfillment." To write a totally disastrous book would be to create a catastrophe (a word meaning both calamity and denouement) marked by careful plotting of the disaster's coordinates. In other words, the totally disastrous book assumes a full recovery of the disastrous. As such, it enacts a dialectical negation of death's negativity. To resist the spell of this totalizing imperative, DeLillo constructs *White Noise* as a shady counterplot. The novel appropriates, only to subvert, two plot structures typically dedicated to unity and closure: the disaster story (in which victims, causes, effects, and cures are *totally exposed*)[2]; the domestic story (in which characters, conflicts, and resolutions are *totally insulated*). Dramatizing Serres' point that in French *parasite* means both social sponge and communications interference, DeLillo feeds off of plots designed to cut out social, semantic, and epistemological static in order to program white noise without reducing it to a clear signal.

In this respect, *White Noise* does more than express what Jean-François Lyotard, in *The Postmodern Condition*, calls an "incredulity toward meta-narratives" (xxiv). The novel is something more than a critique of those plots characterized by a commitment to eliminate all heterogeneity in the name of the homogeneous. I argue that this literary counterplot represents a response to the following question, one raised directly at the end of the novel through the portrait of a nonbelieving nun: What remains of faith in the wake of efforts to eliminate the remainder? DeLillo addresses this question by proposing a different kind of faith in remains. Rejecting consumer culture's fetishism of waste as that which, when properly managed, insures salvation, he models a complex expression of what might (disastrously?) be called *waste respect*, a phrase in which "waste" is but one inadequate name for what is wholly Other, something so exceptional it persistently escapes onto-theological marketing as a stellar essence. For Blanchot, this nonto-talizable dis-aster is a necessarily improper name for God:

> I cannot welcome the Other, not even with an acceptance that would be infinite. Such is the new and difficult feature of the plot. The other, as neighbor, is the relation that I cannot sustain, and whose approach is death itself, the mortal proximity (he who sees God dies: for "dying" is one manner of seeing the invisible, of saying the ineffable. Dying is the indiscretion wherein God, become somehow and necessarily a god without truth, surrenders to passivity). (*Writing* 23)

In DeLillo's new and difficult domestic plot, the only responsible way to entertain the impossible neighbor described as "god without truth" is to try to entertain the notion that one always lives just on the brink of disaster. Anything but a gesture of resignation, such "surrender to passivity" is crucial because it challenges the repressive spell of totalizing thought, because it rejects the deadly promise of a fully present God and a fully self-present Self, because it treats with playful seriousness the vertiginous nature of existence. As one of the bursts of white noise in Gladney's home suggests: "'There are forms of vertigo that do not include spinning'" (56).

2. GARBAGE DISPOSAL

> Things had hardly changed at all. Only materials had changed, technologies; we were still the same nation of ascetics, efficiency experts, haters of waste. We have been redesigning our landscape all these years to cut out unneeded objects such as trees, mountains and all those buildings which do not make practical use of every inch of space. The ascetic hates waste. We plan the destruction of everything which does not serve the cause of efficiency. Hard to believe, he said, that we are ascetics. But we are, more than all the fake saints across the sea.

> Don DeLillo, *Americana*

> Waste is part of the rigorous administration of things which requires a certain slack. It is no longer a sign of failure, but a form of use whereby utility preserves itself by accommodating what is apparently of no use. Thus one cannot speak of loss "pure and simple." Or rather, one cannot speak of anything else, until loss, always inappropriate and impure, reverberates in language as that which never can be said . . .

> *The Writing of the Disaster*

White Noise (mis)spells disaster most imaginatively in those places where it represents modern America's complex conviction about the disastrous effects of waste. The novel is shot through with allusions to the various emissions, transmissions, additives, substitutes, and spinoffs on which critics of the American scene have seized when claiming that the national landscape has become a virtual wasteland. While DeLillo acknowledges the possibility that the products and byproducts of technological advance may make us more susceptible to physical ruin, he finds more disturbing the facile philosophical assumption that with "rigorous administration" of "what is apparently of no use" the infinite disaster of death-in-life can be avoided and lives saved. Paradoxically, he indicts contemporary culture for having too much faith in waste, for producing (or eliminating) waste as a useful sign of the useless. Commodifying waste as absolute negativity, postmodern culture inherits progressive culture's dialectical insistence that the negation (or elimination) of waste results in the realization of perfect positivity. According to this plot, refuse holds the promise of perfect re-fusal. As Gladney puts it: "What we are reluctant to touch often seems the very fabric of our salvation" (31).

To eliminate waste altogether—to express it as an identifiably improper other and then to dispose of it properly—would be to convert virtual waste into something other than untold disaster. DeLillo critiques the shallowness of this conversion logic by showing how both religious and secular versions of such a totalizing plot—through their insistence on absolute narrative closure—necessarily skirt life's inconceivable catastrophe. At the evacuation center, where the townspeople are seeking refuge from the toxic cloud, Gladney is confronted by a Jehovah's Witness who, trying to convert those in flight from toxic waste, confidently deciphers the spill as an apocalyptic sign that the kingdom of God is at hand for those who have learned to eliminate their own leaks: "'All the flashiness of Armageddon is in the rotting. The saved know each other by their neatness and reserve'" (136). The neat, reserved pose is reminiscent of the blank posture assumed by the naturalist cyberconsumer. In both cases, such an antipose or dis-pose is guided by a refusal to entertain disaster as radical epistemological decay, as the all-but-obliterated site where thought collapses: "Is this the point of Armageddon? No ambiguity, no more doubt" (137). Gladney calls into question this idealization of disaster—what Blanchot calls "destruction in view of possible construction" (*Writing* 119)—when he considers the statement made by his New Age ex-wife that we are now living in an "Age of Darkness": "How final is the Age of Darkness? Does it mean supreme destruction, a night that swallows existence so completely that I am cured of my own lonely dying?" (273). The prospect of total dissolution is actually a naively comforting solution since the presence of total darkness brings death out of the shadows. As Gladney's wife Babette quips: "'What is dark? It's just another name for light'" (301). Such an all-illuminating dark/light dichotomy excludes death's darkness, a different dark lit up only as that "which can never be said." In an earlier DeLillo novel, *Ratner's Star*, this nocturnal nothing elicits only a rhythmic cry:

> This was not just complete absence of light but a state of its own, the quality of authentic darkness, that aspect of nightlikeness which makes distinctions impossible. This dark had a special presence. It was far from empty. It was not just nonlight. It had a nature that dated back. . . . He began to wail then. (391)

White Noise illustrates how the spiritual longing to abolish death's darkness by eliminating waste informs the most secular rites of consumer culture. For instance, Babette uses the basement of a local church to teach a class on "correct posture"; the purpose is to facilitate (a)tonement by assuming a dis-pose free of the toxic slouch. Gladney makes literal the culture's belief in the redemptive power of refuse when he sifts through the family garbage looking for the discarded bottle of the drug that supposedly produces freedom from the fear of death. The novel pokes fun at these domestic designs on deliverance not only by having Gladney's own plot end in nothing more than near disaster (his nonfatal shooting of drug supplier Willie Mink) but also by frequently making children the most starry-eyed advocates of the domestic war on waste, adolescent administrators of the household scene. Just as Babette's daughter Denise stands guard over the trash compactor (or garbage disposal), "making sure the mangling din contained the correct sonic elements" (34), Gladney's son Heinrich criticizes his father for not being more efficient in the preparation of his coffee. The son's admonitions lead Gladney to inquire about the salvational benefits of reducing kinetic excess:

"What do you save if you don't waste?"

"Over a lifetime? You save tremendous amounts of time and energy," he said.

"What will you do with them?"

"Use them to live longer." (102)

It is no coincidence that this conversation about the virtues of a scientifically managed, Taylorized life takes place in the kitchen since, throughout the novel, the elimination of waste is intricately bound up with the problem of consumption. Frequently using the projection of a calamity, either in the air or on the air, as the haunting backdrop for a family meal, DeLillo joins anxiety about securing community and home as nonhazardous zones with anxiety about fashioning the body as a waste-free site, an innocent plot, a perfectly kept (up) property. By foregrounding food rituals in times of crisis, he raises the spectre of the ego's endless crisis of want. Indeed, *White Noise* might be said to participate in Auster's aesthetics of hunger since it portrays numerous characters literally and metaphorically starving to recover from the fact that, as Blanchot puts it, death leaves every subject beside itself, "a *subjectivity without any subject*: the wounded space, the hurt of the dying, the already dead body which no one could ever own, or ever say of it, I, *my body*" (*Writing* 30). Contemporary culture's belief that this wound of self-difference can be healed through progressive-style management of food intake explains why Babette also volunteers to teach a class called "'Eating and Drinking: Basic Parameters'" (171) or why the "life after death" tabloid article she reads aloud at the evacuation center (escaping dis-aster by reciting *The Star*?!) claims that those who have successfully regressed to previous lives work as "'food stylists for NASA'" (143). When Gladney responds to the approach of the "airborne toxic event" by asking "'When do we eat?'" (113), he articulates the naive faith that consumption will save us from the disaster of death-in-life by enabling us to ruminate (on) the other properly.

Despite having access to the luxuries of American consumer culture, DeLillo's characters still approach consumption as a life and death matter since consumption raises the issue of how to live with the difference death makes. Faced with the ineffectiveness, irrelevance, and terror marking other death-defying systems—medical technology, anemic Christianity,

Nazi Germany—they try to minimize death's catastrophe by adopting postures of self-denial. Like "Advance Disaster Management," the private con-
sulting firm which carries out simulated evacuations in the community,
Gladney and others attempt to avoid disaster through elaborate rituals of
voidance. They seek to overcome the infirmity of death by making themselves firm through puritanical regimens. They plot strategies of purgation,
reduction, and abstention in an effort to transform the self into what
Heinrich calls "the total package," self-realized Being unafflicted by death's
absent presence. However, these renunciatory practices inevitably turn out
to be no more than simulated evacuation procedures or virtual dis-posals
since all efforts at managing death's "real" disaster are bound to fail, disaster being (and yet not *being*), according to Blanchot, an uncon-firmable
reality to which there is no adequate response: "[T]he impossible real, that
share of disaster wherein every reality, safe and sound, sinks" (*Writing* 38).

Babette is one of the figures who tries to cope with (death's) disaster by
disposing of waste in her life. She treats the family's forced evacuation due
to the "dense concentrations of byproduct" (138) in the atmosphere as an
opportunity to follow through on her plot to eliminate all compromising
byproducts from her diet. Her survival kit includes "snack thins" and other
foodstuffs that produce no flabby fallout: "'I thought this would be a good
time to cut down on fatty things. . . . This is a time for discipline, mental
toughness. We're practically at the edge'" (132). Likewise, Gladney, convinced that "Death has entered" as a result of his possible consumption of
toxic waste, responds by undertaking a frenzied ritual of housecleaning:

> The more things I threw away the more I found. . . . There was an immen-
> sity of things, an overburdening weight, a connection, a mortality. I
> stalked the rooms, flinging things into cardboard boxes. Plastic electric
> fans, burnt-out toasters, *Star Trek* needlepoints. It took well over an hour
> to get everything down to the sidewalk. No one helped me. I didn't want
> help or company or human understanding. I just wanted to get the stuff
> out of the house. (262)

By disposing of the *Star Trek* needlepoints, Gladney only reveals how
bound he is to the astrologic of dialectical thinking. He tries to rid himself
of every sidereal enterprise in order to realize minimalism's aesthetic ideal
of the empty plot or white wall, the final frontier of pure space where the self
is transported from its fallen state.[3] As he puts it: "Let the days be aimless.
Let the seasons drift. Do not advance the action according to a plan" (98).

The family practices a collective version of such self-purification when it
votes unanimously not to let neighbors come over to the house: "'Just keep
them out of here'" (43). By making themselves collectively indisposed, the
family poses as a waste-free unit. It aspires to be a hermetic organism
sealed off from any foreign influence, like the family seen walking togeth-

er during the evacuation "wrapped completely in plastic, a single large sheet of transparent polyethylene" (121). Just as Bernarr Macfadden's display of the physical culture hardbody bears a trace of the racist desire to protect Anglo-Saxon culture against immigrant influx, the family's display of an impenetrable domestic homebody bears a trace of the fascist crowds on which Gladney lectures, those firm columns of Nazi troops that embody the total(itarian) package in order to "'form a shield against their own dying'" (73). Yet the family's supposedly closed system turns out to be open-ended since estranged relatives—outsiders who are also insiders—are always showing up within the nuclear plot to destabilize the boundaries of the family's proper identity. And in a wonderfully ironic twist, one of the figures, Babette's father Vernon Dickey, is someone Gladney initially mistakes, in a predawn fantasy, for death itself.

An equally unsuccessful and potentially disastrous cultural plot is the scheme to eliminate death's virtual wastefulness by means of hyperconsumption. When not participating in rituals of evacuation or exclusion, the characters in *White Noise* engage in acts of manic incorporation. In Gladney's words: "When times are bad, people feel compelled to overeat" (14). On being reminded by a colleague of his fundamental infirmity and incompleteness—"'You're a different person altogether. . . . A big, harmless, aging, indistinct sort of guy'" (83)—Gladney goes on a shopping spree, seeking to acquire "endless well-being" in a frenzy of material consumption. Heinrich's friend Orest Mercator prepares to break the world record for time spent confined with poisonous snakes by both purging and binging. Hoping that the confinement will enable him to "dwell in some angelic scan, able to leap free of everyday dying" (267), he adopts austerities reminiscent of those undertaken by Auster's detective when confined to a stakeout in *City of Glass*. Gearing up to face the snakes in the minimalist space of a "glass cage," he strives to become a still man: "'He's down to two meals a day. He sleeps sitting up, two hours at a time'" (182). And just as Quinn trains for his max work by devouring pulp fiction, Mercator trains for his feat by cramming himself full of carbohydrates, by "loading up, centering himself" (265).[4]

DeLillo's awareness of the ascetic impulse behind hyperconsumption is perhaps made most explicit in his description of the character Bloomberg in the novel *End Zone*. A Jewish left tackle at a small college in Texas who participates in football's rituals of self-denial in an effort to "unjew" himself, Bloomberg tries to starve himself down to a magical playing weight. Yet, as the equally ascetic narrator of the novel suggests, Bloomberg might be able to pursue his dream of self-negation—his desire to exist "beyond guilt, beyond blood, beyond the ridiculous past" (77)—just as well by capitalizing on, even expanding on, his size:

To weigh three hundred pounds. What devout vulgarity. It seemed a worthwhile goal for prospective saints and flagellants. The new asceticism. All the visionary possibilities of the fast. To feed on the plants and animals of the earth. To expand and wallow. I cherished his size, the formlessness of it, the sheer vulgar pleasure, his sense of being overwritten prose. Somehow it was the opposite of death. (49)

Anticipating Mark Leyner's surrealist vision of a physically enormous celebrity author who lets no opportunity for profit go to waste (see Chapter Four), this fantasy about the bulky Jewish ballplayer articulates consumer culture's expectation that relentless consumption promises a way out of exile in the desert and into the end zone of the kingdom.

While many of these hungry efforts to ward off death through hyper-consumption come across as quaintly ineffective, other scenes of excess consumption in *White Noise*—Willie Mink popping Dylar pills "'like candy'" (308); the German teacher Howard Dunlop hoarding in his apartment "items scavenged from the ravine" (173)—carry more unsavory overtones. At the end of the novel, Gladney, having botched the plot to escape his own mortality by committing murder, briefly experiences a rage to introject waste. He convinces himself that his redemption lies in rescuing the man he has just shot, the wounded, wasted figure of Willie Mink. In effect, he strives to dispatch the other by taking it in rather than doing it in: "Get past disgust. Forgive the foul body. Embrace it whole" (314). Yet this prescription for inclusiveness proves to be no more effective than his friend Murray Siskind's pseudo-intellectual mantra for eliminating difference: "'Kill to live'" (291). In the novel's most incisive critique of the dream of total introjection, DeLillo outlines a scientific proposal for cleaning up the airborne toxic event that entails swallowing up the hazardous waste. A rumor spreads among the refugees from the spill that the contaminated material in the atmosphere might be eliminated by dropping into the black mass genetically engineered microorganisms with "a built-in appetite for the particular toxic agents in Nyodene D. They would literally consume the billowing cloud, eat it up, break it down, decompose it" (160). However, as Gladney points out, this imperialist techno-fantasy of subduing a dark other by thoroughly assimilating it has its own dangers: "No one knew what would happen to the toxic waste once it was eaten or to the microorganisms once they were finished eating" (160). Regardless how stellar, the plot to realize total domination or absolute mastery of the other always bears traces of the disastrous.

If DeLillo is telling us that even the neatest geographical, technological, and philosophical plots can prove to be deadly, what kind of plot are we to believe in? Is there another kind of plot available, or is every plot a shitty plot? Perhaps plots geared toward the elimination of waste are not shitty enough. What would a really shitty plot look like? Would it involve approaching the sacred?

3. VOID WHERE PROHIBITED

There was something about waste material that defied systematic naming.

Ratner's Star

I marched a bit longer. Then I saw something that terrified me. I stood absolutely still, as if motion might impede my understanding of this moment. It was three yards in front of me, excrement, a low mound of it, simple shit, nothing more, yet strange and vile in this wilderness, perhaps the one thing that did not betray its definition. I tried not to look any longer. I held my breath, fearing whatever smell might still be clinging to that spot. I wanted my senses to deny this experience, leaving it for wind and dust. There was the graven art of a curse in that sight. It was over-whelming, a terminal act, nullity in the very word, shit, as of dogs squat-ting near partly eaten bodies, rot repeating itself; defecation, as of old women in nursing homes fouling their beds; feces, as of specimen, sample, analysis, diagnosis, bleak assessments of disease in the bowels; dung, as of dry straw, erupting with microscopic eggs; excrement, as of final matter voided, the chemical stink of self discontinued; offal, as of butchered ani-mals' intestines slick with shit and blood, shit everywhere, shit in the life cycle, shit as earth as food as shit, wise men sitting impassively in shit, holy men praying to shit, scientists tasting it, volumes to be compiled on color and texture and scent, shit's infinite treachery, everywhere this whis-per of inexistence.

End Zone

Beyond the Logos College gridiron, in the void of the Texas desert, the half-back approaches an awful secret(ion). An aspiring ascetic, he has enrolled on the desert campus to redeem himself—to escape his checkered past—by fully submitting to the demands of the game and the place: "And it would be all work, pain, fury, sweat. No time for nonessential things. We would deny ourselves. We would get right down to the bottom of it. We would find out how much we could take. We would learn the secrets" (*End Zone* 237). Master the system, punish the flesh, kill the clock. The religion of football. Finding the end zone means eliminating the waste of time altogether. It means running an end around (on) death.

And yet . . . on the outskirts of Logos some untreated waste. Out of the body's end zone, a trace of the void. If death is the void where thought is prohibited, excrement is the voided matter that prohibits avoiding death altogether. Defecation as near disaster, as virtual waste: "Then I saw some-thing that terrified me." Fearful and trembling, the narrator experiences a kind of shit fit. He spits out a fitful, logorrheic response that shows shit to be slippery stuff. Infinitely treacherous, it can't be tackled cleanly. Like food, it moves across the body's borders, destabilizing the boundaries of identity. In *Powers of Horror*, Kristeva describes how shit constantly threatens to de-compose the subject and so has to be classified as hazardous waste, a dangerous other which the upstanding self must avoid if it wants to maintain its composure: "Fecal matter signifies, as it were, what never ceases to separate from a body in a state of permanent loss in order to become *autonomous, distinct* from the mixtures, alterations, and decay that run through it. That is the price the body must pay if it is to become *clean and proper*" (108). Ritually constructed as a dirty, de-filing difference, shit happens (into focus) as a vision of horror: "There was the graven art of a curse in that sight."

However, as DeLillo's meditation on *merde* indicates, shit's spell doesn't end there. In Kristeva's psychoanalytic reading of the matter, the refusal of bodily refuse reenacts the child's painful separation from its *mater*, a once-familiar but now-forgotten maternal presence from which the subject has had to split, in a time before language, in order to begin distinguishing itself as an other:

> Psychoanalysis has indeed seen that anal dejections constitute the first material separation that is controllable by the human being. It has also deciphered, in that very rejection, the mastered repetition of a more archaic separation (from the maternal body) as well as the condition of division (high-low), of discretion, of difference, of recurrence, in short of the condition of the processes that underpin symbolicity. (108)

Neither simply a continuation of self nor simply "the chemical stink of self discontinued," excrement is a spoor of the repressed M-Other. This shit haunts the split subject by eliciting "depraved desire" (73) for a perfect reunion with the "abject," depraved because the reunion can only be organized at the expense of life itself. Longing to escape life's disaster by dying out of a condition of loss, longing to hark back to a lost garden, Gary Harkness, DeLillo's desert wanderer, thus happens on shit as a "whisper of inexistence," a form of white noise which puts him in a double bind by bearing the alluring yet unbearable mark of death, of God, of the death of God. Holy shit!

Kristeva draws out this link between shit and the sacred by making a connection between the individual subject's phobic relationship to waste and society's phobic relationship to waste. Borrowing from Mary Douglas, she finds collective phobia made manifest in rites of defilement and purification practiced by every religion. Borrowing from Freud, she then interrogates this universal phenomenon in light of the critical role the incest taboo plays in structuring religious thought. For Kristeva, the "simple logic of *excluding filth*" is a response to fear of social disorder or chaos that is traceable in turn to a fear of the primordial mother, a fear (mis)spelled as the dread of incest: "[Incest prohibition] cuts short the temptation to return, with abjection and jouissance, to that passivity status within the symbolic function, where the subject, fluctuating between inside and outside, pleasure and pain, word and deed, would find death, along with nirvana" (63–64). Put another way, ritual demonization of the impure and the unclean dramatize a plot carried out against a fugitive "feminine threat" in the name of ontological and theological unity: "In other words, the place and law of the One do not exist without a series of separations that are oral, corporeal, and even more generally material, and in the last analysis relating to fusion with the mother" (94).

Kristeva suggests that in archaic cultures, where the monological Law of the Father has not yet been set in stone, the subject's residual fascination with this prohibited maternal void receives greater expression. Treating waste as a blessing as well as curse, archaic ritual lends it the ambivalent charge of the sacred: "The purification rite appears then as that essential ridge, which, prohibiting the filthy object, extracts it from the secular order and lines it at once with a sacred facet" (65). DeLillo works to reenact this 'primitive' entertainment of waste's double bind by acknowledging the extent to which prohibited matter bears traces of a radically ambiguous, deathly, divine Otherness. Take, for example, Gladney's excursus on his excrement, the shit he has to offer up at his health check: "Alone in the glove compartment rode an ominous plastic locket, which I'd reverently enclosed in three interlocking Baggies, successively twist-tied. Here was a daub of the most solemn waste of all, certain to be looked upon by the technicians on duty with the mingled deference, awe, and dread we have come to associate with exotic religions of the world" (275). Shit is the trace of a dis-aster more dreadful than the "nebulous mass" Gladney may or may not have developed in his system as a result of exposure to toxic waste. It poses an untreatable threat both to clean and proper identity and to the clean and proper authority of modern medicine, authority built, in DeLillo's mind, on phallic confidence in perfect mastery: "Your doctor knows the symbols" (281).

Like DeLillo's desert droppings in *End Zone*, the sacred haunts the margins of every logocentric plot. In his anthropological study *Violence and the Sacred*, René Girard argues that the sacred is assigned a geographically marginal position in so-called primitive cultures because it is identical to violence, a force which presents a threat to order and yet a force which, when harnessed properly, insures the preservation of order:

> The complex and delicate nature of the community's dealings with the sacred, the ceaseless effort to arrive at the ordered and uninterrupted accord essential to the well-being of the community, can only be expressed, for want of the naked truth, in terms of optimum *distance*. If the community comes too near the sacred it risks being devoured by it; if, on the other hand, the community drifts too far away, out of range of the

sacred's therapeutic threats and warnings, the effects of its fecund presence are lost. (268)

Destructive and creative, devouring and fecund, Girard's sacred violence
recalls Kristeva's maternal "pseudo-object." In its struggle to establish a
proximate distance to and from violence, the archaic society recapitulates
the individual subject's struggle to maintain a proximate distance to and
from a (M)other capable of violence. For as Mark Taylor puts it: "A mother's love, after all, can s-mother. The nourishing breast of the mother sometimes appears to be a devouring b(r)east. Milk can make one gag, even
vomit" (*Altarity* 164).

Streams of white rage. Streams of white milk. Streams of white noise.
Girard draws a connection between sacred flows and the seemingly profane
flows generated by modern techno-culture when he points out that in
numerous African societies the metal worker is a sacred figure, one whose
technological products are acknowledged to be instruments of violence
capable of both protecting concerns and wreaking havoc: "For better or for
worse, the metal worker is the master of a potent form of violence. That is
why he is 'sacred' in the dual sense of the word. He enjoys certain privileges but is considered a slightly sinister figure. He is someone to be avoided; and his forge is relegated to the outskirts of the community" (260–61).
Touching on issues important to DeLillo, Girard intimates that in
'advanced' cultures this always fragile psychological and spatial arrange-
ment threatens to collapse. Specifically, he claims that our worship of technology causes us to forsake the quest for optimum spacing *vis-à-vis* the
smithy and therefore to invite disaster: "The specters of nuclear warfare
and industrial pollution that menace our society constitute only one illustration—admittedly a dramatic one—of a law that primitive people regard
as real even if they do not entirely understand it but that we dismiss as fic-
titious: whoever uses violence will in turn be used by it" (261). DeLillo
records this imminent collapse in *White Noise* by calling his fictional town
Blacksmith, a name that illustrates the extent to which the forge has moved
in from the outskirts to become synonymous with the community itself.
The novel's spectre of industrial pollution thus functions as both a literal
and figurative manifestation of what Girard calls "impure violence."

According to Girard, primitive cultures combat the sacred's hazardous
spill into community through the practice of sacrifice, an expression of
violence that serves to check the toxic spirit of vengeance: "The function
of ritual is to 'purify' violence; that is, to trick violence into spending itself
on victims whose death will provoke no reprisals" (36). Put another way,
the social body is restored to health by simulating disaster: "[The] act is
a simulated performance designed to offer a substitute satisfaction." (201).
Unlike the SIMUVAC simulations in *White Noise*—the data displays
and evacuation drills designed to reduce waste by reducing disaster to star-

studded codes—sacrificial simulation is designed to entertain waste by dramatizing violence as something other than a purely negative force. Whereas SIMUVAC's plots move deathward in a sinister way by trying to bind death to a binary system, the sacrificial plot moves deathward with a difference by cutting death loose, staging, on the altar, a life-giving death, the product of what Girard terms "regenerative violence." SIMUVAC represents an unhappy postmodern alternative to sacrifice because its mission simulates what Kristeva calls "a religion of abomination," a belief system geared to diminishing the sacredness of death by subjugating it to the stellar presence of "the One" (Meaning, Identity, God):

> A religion of abomination overlays a religion of the sacred. It marks the exit of religion and the unfolding of morals; or leading back the One that separates and unifies, not to the fascinated contemplation of the sacred, from which it separates, but to the very device that it ushers in: logic, abstraction, rules of systems and judgments. . . . It tempers the fascination of murder; it gets around its desire by means of the abomination it associates with any act of incorporation and rejection of an ob-ject, thing or living being. (111)

DeLillo recognizes that many secular acts of "incorporation and rejection" are governed by the same disastrous drive to abominate or *lay waste to* the sacred. Nevertheless, he insists "fascinated contemplation of the sacred" is not dead in contemporary culture. Indeed, he uses the altar of television to stage acts of sacrificial simulation. An example is the family's contemplation of disaster footage. During "Friday assembly"—a ritual meal consumed in front of the television—the family becomes transfixed by scenes of catastrophe:

> There were floods, earthquakes, mud slides, erupting volcanoes. We'd never before been so attentive to our duty, our Friday assembly. . . . Babette tried to switch to a comedy series about a group of racially mixed kids who build their own communications satellite. She was startled by the force of our objection. We were otherwise silent, watching houses slide into the ocean, whole villages crackle and ignite in a mass of advancing lava. Every disaster made us wish for more, for something bigger, grander, more sweeping. (64)

In one respect, these images are linked to the sacred because they highlight the limitations of technology. As Girard puts it: "The sacred consists of all those forces whose dominance over man increases or seems to increase in proportion to man's effort to master them. Tempests, forest fires, and plagues, among other phenomena, may be classified as sacred" (31). In another respect, the images are linked to the sacred because they highlight the limitations of both spectacle and speculation. The family is aware there remains something just hidden from view, something flickering at the horizon of the conceivable, "something bigger, grander, more sweeping." The electronic spectacle of violence does serve as a kind of sacrificial event binding members of the clan together in a rite of regenerative viewing; the family rejects the phony responsibilities of political correctness, choosing instead to gather in awe ("We'd never before been so attentive to our duty") before an altar (the tube) on which death is being fed. Yet the reel disasters disappoint, even as they inspire, because, they point toward a "real" disaster that, like the messiah, is forever still to come: "The disappointment of the disaster: not answering to expectations, not allowing the point to be made or the appointed sum to be paid in full—foreign to orientation, even to orientation as disorientation or simple straying" (*Writing* 48). Though "whole villages crackle and ignite" with apocalyptic intensity, the conflagration is not all consuming. Something is left over from the fire . . . ambivalent remains . . . sacred ashes. In the failing light of these imperceptible embers, it makes sense that in the story the narrator's first flirtation with the disaster of his death occurs while he and Babette (who has just finished exercising or 'going for the burn') embrace on a ground of scorched matter: "I held her in my arms on the cinder track" (14).

A text whose narrator is haunted by the figure of Hitler, *White Noise* addresses the question: What remains (of the) sacred after the Holocaust? It does so by sifting through ashes for the sacred remainder of the holocaust: "holocaust *n* 1: a burnt sacrifice: a sacrificial offering wholly consumed by fire 2: a complete or thorough sacrifice or destruction esp. by fire" (*Webster's*). Constantly aware of the charred, friable nature of language, DeLillo strives to ignite what Derrida refers to as "*a holocaust of the holocaust,*" (*Cinders* 48) a retreating blaze or backfire that is nevertheless immeasurably intense because it puts logocentrism's enthrallment with the "all" *at stake*: "In this sacrifice, all (holos) is burned (caustos), and the fire can go out only stoked" (*Cinders* 46). One way DeLillo tends to the "*all-burning*" but ever-extinguished scoria of the sacred is by staging a fire in Blacksmith. Crowds gather to watch the local insane asylum go up in flames. The fire is treated in ceremonial fashion—"The great work of containing the blaze went on, a labor that seemed as old and lost as cathedral-building . . ." (240)—and includes a contemporary version of a sacrificial victim: "A woman in a fiery nightgown walked across the lawn. We gasped, almost in appreciation. She was white-haired and slight, fringed in burning air, and we could see she was mad, so lost to dreams and furies that the fire around her head seemed almost incidental. No one said a word" (239). The madwoman resembles the traditional scapegoats of ancient sacrifice (children, misfits, criminals, slaves, livestock) in that she is a marginal figure—in Girard's words "a monstrous double"—whose relationship to the community proper, like shit's relationship to the self, is marked by continuity and discontinuity (the asylum is nestled in a shady residential street). She is a latter day *pharmakos*, a figure "fringed" with an aura of the sacred by virtue of being both poison and antidote, both a symbol of impurity threatening the health of the social body proper and a force of decontamination whose sacrifice purges the social body of toxins. As Derrida puts it: "The origin of difference and division, the *pharmakos* represents evil both introjected and projected. Beneficial insofar as [s]he cures—and for that, venerated and cared for—harmful insofar as [s]he incarnates the powers of evil—and for that feared and treated with caution" ("Plato's Pharmacy" 133).

For DeLillo, the spectacle of combustion has the quality of an "ancient, spacious, and terrible drama" not only because it dramatizes a watered-down version of ancient sacrifice but also because it recapitulates the darkly dazzling backfire of the maternal abject. The blaze astonishes because it produces a profoundly ambivalent reaction, its sweetly resinous odor of "smoke and charred stone" mixing with a "sharp and bitter stink" (240). Given the strength of this double bind, is it any accident that, unable to stomach this primal scene any longer, Gladney and Heinrich return home to discuss "the noise of the conflagration" over "warm milk" (241)? By burning the *insense[é]* (Fr. insane person, madwoman, maniac), by lighting the incense of the *insenseé*, DeLillo offers up a reminder of an ineffable feminine power that elicits a blend of attraction and repulsion: "We gasped, almost in appreciation. . . . No one said a word." Like Peter Stillman, Jr., the ghostly, white-outfitted, deranged speaker of "'numb noise'" who is released from his father's crazed theological experiment by means of a conflagration, the immolated madwoman is a spectral embodiment of the (M)Other's milky white noise: "She went down in a white burst." Ultimately, DeLillo's fiery scenes of destruction on TV and in the community show him to be engaged in a practice Derrida labels "pyrotechnical writing." Just as the novelist adopts a disaster narrative in order to investigate the (un)real disaster invariably left out of the genre's speculations on catastrophe, he sets fires in his narrative in order to inspect unrecognizable ruins blanketed by the all-consuming fires of speculative philosophy: "Pyrotechnical writing feigns abandoning everything to what goes up in smoke, leaving there only cinder that does not remain" (*Cinders* 61).

Death . . . Disaster . . . Remainder . . . Cinder . . . (M)Other . . . These various (mis)spellings of virtual waste overlap in a vertiginous scene in which Babette suddenly appears to Gladney on television teaching her class on posture. In other words, she appears on the same altar where the family has witnessed natural disaster:

> A strangeness gripped me, a sense of psychic disorientation. . . . It was but wasn't her. . . . Waves and radiation. Something leaked through the mesh . . . . The kids were flushed with excitement but I felt a certain disquiet. I

> tried to tell myself it was only television—whatever that was, however it
> worked—and not some journey out of life or death, not some mysterious
> separation. (104–05)

It was but wasn't her. Present as virtual absence, the (un)familiar mother is
an eerie reminder of the "mysterious separation" the individual subject
undergoes even before it gets fashioned, according to the law of monolo-
gism, as an autonomous, self-present ego subject to an autonomous, self-
present God. Sharing the screen with catastrophe, challenging the most
basic oppositions (self/other; life/death; reality/appearance; inside/outside;
intimate/alien) that set up the "mesh" of phallogocentric culture, Babette's
uncanny image provides a glimpse into the prohibited void of an archaic
feminine power. Like DeLillo, Gladney refuses to censure completely the
awful subject matter of the *mater* even as he registers his impulse to abject
it, to trash it as being "only television." He thus experiences this deathly
program, this *mummy* show—"There was no sound, no voice, nothing"
(105)—as a blast from an unimaginable past that sends him reeling toward
the edge of an abyss marking the very limits of language, knowledge, being:
"A two-syllable infantile cry, *ba-ba*, issued from the deeps of my soul"
(104). Heard elsewhere in the novel as Wilder's "huge lament"—the
Gladney toddler's long, inexplicable fit which includes his "crying out,
saying nameless things" and ends with his consuming a glass of milk in
a "single powerful swallow"—this wail confirms Kristeva's assessment
that "narrative yields to a *crying-out theme* . . . when it tends to coin-
cide with the incandescent states of a boundary-subjectivity that I have
called abjection . . ." (141).

   If the phantasmagoric image that prompts Gladney to cry out stands in
for the sacred, it also stands in for writing, appearing as it does "in black
and white, framed in formal borders" (104). Babette's abject projection
and the babble it elicits suggest writing itself may assume the status of the
sacred in contemporary culture insofar as it calls attention to modernity's
"Crisis of the Word" (Kristeva 208). On one hand, these babblings express
the instability of the signifying process. Like Auster's glassy prose, they are
slippery reminders that language and subjectivity are always already ravaged by want. On the other hand, they expose the mechanisms of patri-
archical repression at work in every plot—be it political, psychological,
fictional, or religious—geared toward the establishment of Meaning and
Identity. DeLillo fits Mark Taylor's definition of the modern writer in that
he scavenges from the secularized realm of mass media in order to explore
essentially religious crises: "In the absence of religious rites, the w-rite-r
becomes the high priest who undertakes the impossible task of writing the
unnameable" (*Altarity* 178). While DeLillo is a literary plotter always sen-
sitive to his own complicity in the scheme to dispose of difference, his sustained inquiry into what inevitably gets covered up by plots shows him to

be someone who believes the death of God is not a disaster, or, rather, someone who believes God to be a most imaginative way of (mis)spelling death's disaster. He approaches his fiction as a sacrificial act of generative violence in which meaning is *cut open* to provide a blinding glimpse of God as virtual waste. His writing functions as a ritual of destruction/creation designed to honor what (dis)appears in the babble: "This is what we bring to the temple, not prayer or chant or slaughtered rams. Our offering is language" (*The Names* 331).

The media-generated bursts of white noise interrupting the narrative of *White Noise* are particularly striking examples of this kind of offering. Originating just as often from an unspecified source as from what Gladney at one point calls "[t]he voice upstairs" (226), these (a)theological traces are profoundly ambiguous. In one respect, they appear to be radically decontextualized fragments of language whose significance has been lost. They come across as sheer detritus of the information age. There would seem to be no virtue to them. However, a number of them present the teasing possibility of being more than merely electronic dead letters. They almost seem to be encrypted transmissions conveying some crucial message about the risks and rewards associated with consumption: "'This creature has developed a complicated stomach in keeping with its leafy diet'" (95); "Lead, unleaded, super unleaded" (199); "'A California think tank says the next world war may be fought over salt'" (226); "Clorets, Velamints, Freedent" (229); "'Excesses of salt, phosphorous, magnesium'" (236); "'The pet under stress may need a prescription diet'" (307). Falling somewhere between the operative and the inoperative, between sense and nonsense, between speech and silence, this noise is narrative virtual waste, hazardous to the system because it carries the death of Meaning. Such techno-babble is the linguistic equivalent of Bartleby the scrivener. Dispatched from no traceable (employment) agency, it occupies the legal premises of the narrative and yet prefers not to do the work of dispatching significance. The pithy, paratactical scraps break in on and break open the narrative. They bear witness to an aphoristic sensibility at play in much of the novel. As Norman O. Brown indicates, aphorism tries to spell out what is excommunicated by systematic thought. It is a superabundance edged by incompletion, a life edged by death: "Aphoristic form is suicide, or self-sacrifice; for truth must die . . . . Systematic form attempts to evade the necessity of death in the life of the mind and the body; it has immortal longings on it, and so it remains dead" (187–88). Like disaster footage, the sacrificial language of aphorism disappoints those with "immortal longings," those convinced a "voice or noise would crack across the sky and we would be lifted out of death" (*White Noise* 234).[5] Crucial to his darkly comic vision, DeLillo's white noise is not simply a series of authorial wisecracks aimed at the excesses of late capitalist culture. More than anything else, it is a series of cracks in the text signaling what Kristeva calls "a laughing apocalypse . . . an apocalypse without God. Black mysticism of transcendental collapse" (206).

The black mysticism of white noise. Composed in these very different black and white terms, DeLillo's novel represents what might be called *nebular writing*: "**nebula**: [fr. L, mist, cloud] **1 a** : any of many immense bodies of highly rarified gas or dust in the interstellar space of our own Milky Way and other galaxies that when located in our own Milky Way may by absorption of light from objects farther away be observed as a dark cloud or may by reflection or reemission of light from associated nearby stars be observed as a bright cloud **b** : galaxy; specif. : a galaxy outside the Milky Way galaxy **2** : a white spot or a slight opacity of the cornea **3** : a liquid preparation intended for medicinal spraying" (*Webster's*). Neither intrinsically dark nor light, black nor white, nebular writing offers an imperfect antidote to the spell of transcendental signification by calling attention to the white spots occluding every perception, to the white noise distorting every communication. Nebular writing offers a subversive alternative to what the author, in his novel *Ratner's Star*, calls "interstellar vocabulary" or "cosmic discourse," an abstract medium purged of semantic excess being developed by fictional scientists hoping to decipher the origin and meaning of a cryptic signal, apparently from outer space: "'Think of it. A transgalactic language. Pure and perfect mathematical logic. A means of speaking to the universe'" (274). Called Logicon, this imaginary language expresses the logocentric fantasy of waste-free transmission. No wonder, then, that the obscure source of the message gets spelled out with the help of an acronymic allusion to the anal: "'And let's find a more precise name for the so-called beings who are presumed to have initiated the transmission. How about 'artificial radio source extants'? ARS extants. Just so we know what's what'" (274). Holed up underground, the mathematicians and astronomers in *Ratner's Star* are techno-ascetics frustrated in their efforts to crack the code by tracing excremental extraterrestrials back to some cosmic end zone. DeLillo is rightfully suspicious of such a project, and he playfully suggests that the message may have originated from a cosmic disaster zone called a mohole. Neither bright star nor black hole, neither matter nor anti-matter, a mohole is a nebular near vacuum which ironically only serves to amplify the noise of language:

> Incidentally it's no good trying to visualize a mohole. I've already tried and it can't be done. Nobody knows what it looks like because it doesn't look like anything. And we can't pinpoint its location because it seems to have many locations—another way of saying there are moholes numbering n—and they all seem to shift, affecting different parts of the computer universe for varying amounts of time. The sum total of all moholes is what I call the value-dark dimension. All the key words in this explanation, by the way, are totally misleading due to the everyday quirks of language. (180–81)

Like death, the mohole is value dark. Like the primordial partial-object called mother, the mohole is a starless Milky Way. Through such nebulous articulation of the holeyest of holes, DeLillo undertakes the hazardous task of having faith in virtual waste.

4. TRASH RECOLLECTION

The babbling book. Nebular writing. Is there any virtue in all of this? Is such discourse at best forgettable, at worst irresponsible? Or is it somehow a responsible response to the issue of forgetting? Is it possible that *White Noise* represents the most responsible kind of writing precisely because it treats forgetting seriously?

In fact, the novel is preoccupied with the problem of forgetfulness.[6] Characters continually express fear that they are forgetting, will forget, or can't forget. Gladney, attempting to alleviate Babette's worries about her tendency to forget, says: "'Forgetfulness has gotten into the air and water. It's entered the food chain'" (52). Forgetfulness, in other words, is a particularly hazardous form of waste, one to which we are forever exposed no matter how ascetic our lifestyle, yet one that cannot even guarantee the disastrous relief of total oblivion. The relief forgetfulness cannot guarantee is relief from the knowledge that, before we know it, we die. Babette takes Dylar because it is supposed to repress the fear of death. It is supposed to make her forget what she is unsuccessfully trying to forget through forgetfulness: "'Mr. Gray said my loss of memory is a desperate attempt to counteract my fear of death. It's like a war of neurons. I am able to forget many things but I fail when it comes to death'" (202). A drug for forgetting death can't work since, paradoxically, death is bound up with a supplementary forgetting which renders inadequate the distinction between the remembered and the forgotten. As Blanchot puts it: "Inoperative forgetfulness, forever idled, which is nothing and does nothing (and which not even dying would reach): this is what, hiding itself from awareness and from unawareness too, does not leave us alone, nor does it disturb us, for we have covered it over with consciousness-unconsciousness" (*Writing* 85-86).

Dylar is a little white pill advertised as being able to block out the white noise of death. To take the drug is to practice a form of asceticism, not least because the tablet is designed to work in the body without any waste of its chemical ingredients and without any wasteful side effects: "'You don't get a burst of medication followed by the merest trickle. No upset stomach, queasiness, vomiting, muscle cramps, et cetera. This system is efficient'" (188). An alternative to nonconsumption and to hyperconsumption, Dylar recalls Progressive Era cyberconsumption. Its streamlined action makes it the hi-tech equivalent of the "Industrious Munching" promoted by Horace Fletcher. The black market pharmaceutical would thus appear to be a beneficent or white *pharmakon*, a remedy freeing one from physiological and metaphysical waste. After all, Babette, in her attempt to hide her addiction, insists the object she has swallowed is "'a Life Saver'" (123).

However, this analysis of the drug is, like the drug itself, developed according to a prescription for forgetting death. In the case of the analysis, forgetting involves whiting out alternative, shrouded, morbid meanings of both "white" and "*pharmakon*." In "Plato's Pharmacy," Derrida calls attention to the suppressive nature of this white logic, doing so by unraveling Plato's identification of writing as a *pharmakon*, an identification rooted in the problem of forgetting. "Writing's case is grave" according to Derrida because, like death, it falls somewhere between the integrity of memory and the disintegration of amnesia. Like the sacrificial *pharmakos*, writing is both antidote and poison. On one hand, writing would seem to be an ideal mnemonic structure built to house the living essence of the thing itself. From this perspective, memory is at home in writing because the act of recording or imprinting insures memory never errs. On the other hand, writing would seem to be an agent of forgetting since it enables the writer to drift (off) from the scene of his communication. From this perspective, memory's home life is troubled by writing because writing makes it so that memory does not have stick around and support the truth. Giving over to writing its supervisorial role, memory goes astray, shambles off, gets strung out, becomes lethargic:

> Confident of the permanence and independence of its *types (tupoi)*, memory will fall asleep, will not keep itself up, will no longer keep to keeping itself alert, present, as close as possible to the truth of what is. Letting itself get stoned [*médusée*] by its own signs, its own guardians, by the types committed to the keeping and surveillance of knowledge, it will sink down into *lēthē*, overcome by non-knowledge and forgetfulness. ("Plato's Pharmacy" 105)

Just as the *pharmakos* neither fully belongs to, nor is completely excluded from, the membership of the community, the *pharmakon* is neither a perfectly legitimate nor a strictly illegitimate form of remembering. Writing simulates the virtue of unaided, direct, authentic memory and the vice of forgetfulness: "The *pharmakon* and writing are thus always involved in questions of life and death" (105). A virtually wasted medium, writing challenges the redemption-bound belief that simulation or representation can re-present the Real.[7] As a result, a metaphysics of presence, in an effort to sustain the vision of a good home where memory, truth, and knowledge are always present (to themselves), abjects writing. In Derrida's formulation, logocentric philosophy constructs writing as a dangerous intruder or form of white noise breaking in from outside to wreck an otherwise tranquil domestic scene:

> Apprehended as a blend and an impurity, the *pharmakon* also acts like an aggressor or a housebreaker, threatening some internal purity and securi- ty . . . The restoration of internal purity must thus reconstitute, *recite* . . . that to which the *pharmakon* should not have had to be added and attached like a literal parasite: a letter installing itself . . . to distort {like static, = '*bruit parasite*'} the pure audibility of a voice. Such are the rela- tions between the writing supplement and the *logos-zōn*. In order to cure the latter of the *pharmakon* and rid it of the parasite, it is thus necessary to put the outside back in its place. To keep the outside out. ("Plato's Pharmacy" 128)

Seeking to realize a perfectly secure domestic environment, the main char- acters in *White Noise* hit on a drug whose brand name, Dylar, bears with- in it the etymological trace of divine protection of domestic space: "**lar:** Pl. **lares** Roman Myth. **a.** *pl.* The tutelary deities of a house, household gods, hence, the home. **b.** *sing.* A household or ancestral deity" (OED).

For Don DeLillo, the writer's responsibility lies in challenging logocen- tric claims to "internal purity and security." In *White Noise*, he accepts this responsibility by presenting domestic static that cannot easily be seized on as the sign of an external threat. In one instance, it even breaks out within the home as a signal of invisible smoke from undetectable cinders: "The smoke alarm went off in the hallway upstairs, either to let us know the bat- tery had just died or because the house was on fire. We finished our lunch in silence" (8). This technological backfire bears the trace of a theological backfire that has been systematically forgotten through attempts to fix the sacred as an identifiable blaze. In Bataille's words: "Christianity has made the sacred *substantial*, but the nature of the sacred, in which today we rec- ognize the burning existence of religion, is perhaps the most ungraspable thing that has been produced between men: the sacred is only a privileged moment of communal unity, a moment of the convulsive communication of what is ordinarily stifled" ("The Sacred" 242). DeLillo critiques idealiz- ing seizures carried out in the pursuit of full substantiality or utter insub- stantiality. He does so by offering prose that communicates convulsively. In this regard, his work embodies Blanchot's notion of a "surrender to pas- sivity," a posture which must not be read as an expression of indifference. Indeed, this surrender actually constitutes the most vigorous challenge to the repressiveness of totalizing activity. As Blanchot says:

> Passivity is a task—but in a different language: in the language of the non- dialectic drive—just as negativity is a task in the language wherein the dialectic proposes to us the realization of all possibilities, provided we know how (by cooperating with time through power and mastery in the world) to let time take all its time (*Writing* 27).

DeLillo is an artist ever suspicious of "the realization of all possibilities." His plots move deathward under the spell of the Absolute or the Whole and yet are altered just slightly by a nondialectic drive to approach altarity. Believing it to be literature's responsibility to investigate "the half-concealed disasters that constitute a life" (*White Noise* 228), he espouses a difficult faith in virtually uncollectable trash.

CHAPTER FOUR

Figuring Out Mark Leyner:
A Waste of Time

1. THE RUSH OF SCANDAL

> Paradoxically, for a negation to be 'truly' negative, it cannot be true, since
> this will always make it a kind of positive. Positivity is resisted, therefore,
> not by negativity, but by indeterminacy (which, therefore, naturally can-
> not 'resist' it). . . . If it is always the case that a negative can be cashed in
> as a positive, there is always the uncertainty as to what that value will be,
> which may amount to an uncertainty about whether or not it is a positive
> value.
>
> Steven Connor, "Absolute Rubbish"

What good is Mark Leyner? Is his writing positive or negative? Is it a waste
of time? One cannot begin to figure out Mark Leyner's novel *Et Tu, Babe*
without addressing these concerns about evaluation since the text itself
spends much time figuring up Mark Leyner's value. In the novel—a first-
person narrative about a massively built and hugely famous writer named
Mark Leyner[1] who thrives on the fast-lane lifestyle and image-oriented culture of celebrity—nothing about the larger-than-life author is a waste of
time. In fact, the marketplace rushes to cash in as positive the fictional
author's seemingly most inconsequential and scandalous issuances. For
instance, one of his "discarded deodorant sticks with a stray armpit hair"
(79) is bought by a Japanese industrialist at a Sotheby' s auction for an outrageous sum. Likewise, the novel's title suggests that the real Mark Leyner's
fictional issuance, no matter how critical it may be of contemporary culture's drive to aestheticize the commodity and to commodify the aesthetic,
is bound to be made fit for consumption with the same ease, if not for
the same price. The title's blend of lofty Shakespearian rhetoric and
Hollywood-agent smarminess would seem to announce a transgressive

postmodern text whose aesthetic value cannot be easily determined or positivized since it collapses distinctions between high and low forms of culture. Yet its tone is accusatory, implicating the reader in a plot to submit the text to the normalizing mechanisms of the marketplace. The title seems to say to the reader, "You too, as soon as you invest in this book, conspire to commodify Mark Leyner."

In one respect, then, *Et Tu, Babe* details the impossibility of making art that is a total waste of time or that is truly outrageous. In other words, it rejects as idealistic the goal of producing cultural activities or events that remain uncontaminated by economic principles of objectification and utilization. Steven Connor, in the essay cited in the epigraph, outlines how the twentieth-century preoccupation with creating absolute rubbish—a preoccupation evident in such texts as disposable dadaist ready-mades and transient performance art pieces—marks a recent manifestation of the longstanding desire to conceive of art as a sanctuary for self-grounding value, as a cradle of noneconomic activity uncorrupted by the grubby forces of investment and calculation. He then stresses that the notion of art as a realm of sublime uselessness or absolute negative value has become increasingly difficult to hold onto when, in his words, "the rise of the mass-cultural market and increasing commodification of the cultural sphere threatens more and more to contaminate its autonomy" (58).

Et Tu, Babe takes this threat one step further by appearing to abolish altogether the idea of art's autonomy. Specifically, it depicts late capitalism's implementation of what Connor calls the "law of positive value," a law that defines as economic even the most degraded or dis-integrative attempts to escape "the contingency of economic exchange" since such projects are assumed to realize a goal, to secure some kind of benefit, or to produce a valuable (i.e., positive) outcome. Leyner cleverly documents the way cultural products and activities are now instantly subjected to such capitalizing impress. At one level, his narrative reads like the manic manifesto of a writer who treats his craft as a corporate enterprise. The text incorporates numerous images of elements considered refuse by official culture—bodily discharges, social discards, media tawdriness—in order to show how even the most seemingly negativized stuff gets quickly positivized for profit. As a result, Leyner's surreal collage—a cut-up text complete with Samuel Beckett "writing brochure copy for the Hyatt Regency Hotel on Maui" (162)—appears to be a positive illustration of the failure of projects like surrealism to be adequately unreasonable or sufficiently scandalous.

Yet, in another respect, Leyner's work comes close to being a waste of time by attempting to defer rather than defy appropriation by critical and financial economies. As Connor points out, what late capitalist economy values most is the ability to ascribe value with as little waste of time as possible: "Value therefore comes to consist, especially in advanced multinational capitalism, not in specific yields or products but in the very speed of the economic process itself—literally the 'rate' of exchange rather than the objects of exchange" (93). The emotional rush of the scandalous will give way, almost instantaneously, to the rush to capitalize on scandal. But *Et Tu, Babe* turns out to be scandalous not so much because it is shocking (though some may find it so) but rather because it seeks to assert itself as an obstacle holding up the arrival of its own value: "**scandal:** L *scandalum* cause of offense or stumbling **1.** In religious use. **a.** Discredit to religion occasioned by the conduct of a religious person; conduct, on the part of a religious person, which brings discredit on religion. Also perplexity of conscience occasioned by the conduct of one who is looked up to as an example **b.** Something that hinders reception of the faith or obedience to the Divine law; an occasion of unbelief or moral lapse; a stumbling-block" (OED). The author attempts to shake faith in the divine law of positive value by making it hard to figure out whether his book is positive or negative. While Mark Leyner delivers a wicked attack on the marriage of art and commerce, he does so by employing a rapid-fire form that depicts Mark Leyner converting his figure into sales figures as fast as he can. The novel thus wastes time by refusing to be quickly evaluated as either a simple sellout to the economic (a critically negligible commitment to positivity) or an outright rejection of the economic (an act of negating positivity reclaimed as positive critique).

I will argue that by trying to situate his text in a (non)position of indeterminacy Leyner exposes the repressive effects of an economy founded on the dialectical imperative to secure absolute value. As *Et Tu, Babe* demonstrates, contemporary culture rushes to repress aesthetic difference by rapidly assimilating all artifacts and events within a positive/negative framework. In order to retard this reductive, homogenizing work, Leyner attempts to fashion a text resistant to rapid seizure. In the effort to be a waste of time, he recalls the work of Bataille whose concept of *dépense* seeks to identify radical heterogeneity (in economic terms: nonproductive dissipation, expenditure without return; in philosophical terms: the unthinkable, the irreducibly Other) which cannot be tolerated by the totalizing systems of capitalist utilitarianism and scientific reason. But while Leyner values the idea of an absolute negativity necessarily left out by economies—aesthetic, philosophical, psychic—committed to absolute positivity, he also recognizes the impossibility of isolating truly negative value. Forced to resist the law of positive value otherwise than by adopting an easily co-opted oppositional posture, the best (which ideally is a not-quite-best or not-quite-worst) he can do is to mark his time by hiding in the shadow of Mark Leyner, masking his resistance by mimicking the principal values of late capitalism: a devotion to speed and a worship of image.

2. THE WARPED WRITER

> Speed creates pure objects. It is itself a pure object, since it cancels out the
> ground and territorial reference-points, since it runs ahead of time to
> annul time itself, since it moves more quickly than its own cause and oblit-
> erates that cause by outstripping it. Speed is the triumph of effect over
> cause, the triumph of instantaneity over time as depth, the triumph of the
> surface and pure objectality over the profundity of desire. . . . Its only rule
> is to leave no trace behind. Triumph of forgetting over memory, an uncul-
> tivated, amnesiac intoxication. . . . Speed is simply the rite that initiates us
> into emptiness: a nostalgic desire for forms to revert to immobility, con-
> cealed beneath the very intensification of their mobility.
>
> Jean Baudrillard, *America*

Et Tu, Babe sketches a portrait of the artist as cult figure. In this case, what
has made the author an "instant icon" (25) is his ability to cultivate an
image that embodies the myth of instantaneity. In his panic quest for currency—for money and for maximum exposure—Mark Leyner is obsessed
with, or addicted to, speed: "I work and I play at one speed: hyperdrive—
Mach 9, adrenaline OD, total warp. It's the only way I know how to live"
(77). Bent on obliterating time for the same reason he is bent on manipu-
lating his physique, Leyner represents what could be called a *warped
writer*. He saturates the market with his presence by capitalizing on the
longing for liberation through speed, a longing currently stimulated by the
electronic currents of information technology, by the promise of time and
space annulled, by the fantasy of instant access and zero delay. His pro-
file of inexhaustible energy and perpetually peak performance has a self-
proclaimed "inspirational" appeal insofar as it taps into capitalism's dream
of redemption through acceleration. In our fantasies about speed, we neither waste time nor are wasted by time. The fictional author hypes his
hyperkinetic life in order to sell the concept of saving time and being saved
from time. Leyner makes this *current* rage for salvation outrageously
graphic when he describes his namesake's bodyguards, "arthritic nonage-
narian widows" whom Leyner rapidly rejuvenates by injecting them with
"large doses of synthetic human growth hormone and testosterone" and by
graphing onto them "powerful artificial muscles made out of polymer gels
that contract when electricity is applied and expand when the current is
turned off" (16).

Like his bodyguards, the warped writer is what Baudrillard calls a "pure
object," a figure seemingly jettisoned out of the flow of time by his own
turbocharged transformations. To stay current, Leyner continually tries to
slip his own traces, "'compulsively altering'" his body, his biography, and
his books to match patterns of mass consumption. These rituals of "self-
surgery" or self-erasure are profit making because they re-create the

celebrity as a kind of contemporary ascetic hero. Leyner resembles Roland Barthes' "*jet-man*," the pilot of supersonic flight whose exacting devotion to velocity reactivates the myth of the "glamorous singularity of an inhuman condition" (72). The *jet-man*, like the warped writer, radiates an aura of what Barthes calls "semi-divinity" through his austere determination to reduce the drags of desire and memory by becoming weightless. Both figures seek speeds that are out of this world, Leyner even using supersonic travel to *take time off* from his schedule: "I'm in the XXT7, a top-secret, experimental hyperspeed jet fighter that does about Mach 8. I just had to get away from it all . . ." (89). In the process, they appear to achieve a transcendent state of emptiness, becoming pure objects by paring themselves down to a series of streamlined surfaces: "The anti-G suit of inflatable nylon, the shiny helmet, introduce the *jet-man* into a novel type of skin in which '*even his mother would not know him*'" ("Jet-man" 72).

However, the *jet-man*'s strategies for eliminating the wasteful effects of time are much different than those of the warped writer. The *jet-man*, according to Barthes, purifies himself in part by adopting a position of "pure passivity." Strapped in, propelled by mechanical thrust, the *jet-man* is "inert" and "dispossessed" (73). The warped writer, according to Leyner, purifies himself by being hyperactive. As illustrated by the following passage from his previous novel *My Cousin, My Gastroenterologist*, Leyner represents the warped writer as hyperproducer, in this case someone literally high on speed:

> As I iron a pair of tennis shorts I dictate a haiku into the tape recorder and then dash off to snake a clogged drain in the bathroom sink and then do three minutes on the speedbag before making an origami praying mantis and then reading an article in *High Fidelity* magazine as I stir the coq au vin. These Methedrine suppositories are fantastic! . . . I'm an exploding skeleton of kinetic vectors. I stand upon a peak in Darien like stout Cortez shouting I write the songs! I rupture into afterimages like the nude descending a staircase. (49–50)

Speed kills . . . time. Fast-acting, speed stimulates the dream of eliminating waste, the fantasy of discharge without delay: "These Methedrine suppositories are fantastic!" Speed promises instant relief . . . the relief of instantaneity. Like Duchamp's nude, the speed junkie generates the illusion of negating time and space by being everywhere at once. More than anything else, Mark Leyner's portraits of manic intensity advertise identity purged of what Derrida calls *différance*, the play of difference over time and in space that prevents the self from being fully self-present as Being. Such frenzied expenditure of energy appears to restore the subject to a condition of perfect self-possession by negating the temporal and spatial intervals dividing the self from itself. Like the hypermasculine physical culturist, the hypermasculine warped writer thus aims, paradoxically, to become a living still life. As Barthes puts it: "This paradox is that an excess of speed turns into repose. . . . The *jet-man* . . . is defined by a coenaesthesis of motionlessness . . . as if the extravagance of his vocation precisely consisted in *overtaking* motion, in going faster than speed" (71).

For the traditional ascetic, the "repose" of full Being is realized only through submission to regimens of abstention and isolation. The *jet-man* performs such rituals of self-denial in his effort to meet the demands of aerodynamics: "Mythically, the *jet-man* is defined less by his courage than by his weight, his diet and his habits (temperance, frugality, continence)" (71–72). The warped writer, in comparison, reworks the logic of asceticism, marketing himself as an ascetic hero who is made whole through the practice of hyperconsumption. Favoring "hulk couture"[2] over hermitic culture, Mark Leyner keeps his warped figure by eating as relentlessly as he works, even undertaking these activities simultaneously so as not to waste time: "He'd devised a small trough that hung from his neck from which he ate continuously while he typed" (151). Instead of fasting for plenitude, the warped writer just eats fast. Not coincidentally, this postmodern author's habit of hyperconsumption reenacts a naturalist author's habit of cyberconsumption. Like Leyner's manic intake, Upton Sinclair's supposedly hassle-free ingestion of raw foods is based on a desire to dispatch (with) the difference time makes. In *Et Tu, Babe*, this metaphysical hunger is dramatized in a fantasy Leyner has of "an inconceivably immense being" capable of eating a sandwich with "literally 'everything' on it." Like hyperspeed, such consumption is redemptive because nothing is wasted; no leftovers remain. To consume everything is to assume absolute self-consciousness, to negate otherness by incorporating it into the self. By dispatching the "hypothetical hoagie," the "colossal" subject makes itself full and fully self-present. As Leyner puts it: "And would not this meal, by its very nature, exhaust time itself?" (5–6).

3. THE ART OF DISPATCH

> **dispatch** *vt* **1 a** : to send off or away (as to a special destination) with promptness or speed often as a matter of official business **b** : to perform the job of dispatcher of **2 a** : to get rid of (as by sending away): dismiss, discharge **b** : to put to death: kill **3 a** : to dispose of rapidly or efficiently (as a piece of business); execute quickly **3 b** : to eat with avid concentration: clean up by eating.
>
> *Webster's Third New International Dictionary*

Both hyperproducer and hyperconsumer, the warped writer demonstrates what might be called the *art of dispatch*, a practice designed "to get rid of" temporality—to exhaust time—and thereby to "dismiss" traces of the other. To dispatch is thus to repress difference. Mark Leyner depicts an artist dedicated to the art of dispatch in order to draw a parallel between the current rage to repress ontological difference and the current rage to repress aesthetic difference. He then challenges the repressiveness inherent in the culture's devotion to speed by fashioning a text that imitates the art of dispatch in order to expose the scandalous faults in its totalizing structure.

To duplicate a discourse whose "special destination" is full identity or pure presence, he produces a high-speed form that appears to dispatch the difference between author and character. Specifically, Mark Leyner looks identical to Mark Leyner by virtue of the fact that the form of *Et Tu, Babe* has a 'hyper' feel to it. In one respect it is a hypertrophic text, straining and bulging with a mass of allusion to the world of advertising, popular culture, and medical technology. The body of his fiction—like the body of his fictional character—is injected and swollen with the synthetic extracts of image culture. In another respect it is a hypermetabolic text, processing with remarkable rapidity an array of discourses culled from mass media—including game show contest, commercial endorsement, celebrity interview, fan mail, presidential news conference, public relations directive, and autobiography—spliced together in the hyperkinetic, jump-cut style of music video. Leyner's prose is thus a kind of hyperfiction—though the text is not constructed for interactive consumption in the corridors of cyberspace—because it reflects a voracious appetite while conveying a feeling of relentless acceleration.

In crafting this high-pitched, jam-packed, manic style, Leyner simulates what Baudrillard calls "the ecstasy of communication." Used to describe the dense and high-speed flow of data generated by communication networks and information highways, the term carries a negative connotation, identifying as "obscene" the impression that all lives, events, environments are now brought to the screen and made "transparent," that "all secrets, spaces and scenes [are] abolished in a single dimension of communication" ("Ecstasy" 131). Baudrillard laments the way the volume and velocity of this information produce a kind of "superficial saturation"—a pornographic overexposure—in which nothing is left unseen or unheard. With our virtual bulletin boards, our tell-all talk shows, and our courtroom cameras, we are left to witness "the obscenity of the visible, of the all-too-visible, of the more-visible-than-the visible" (131).

It is precisely this sense of hypervisibility that Leyner strives to re-create through his hyperfictional form: "'The goal was to make every sentence seem like a tabloid headline, so to speak, to turn up the volume on every sentence, to deliver a constant surprise'" (Grimes 64). The novel is obscene not so much because of the clinical and carnivalesque references to masturbation, bodily secretions, and grotesquely enlarged organs but rather because of the ways in which Mark Leyner makes himself into a phenomenon by means of a nonstop campaign to render visible the product of his own personality. Hyperfiction as aesthetic hyperactivity becomes conflated with hyperfiction as the aesthetics of hype. *Et Tu, Babe* unfolds as a literary infomercial designed to inflate and circulate the commodity Mark Leyner.[3]

By blitzing the reader, by precluding pause for reflection, Leyner endeavors to create an ecstatic experience in which the reader surrenders the right to differ or defer in the ascription of value. In other words, the text sets out to reproduce in the reader what Baudrillard refers to as a schizophrenic experience, the contemporary consumer's inability to resist the media's electronic manipulation of historical and monetary currents:

> Too great a proximity of everything, the unclean promiscuity of everything which touches, invests and penetrates without resistance, with no halo of private protection, not even his own body, to protect him anymore. . . . the total instantaneity of things, the feeling of no defense, no retreat. ("Ecstasy" 132–33)

Dubbed "the poet laureate of information overload" (Grimes 51), Leyner comes off as a warped writer bent on eliminating axiological uncertainty by achieving "total instantaneity." In an interview, Leyner even describes his cultivation of a hyperfictional form as an ascetic commitment to producing prose from which all the slow parts are cut or from which all the narrative waste is dispatched: "'[In traditional narratives] there's always 14 pages describing a lawn that you skip over. . . . I wondered, can you write a kind of fiction that the reader can't skip, because it's so dense with pleasure, so unrelentingly enjoyable, so packed with event'" (Grimes 64).

Yet while the novel appears determined to waste no time securing an investment of value, it also appears to support Baudrillard's claim that such investment is "unclean," defiling, scandalous. Though they share an adrenaline-based approach to art, Mark Leyner proves to be somewhat different than Mark Leyner, weaving into his warped prose a satire on the fate of the aesthetic in what the critic Ben Agger calls the age of "fast capitalism." For Agger, as for Baudrillard, the late capitalist marketplace—defined by accelerating production rates, refined distribution techniques, and streamlined flows of electronic credit—creates a set of conditions in which written texts undergo a nearly instantaneous conversion into disposable commodities.[4] In this system built for speed "books become things provoking their thoughtlessly ready readings" (Agger 5) by being packaged and pitched in easy-to-digest ways which confiscate the texts' critical complexity. Regardless how opposed to the ideological tenets of this system, texts are appropriated and neutralized by it. They suffer a "degradation of signification" by being swept up into fast capitalism's raging current. As Agger puts it: "The more prose is degraded into slogans, clichés, and codes, particularly on the model of advertising, the less writing can construct imaginatively the possibility of a very different world" (17). In aesthetic terms, accelerated culture's commitment to the art of dispatch results in a commitment to art as dispatch. Since its ability to express difference is eliminated by a rapid process of reification, the artwork appears as nothing other than an official message or press release *expressing* the values of the dominant social order.

While both writers acknowledge the homogenizing effects of speed, Leyner and Agger differ in their conception of how to exceed the limits of this economy in order to make time for heterogeneity or difference. Agger's opposition to the art of dispatch rests on his belief in the possibility of fashioning texts capable of remaining uncontaminated by fast capitalism. Speculating that "books do not exist" in a marketplace consumed with speed, Agger defines true books as those that provide "examples of critique's ability to stand apart in order to think the world differently" (4). Leyner's opposition to the art of dispatch rests on his recognition of the purist pretension—the fantasy of being waste-free—informing the desire "to stand apart." Acknowledging the impossibility of situating a text wholly outside fast capitalism's restricted economy, Leyner rejects Agger's quick fix by adopting a form of dispatch art—the hyperfictional novel—in order to challenge the structure from within.

Et Tu, Babe begins to resist this totalizing system by exploiting the reproachable, scandalous efforts of an artist who exploits rather than resists the forces of totalization. A speed demon committed to the art of dispatch, Mark Leyner produces what Andrew Haase calls "panic art." While he appears to embrace recklessness and excess—witness his "kamikaze-like" workouts and his fascination with effluvia—Leyner is far from embodying Bataille's ideals of baseless expenditure, nonproductive prodigality, and excremental value. Instead, his frenetic lifestyle and his attraction to the abject constitute carefully calculated strategies devised to insure financial success. The warped writer resembles Mark Kostabi, a self-aggrandizing visual artist who conceives of aesthetic practice as a corporate campaign to stay current and to generate currency:

> As far as I know I am tops in my field. I haven't met another individual who possesses as much genius as I do. I employ assistants to execute my ideas. I hire people to create sub-ideas. . . . Everything is sales, whether it's painting or chit-chat or lunch. I don't paint with a brush between my fingers. I paint in the same way Donald Trump builds when he causes the Trump Tower to come into existence. (Haase 21)

Choosing the power lunch over the posture of self-effacement, the panic artist is nevertheless an ascetic figure made apprehensive by the threat of wasted time, by indeterminacy and conflict which delay prompt settlement of aesthetic value. The panic artist responds to this anxiety by being a corporate monster who incorporates—assimilates, digests, dispatches—at a panicky pace. Panic art assumes that nothing remains unfit for consumption by the economic system. Nothing is refused as refuse because "Everything is sales." In *Et Tu, Babe,* images of devouring monsters abound, including a giant who eats "postmenopausal crossing guards." The book is dedicated to Leyner's editor, a figure identified as "The Monster Maker." Moreover, Mark Leyner acts and looks like a monster, one who hypes his own aesthetic by continually incorporating reference to the irresistible, indomitable body of his work and work of his body: "Today I *am* the most intense, and in a certain sense, the most significant young prose writer in America. And I have the body of a grotesquely swollen steroid freak" (16).

This statement is remarkable not only for its blatant self-inflation but also for the fact that it incorporates a variation on a laudatory blurb generated by the critic Larry McCaffery which appears on the back cover of Leyner's second work, *My Cousin, My Gastroenterologist:* "Establishes Mark Leyner as the most intense, and, in a sense, the most significant prose writer in America." Leyner (as Leyner?) resorts to this real-life strain of critical hype several times, injecting it, like an illegal growth hormone, into the stream of his hyperdiscourse in order to swell his figure(s). Such monstrous self-enhancement reaches absurdly exaggerated proportions in a dispatch sent to Leyner from the V.P. of marketing at Columbia Records concerning promotional material the panic author has written for pop singer George Michael's (real) album *Listen Without Prejudice, Vol. 1:* "He loves the liner notes and in fact called them the most intense and, in a certain sense, the most significant liner notes he'd ever read" (36). *Et Tu, Babe* thus presents a *mise en abîme* in which all distinctions between art and advertisement, primary text and promotional gloss, inside and outside collapse. McCaffery's language, used to hype the real Mark Leyner, is supplementary material incorporated into *Et Tu, Babe* to describe Leyner's language which, used to hype George Michael, is itself supplementary material (liner notes) packaged as part of the aesthetic product, a product whose originality and integrity are, in turn, open to question, Michael's success being, arguably, attributable to the way his image was packaged on MTV (As Michael himself says, in a lyric from the album, "To win the race? A prettier face!/ Brand new clothes and a big fat place/ On your rock and roll TV" ["Freedom '90"]).

Given this system of relentless incorporation, in which nothing is so saccharine or so tasteless that it cannot be profitably ingested, there seems to be no possibility of producing artwork that succeeds as disgusting negativity or unswallowable shit. Nevertheless, Leyner does attempt to slacken such intensity or to slow down the digestive process by expressing what Steven Connor refers to as an "embarrassed awareness of the recursion of value in non-value" (75), an awareness made manifest in the novel's preoccupation with images of expulsion, secretion, and refuse. The text is full of references to bodily excretions or byproducts: vomit, semen, sweat, shit, smegma, and even "a large piece of pinkish-white brain tissue extruding from one ear—the equivalent of a cerebral hemorrhoid" (100); however, this seemingly heterological stuff is always being assimilated or metabolized by the corporate monster. The way these residues are processed within the text illustrates what Connor calls the "recoil of negativity into positivity" (76) that occurs in any economic structure but occurs with overwhelming rapidity in an economy based on speed dialing and superconduction.

The book opens with an example of reclaimed marginalia, a private letter from Leyner to his editor that serves as a sales pitch for the text. Anticipating the academic industry and art world's hunger to recuperate any scrap of authorial production, Leyner redeems the form of the private note as self-promoting dispatch: "*ET TU, BABE* . . . will undoubtedly be, page by page, and line by line, the most entertaining book that Vintage has ever published" (4). The letter also advertises his ability to capitalize artistically on subjects or materials traditionally considered unpalatable, unusable, anti-aesthetic:

> The unwashed armpits of the most beautiful women in the world . . . a urinal with chunks of fresh watermelon in it . . . a retarded guy whining "Eddie, Eddie, get me an Ovaltine"—almost anything inspires me. Immediately after finishing MY COUSIN, MY GASTROENTEROLO-GIST, I outlined a new book about people with trichotillomania—people who compulsively pull out their hair. (4)

According to this aesthetic, there is no irretrievable loss. Everything that once was cut out or pulled out is put back in for profit.

Leyner's investment in waste is made literal and graphic by his pleasure in consuming the excremental. He delights in dispatching a drink called a Stinky Pinky: "Two parts gin, one part strawberry schnapps, one part O amino acetomphenome, which is the primary odor component of extract from the anal sac of a Japanese weasel" (22). The most extended example of profiting from effluvia by devouring the disgusting is an outrageous scenario in which Leyner steals a vial of "Abraham Lincoln's morning breath" from the National Museum of Health and Medicine in order to get high from the "overwhelming stench" of the fumes. The concept of preserving such mephitic exhalation signifies the culture's rage to appropriate even the most degraded or insubstantial artifact, while the act of "inhaling the gaseous relic of the Great Emancipator" produces a heightened awareness of the way in which the noneconomic automatically gets converted into the economic:

> Do you know the commercial where the heavily mustached old woman in
> a black shroud drinks strawberry Nestlé's Quik and turns into this buxom
> bombshell in pasties and G-string, and she squats down for a second in a
> mud puddle, and when she gets up, her buttocks are covered with leeches,
> and Jesus appears holding a Barbie, and two beams of sparkling particles
> shoot from the eyes of the Barbie and vaporize the leeches, and the bomb-
> shell gets on her motorcycle, and pink florets of exhaust spurt from its
> tailpipe spelling out the words *Be All That You Can Be?* Try watching that
> on Lincoln's morning breath. It's un-fucking-believable. (74)

The commercial is an accelerated account of how nothing, in postindustrial culture, remains out of circulation; nothing is absolute rubbish. Rather
than selling any particular product, it advertises the transformation, without delay, of the marginalized (the heavily mustached old woman), the
unclean (the mud puddle), the unproductive (the leeches), and the toxic
(the exhaust) into sellable images.

Perhaps the most severe indictment of this totalizing structure occurs in
the depiction of a presidential news conference at which the commander in
chief encourages "poor Americans to nutritionally supplement their food
with their own hair and nail clippings" (67). Recalling Melville's morally
bankrupt Poet Blandmour, who promotes the salutary properties of the
landlord's leftovers by calling them "poor man's pudding,"[5] the president
proposes a program based on the idea that the poor rush to redeem their
own rejectamenta:

> Our bodies are like farms—we're growing this perfectly good source of
> protein right from our scalps and our fingers and our toes—and what do
> we do with it? We throw it away. I think that especially for parents hav-
> ing trouble providing their children with three square meals a day, this is
> an economical—and I've been assured by the Surgeon General, healthy—
> solution. Using an industrial grinder, you simply pulverize the clippings
> into a fine powder. Then you can add the powder to soups, cereals,
> shakes, chopped meat, whatever. (67)

Saving slough. Eating excreta. Dispatching detritus. With a maximally efficient economy, there are no recalcitrant residues, no uncooperative parings
to challenge the integrity of the body proper. Waste works in this scenario
because it is useful and because it guarantees the utility of those who use
it. If they ingest their own egesta, we don't have to throw away time and
money on them to make them productive, to insure they won't waste time
and money.

The domesticating, subordinating effects of this all-consuming system
are embodied in the figure of Leyner's friend Jorge who becomes fed up
with his job at an ant farm where he pukes for profit: "'They'd feed me
steak or chopped meat which I'd digest, and then they'd force me to regur-

gitate to feed the queen and her larvae'" (17). He decides, in a moment of anarchist despair, to rebel against this gross cycle of dispatching by interrupting one of fast capitalism's mail dispatch services. He goes postal. Targeting the company whose motto is *When it absolutely, positively has to be there overnight*, he heads out to "a desolate industrial dump" and proceeds to blow a Federal Express jet out the sky with a "shoulder-held Stinger antiaircraft missile launcher" (17). Ultimately, though, Jorge represents the futility of trying to stand apart from a system in which even vomit has a positive value. He is dispatched to death row where he dies ranting, without consequence, against those "'whose ultimate purpose is to further enrich the ruling elite or solidify the hegemony of the state . . .'" (18).

How then best (or perhaps worst) to resist the culture's commitment to the art of dispatch and to art as dispatch? Leyner's message appears to be that if the currents of fast capitalism are to be slowed at all, however temporarily, the task cannot be accomplished from a waste site outside the official limits. In aesthetic terms, it is impossible to produce an art of *depénse* which, refusing to be delivered or positivized at any time, would undermine the hegemony of art as dispatch. The futility of occupying such a purely wasteful position is made evident by the fact that if one holds fast to the foregoing analysis of the way waste works in *Et Tu, Babe*, the novel gets easily dispatched as something other than a waste of time. To reify this reading would be to label the text a positive exercise in negativity, a satire laboring in hilarious excess to depict the difficulty of mounting aesthetic resistance to speed. Insofar as he ridicules the relentless negation of negativity, Leyner repeats the ascetic impulse to withdraw neatly in order to critique fast capitalism's repression of difference. However, while he does participate in the literary equivalent of Jorge's isolated assault, he also recognizes the speed with which such acts of negation are neutralized. Given the system's imperative of appropriation, Leyner seeks to demonstrate that hope lies not in suddenly blasting the economy from without but rather in patiently displacing it from within. But how does the artist put off the determination of value and not become sold as a total put-off?

4. PUTTING OFF

Logo, derives from the Greek *logos*, which indicates word or speech. More recently, *logo* has been used to designate an emblem, figure, image, or sign—especially one that identifies a product or business for the purposes of advertising. The effectiveness of the logo depends upon its transparency and the immediacy of its meaning. The logo is designed to be grasped in an instant. Logo centrism designates the centrality of the logo—the figure, image, and sign. Within a logo centric economy, signs do not refer to a more basic, fundamental, or essential reality but are signs of signs, figures of figures, images of images. Since everything appears to be image, nothing appears but appearance.

Mark C. Taylor, *Disfiguring*

The overlap of philosophical, aesthetic, and economic commitments to eliminating the waste of time is made clear in Taylor's concept of logo centrism. As the passage indicates, the logo figures centrally in fast capitalism because it is a sign built for speed. "Designed to be grasped in an instant," the logo exemplifies the principles of an economy determined to repress otherness by precipitating evaluation and exchange. Nowhere is this ascetic paradigm governing logo centric culture more in evidence than in the logo of the Nike swoosh. A sign of speed, a sign of a rush, it has become an instantly recognizable icon, the trademark of both a waste-free corporate body and a waste-free individual body as long as we don't put off, as long as we Just Do It.

Taylor speculates that the logo stimulates consumption by selling salvation. Like speed, the logo delivers us from the waste of time by making utopia available now. The logo redeems us from the fragmentation and contingency of modern life by teaching us, in the words of the old Coca-Cola song, "to sing in perfect harmony." In the absence of God—in the absence of a divine Logos embodying absolute, immutable Reality beyond the worldly play of appearances—the logo sells itself as logos present in the world. By buying into image, we buy into the "The Real Thing." In a simulated world where "signs do not refer to a more basic, fundamental, or essential reality," signs are constructed to be spectacular re-presentations of total fitness. As the tennis player Andre Agassi said, when selling his image in an advertisement for an image-making product, the Canon camera: "Image is everything." Logo centric economy capitalizes on the logocentric longing for presence by making the ephemeral appear essential, by making the insubstantial appear substantial:

> While logocentrism struggles to erase signifiers in order to arrive at the pure transcendental signified, logo centrism attempts to extend the sign to infinity by collapsing the signified in the signifier. Union with the real—regardless of how the real is understood—holds out the promise of overcoming alienation and achieving reconciliation. (*Disfiguring* 222–23)

It makes sense, in this context, that God appears in Leyner's novel but does so as a logo-sporting Madison Avenue model. Like the panic author, God is no detached, otherworldly Author-ity, no "pure transcendental signified." Instead, he shows up in the sky as a preppy poster boy—a literally floating signifier—vying for market supremacy with Mark Leyner: "There was God, wearing a pink polo shirt, khaki pants, and brown Top-Siders with no socks, his blond hair blowing in the powerful wind of charged particles and intense ultraviolet radiation from the galactic center. I hated him. And he hated me" (13). Image is "the real" and the Real is image.

Taylor offers the pop art movement as the prime example of a logo centric aesthetic, a movement to which Leyner owes a certain debt. He argues that the foregrounding of image or figure in pop art actually reasserts the logocentric aim of much high modernist art—particularly abstract expressionist painting and International Style architecture—to "dis-figure" texts. According to Taylor, the modernist aesthetic is dedicated to a "theoesthetic" program of "union with the Absolute or Real, which underlies or dwells within every person and all phenomena" (52). Union is achieved by rejecting rather than embracing the logo, "by removing figures, symbols, designs, ornaments" (9). Modernism dis-figures or refuses figures because it sees figures as refuse. Representation is off-putting because it claims to represent the theological purity of the Intelligible or the Universal but does so in the impure form of the sensual or the particular. In their play of difference, signifiers put off access to a transcendental signified. Like the *jetman*, the painter of abstract art and the architect of the white wall seek to overcome the off-putting effects of differing and deferral through an ascetic practice of purgation. Modernist iconoclasm claims that the Real can be realized only through the discipline of negation, only through an allegiance to Mies van der Rohe's declaration that "Less is More." The geometric austerity of a blank canvas and the crystalline essence of an architectural glass curtain thus share a commitment to eliminating the waste of image.

Pop art would seem to resist modernism's ascetic aesthetic—and its sympathy with capitalism's principles of efficiency, rationality, and standardization—by employing figures drawn, literally and metaphorically, from the trash. Like Leyner, painters such as Andy Warhol, sculptors such as Claes Oldenberg, and architects such as Michael Graves recycle images reclaimed from the domains of the 'low'—from the landfill as well as from the worlds of advertising, fashion, and popular entertainment—in order to subvert the purist conceptions of high modernism.[6] However, Taylor insists that pop art embodies what he calls "modernist postmodernism." It reproduces the modernist pursuit of presence in its postmodern appropriation of figure:

> Contrary to popular understanding, pop art is idealistic—it is the *idealism of the image*. Since there is nothing outside the image, the image is (the) "real." Within this specular economy, the "real" is ideal and the ideal is "real." For those who dwell in this utopia of the simulacrum or the simulacrum of utopia, there is nothing for which to hope and *nothing* to fear. Redemption is at hand. "Pop art," Warhol avers, "is liking things." (181)

In this reading of pop art, the hyperproduction of figure or logo—think of Warhol's Campbell's soup cans—simply encourages the hyperconsumption of image characteristic of fast capitalism. And as the warped writer demonstrates, hyperconsumption is ultimately no different than the refusal to consume. Both are puritanical regimens undertaken in the hope of realizing whole-some identity. As Taylor puts it: "Compulsive consumption and rig-

orous asceticism are not merely opposites but are alternative strategies
directed toward the same end. . . . While the ascetic seeks union with
the Real by self-denial, the consumer seeks union with the Real by self-
indulgence" (224).

Mark Leyner is perhaps the ultimate literary embodiment of logo centric culture. Megasuperstar writer, fanatical bodybuilder, ultramacho com-
petitor (he has his "insignia" or logo literally "branded on the buttocks"
of rival authors), and shamelessly self-promoting personality, Leyner is a
cult author who offers redemption not only through exhibitions of speed
but also through exhibitions of his massively muscled figure. Re-creating
the excessive proliferation of signs that characterize celebrity culture, *Et
Tu, Babe* pumps up the Leyner figure—the name as well as the body—to
the point where the artist figuratively and literally disappears behind the
screen of his image. In Taylor's words, "Nothing appears but appearance."
No wonder Leyner elsewhere represents a writer as one who manipulates
image in his spare time:

> Whereas some guys like to go off fly-fishing or spelunking or cuckolding
> Iowans, I like to catch some R and R by renting a small office in some
> sleepy southern town and posing as a dermatologist. Give me a week of
> excising cysts, incising carbuncles, chemabrading acne scars and lasering
> away spidery veins, and I'm completely refreshed, revitalized—eager to
> plunge back into the slash-and-burn, eat-your-young, kill-'em-all-and-let-
> God-sort-'em-out battlegrounds of the New York literary scene. ("Great
> Pretenders" 126)

Like dermatology, panic art is dedicated to the alteration of the superficial.
The "slash-and-burn" artist treats surfaces in order to construct an ideal
body and an ideal text from which the disfiguring marks of time have been
removed.

Undermining modernism's work of negating figure—its effort to represent an image-free Real, a de-formed Form, a bodiless text—Leyner's postmodern work dramatizes a ferocious flaunting of figure in the deformed
form of a hyperbolic body-text. An example of such flaunting or figuring
out is Mark Leyner's glossy collection of portraits titled *The Celestial
Voyeur: Heavenly Views of an Earthly Body*, a piece of coffee table eroti-
ca which, like Madonna's book *Sex*, collapses the distinction between
transgressive artwork and blatant self-advertisement:

> The book I was scheduled to sign—which had just been published by
> Rizzoli—was a $75 oversized volume of nude photographs of myself
> taken by a spy satellite in geostationary orbit over New Jersey. Annie
> Leibowitz, famed Rolling Stone photo-journalist, upon learning that the
> satellite was capable of providing high-resolution images down to the

brand name on a golf ball, contacted the Department of Defense and suggested that they collaborate with her on a book of photographs of me
lolling about the headquarter's rooftop patio, au naturel, basted with oil,
and flexing. (47)

What makes this book pornographic is not the naked flex of a weighty subject. Instead, it is the fact that such ex-orbitant pricelisting, technology, and
scrutiny inflate or flex the subject to the point of weightlessness. Just as
Annie Leibowitz surrenders her artistic autonomy to an anonymous mili-
tary-industrial complex, Leyner surrenders his anatomy to the geostation-
ary gaze of the media. In the star wars competition of celebrity exposure,
the author, despite being launched into orbit, remains a grounded and
grounding Author-ity, only now it is sanctification of the writer's physical
figure, rather than sanctification of the writer as hidden dis-figure, that
establishes him as the origin of Meaning, the site of the Real. The author
thus undergoes what Baudrillard calls "the satellization of the real"
("Ecstasy" 128) which occurs when the opposition between public and private life or between surface and depth gets effaced by the hypermagnifying
currents of electronic communication. As Leyner proudly puts it: "Do I
make any distinction whatsoever between my personal life and my career?
No, sir, I do not" (77).

To satirize the superficiality of logo centrism, Leyner turns up the reso-
lution on every image of his alter ego. One way he emphasizes the panic
artist's hyperreality is by showing him to be a figure whose work centers
around the seductiveness of his logo. So while Leyner incorporates his
name into the novel, **Leyner** incorporates his name by making it a regis-
tered trademark. The "Leyner" brand name is used not only to sell the lat-
est **Leyner** line (of clothing and dolls as well as prose) but also to sell the
"*LeynerHead Sublingual Software Lozenge* that, placed under the tongue,
provides you with the sensation of being a sinewy and licentious pop icon
. . ." (116). The logo may create an appetite for the author's words, but,
more importantly, it stimulates an insatiable desire to consume—literally in
the case of the LeynerHead Lozenge—the author's image.

Leyner makes explicit the link between the contemporary artist's reduction to corporate logo and the contemporary body's reduction to *corpus* as
logo in the wild description of **Mark Leyner's** decision to get a "visceral
tattoo" (54). The warped writer goes to Mexico to have the Team Leyner
insignia—"a guy surfing on an enormous wave of lava"—tattooed on his
left ventricle. By imprinting the logo on his heart, **Leyner** parodies the idea
that the heart is a symbol of the real, innermost self. By internalizing the
surf-iciality of the logo—the logo of the surfer—**Leyner** unsettles the oppositions surface/depth, image/reality, exterior/interior. The heart is now an
emblem of surfing, of riding the surface of the image, just as the logo itself,
with "an erupting volcano in the distance in the upper right-hand corner"

(54) signifies an upheaval confounding the distinction between the superficial and the authentic. The visceral tattoo, which literalizes Baudrillard's notion of the "more-visible-than-visible" since it can only be viewed by X-ray, demonstrates just how the author has become "*image all the way down*" (*Disfiguring* 179).

In view of his insubstantiality, it makes sense that Leyner literally vanishes toward the end of the novel. Subject to having one item removed from his house each week as penalty for stealing Lincoln's morning breath, he is gradually stripped of all his material possessions; nevertheless, he continues his manic pace of composition at his fortified compound until the Federal Punitive Confiscation Tactical Division comes to take away his laptop computer, at which moment "he di." There is, finally, nothing there behind the screen-text-logo through which the panic artist appears. Not surprisingly, then, Leyner threatens to become even more current or present by virtue of his absence. The penultimate chapter is "An Oral History," a riotous send-up of the "last to be with" and "what it was really like" *Current Affair* claims to origin-ality and authenticity. In *Et Tu, Babe*, a number of real-life celebrities—many of whom owe their own celebrity, at least in part, to the image industry (e.g., Connie Chung, Joan Jett, Jessica Hahn, George Plimpton)—describe their privileged access to his presence at the end and giddily recount his creative and physical prowess. Moreover, his disappearance results in the composition of an anonymous dispatch, a final publicity flyer that functions both as a message to keep the Leyner spirit alive and as a sales pitch for the novel it concludes: "*There's no better way to register your support for Leyner and everything he stands for than by urging—and, if necessary, coercing—your family, friends, and co-workers to bulk-order* Et Tu, Babe *from their local bookstores*" (168). The real Mark Leyner disappears in a climactic hypersynthesis of art and advertisement.

The image of depthlessness that figures most prominently in the novel is, ironically, the hulking physique of the bodybuilder. Disfigured in its hugeness, the author's frame represents an excessive or distended display of figure. Alphonso Lingis, in his study *Foreign Bodies*, proposes the idea that the bodybuilder embodies the logo centric play of surfaces in postindustrial society. Rarely cultivated for athletic competition, no longer developed for workplace instrumentation or wartime heroism (these two functions made obsolete by cybernetic machines), the fretted fibers and sculpted contours act solely as "organs-to-be-seen." Lingis suggests that the cult of bodybuilding may dramatize our evolution into "mammalian orchids," creatures attempting to disguise, through a show of flowery splendor, our bodies' atrophy in the electronic age. Moreover, such exotic externalization signals not only the withering of the body but also the disintegration of a private, interior self. The bodybuilder metamorphoses to the extent that identity, no longer located in the depths of the soul, now appears right on the surface:

The homogeneity of the steel drives out the principle of individuality in the bodies that devote themselves to it. It does away with the eccentricities—the dry and irritable skin, the concave faint-hearted chest, the indolent stomach, the furtive hand, the shifting eye—by which movements of retreat set up the as-for-me of individuality and leave their marks on the body. On his-her contours the body builder watches emerging not the eccentricities his or her tastes and vices leave in his or her carnal substance, but the lines of force of the generic *human animal*. (43)

Bodybuilders make the logo flesh and the flesh logo, incarnating the conformity and superficiality of image culture by inscribing their "generic" identities on their skin. Devoting themselves to realizing the reality of image, they strain to become depersonalized, two-dimensional demigods, similar to the life-size cardboard cutouts of the famous with 'whom' tourists pose for pictures.

Leyner tries to distance himself from logo centrism by situating the flattening effect of pumping iron in a broader social context. Equating the bodybuilder's repression of difference with fast capitalism's repression of difference, he identifies in bodybuilding a metaphor for the homogenizing or McDonaldization of culture, the global flexing of golden arches.[7] He parodies the culture industry's marketing of muscle by describing a "'digital video image synthesizing unit'" that automatically dispatches the figure of the archetypal bodybuilder into any film by enabling one "'to take any movie and insert Arnold Schwarzenegger as the actor in the lead role . . . . *It's a Wonderful Life* with Arnold Schwarzenegger instead of Jimmy Stewart, *Gandhi* with Arnold Scharzenegger instead of Ben Kingsley, *Bird* with Arnold Schwarzenegger as Charlie Parker instead of Forest Whitaker . . .'" (50–51). Just as the anonymous bodybuilder attempts to eliminate corporeal eccentricities in a search for "the force of the generic," the computer-aided hyperpresence of Schwarzenegger erases cinematic individuality or particularity, reducing the cultural to a state of uniformity.

As an artist warped by his trips to the Universal gym and by his desire for universal recognition, Mark Leyner personifies this double dedication to dispatching difference in the name of the same. His pumped up figure promises self-presence as well as perpetual presence in the public eye. In *Et Tu, Babe*, one of the spokespersons for homogenization is the actor/director Ron Howard, himself a somewhat hyperreal and homogenizing figure, having grown up in front of the camera and having become a director of such big-budget Hollywood films as *Apollo 13*, a certain kind of investment in ex-orbitancy. Howard fantasizes in gee-whiz, adolescent fashion about a Leynerized world, one in which the satellization of the real and the homogenization of the cultural link up, appropriately enough, in the figure of a logo: "Actually, you know what I'd like to do with the Team Leyner sign? I'd put it into orbit, so it could be like the earth's Statue of Liberty—so it would be the first logo of humanity that the extraterrestrial aliens see

when they immigrate here" (164). For Leyner, as for Taylor, the logo centric aesthetic is ascetic; it endorses physiological and cultural practices
aimed at fashioning an undifferentiated identity, a standardized subject.

In this context, what makes *Et Tu, Babe* a socially responsible waste of
time is the fact that it tries to resist these repressive forces of incorporation
by putting off an easy assessment of its value. Despite the hyperpresence of
Mark Leyner's figure, Mark Leyner is hard to figure out because he under-
cuts both modernism's positive negation of figure and modernist postmodernism's positive negation of ground. He simultaneously revels in and
rejects contemporary culture's obsession with image. From one perspective,
the novel looks like a witty, Duchampian display of popular images—
beginning with the image of celebrity—designed to register as useless work
which calls into question the value of art and the art of evaluation while
maintaining an autonomous position of pure transgressiveness. By engag-
ing in a nonstop treatment of superficiality, Leyner tempts readers to treat
Et Tu, Babe as disgustingly superficial stuff, the aesthetic equivalent of
"'the furfuraceous eczema that covers/ the buttocks of a moribund mule'"
(166). His warped writing seems to beg to be evaluated as a literary
ready-made, an off-putting alternative to modernism's static abstractions.
The title itself insinuates that the reader will turn on the text, just as
Leyner's staff members eventually abandon him. The reader's experience of
revulsion even gets anticipated within the novel by Joe Casale, Leyner's
aide-de-camp, who quits because, as he says: "'I just can't handle it any-
more. . . .'" (147).

Yet the effect of such a betrayal, as the success of Leyner's subsequent
"sensational disappearance" indicates, is merely to speed the reappropriation of the rejected. Leyner's transgression—his theft of Lincoln's valuable
waste—leads to defections and federal seizures which nevertheless enable
him to be to remarketed as a misunderstand *historic visionary.* Likewise,
Leyner's transgressive text will be made subject to an interpretive program
of punitive confiscation, a strategy of axiological repossession exemplified
by Baudrillard's statement that the commodification of the aesthetic makes
for total dreck:

> All original cultural forms, all determined languages are absorbed in
> advertising because it has no depth, it is instantaneous and instanta-
> neously forgotten. Triumph of superficial form, of the smallest common
> denominator of all signification, degree zero of meaning, triumph of
> entropy over all possible tropes. ("Absolute Advertising" 87)

Read in the spirt of this reductive logic, *Et Tu, Babe* actually becomes valuable nonvalue. It works as an example of art as dispatch, succeeds as a "tri-
umph of superficial form." Seen to be aspiring to the instantaneity of the
logo, the book gets positivized as a put off, a no good waste of time.

But Leyner puts off or delays all such quick critical fixes by simultaneously embracing and indicting a logo centric aesthetic. On one hand, his hyperfiction constitutes a pop critique of modernism's vacuous attempts to re-present presence by making figure absent. On the other hand, it constitutes a critique of modernist postmodernism's attempt to re-present presence by making figure all there is. Calling attention to the off-putting, repressive effects of both projects, the novel slides toward what Thomas Pynchon, in *The Crying of Lot 49*, calls an "excluded middle." This (no) place is the scandalous 'lot' of *différance*, a neither/nor location from where the text begins to dislocate the binary oppositions structuring logocentric philosophy and aesthetics: presence/absence, positivity/negativity, sameness/difference, productivity/waste, art/rubbish. Unlike the logo centric author who dies by disappearing into a simulacrum, Leyner enacts a death of the author that is, in Barthes' words, "properly revolutionary" because it suggests the possibility of "refusing to assign to the text (and to the world-as-text) a 'secret,' i.e., an ultimate meaning . . ." ("Death of the Author" 54). Put another way, Leyner tries to be pointless—a waste of time—by putting off his arrival at one of the alternate points structuring restricted economy.

Or perhaps still closer to the point—since the attribution of total pointlessness invests him with "ultimate meaning"—Leyner appears to be (and to make) a continually receding point, a point made in *Et Tu, Babe* by the slippery significance of the name "Mark Leyner." As the duplicity of that sign or figure indicates, Mark Leyner is hard to figure out because his writing points toward the irreducible difference structuring identity. In other words, he exploits those faults—in axiological as well as in linguistic economies—where logocentrism's confidence in authoritative presence begins to crack. But what then might such a nearly pointless, hard-to-figure figure look like? Feigning absolute positivity and absolute negativity, Leyner figures to be an elusive trace, like the surreal narrator of *My Cousin, My Gastroenterologist* who claims to be a rather ungraspable point: "I was an infinitely hot and dense dot" (5).

•

The importance of the cultural commitment to putting off—to enacting what Connor calls "the rhythm of delay, the delay of rhythm" (98)—is taken up by Pynchon in an article titled "Nearer, My Couch, to Thee," an essay in which he considers wasting time by addressing the subject of sloth, a subject ostensibly at odds with the hyperfictional subject of speed.[8] I turn to Pynchon again because he shares with Leyner a desire to inscribe a waste of time, one example being his description, in *The Crying of Lot 49*, of the secret postal service known as W.A.S.T.E. A shadowy organization of otherness—one which seems to surface periodically to disrupt official delivery routes yet one which the heroine Oedipa Maas cannot even prove positively exists—W.A.S.T.E. represents a scandalous (non)system of difference.

It refuses to dispatch (the mail) with regularity and refuses to be regulated by being dispatched with (i.e., suppressed or approved). Like Leyner's writing, the W.A.S.T.E. system delays settlement of its lot by putting off the apprehending forces of law, logic, and evaluation. It remains at large, resisting logocentrism's binary logic by refusing to come out in the open. As Pynchon puts it: "The waiting above all. . . . waiting for a symmetry of choices to break down, to go skew" (181).

Pynchon's nonfiction piece is a shifty, probationary paean to what he calls "the venerable sin of sloth." In the *Oxford English Dictionary*, sloth is defined as follows: "1. Physical or mental inactivity; disinclination to action, exertion, labor; sluggishness, idleness, indolence, laziness; 2. Slowness, tardiness." Sloth seems to be, first, an assertion of negativity, a "disinclination" to work, a rejection of the economic will to increase or conserve, a desire to waste time. However, Pynchon argues that in the modern world sloth has repeatedly been put to work by conservative forces. Specifically, it has been used to repress aesthetic and social difference: in the entertainment industry where "idle exercises in poolside loquacity have not infrequently generated tens of millions of dollars in revenue"; in the political arena where "a failure of political will" has allowed "the introduction of evil policies and the rise of evil regimes, the worldwide fascist ascendency of the 1920's and 30's being perhaps Sloth's finest hour, although the Vietnam era and the Reagan-Bush years are not far behind" (57). Even the sloth of the contemporary couch potato is not a waste of time because it has taught us how to manipulate, even conquer, time through our remote control ability to rewind and channel check at will.

In order to challenge, though never with unqualified success, the government of positivity to which Pynchon sees sloth having been harnessed, sloth must be considered in terms of its second definition, as slowness or tardiness. At the end of his meditation, Pynchon speculates about a different scenario in which humanity hesitates to side with either sloth or its opposite (Work, Productivity, Reason, Utility etc.):

> Perhaps the future of Sloth will lie in sinning against what now seems increasingly to define us—technology. Persisting in Luddite sorrow, despite technology's good intentions, there we'll sit with our heads in virtual reality, glumly refusing to be absorbed in its idle disposable fantasies, even those about superheroes of Sloth back in Sloth's good old days, full of leisurely but lethal misadventures with the ruthless villains of the Acedia squad. (57)

Sloth might be a waste of time after all to the extent that it resists, without rejecting, technology's promise of instantaneous exchange or virtual interaction and to the extent that it defers the determination of value, "refusing" both absolute nonvalue (the superheroes of Sloth) and absolut(ist) value (the Acedia squad). This futuristic setting is where Leyner's book already situates the reader, strapping him/her into a wired text projecting a hyperreal world, generating a barrage of disposable Leyner fantasies, but at the same time encouraging the reader to commit the sin of sloth by putting off being sold on either Mark Leyner or Mark Leyner.

I realize that by winding up my discussion of Mark Leyner this way I run the risk of producing a critical endorsement that conspires to hasten the positivization of his work; however, as I have argued, the strength of *Et Tu, Babe* lies in its ability to forestall, through hyperanticipation, just such a determination of its value. In this context, I will conclude, without further delay, by saying that what *may* make Mark Leyner "in a sense, the most significant young prose writer in America" is his ability to produce slothful hyperfiction. He does the hard work of wasting time.

BACKFIRE III

Hitting on *The Sopranos*

Are drugs in some way linked to the management of remains?

Avital Ronell, *Crack Wars*

At the back end of a project concerned with the dangers of consumer culture's determination to manage remains—its obsession with getting a fix on and from waste—something needs to be said about drugs. To remain silent on the subject would be to imply that there is no connection between narcotics and the works I have placed under consideration. Yet the case is otherwise, as the title *The Waste Fix* implies. Whether it be Upton Sinclair's health food habits, Bartleby's compulsive copying, Babette's hankering for Dylar in *White Noise*, or Mark Leyner's maniacal injection of synthetic hormones, the literary figures I have examined are bound up with addiction. Since I have tried to suggest that certain narratives work through consumer culture's expectations of waste in an effort to address and entertain the sacred, it is tempting to conclude that such addictions are simply the mark of a craving for some kind of mystical high. However, as Avital Ronell claims in her study of *Madame Bovary* entitled *Crack Wars*, such a reading actually issues from of an overly sober philosophical viewpoint: "Precisely due to the promise of exteriority which they are thought to extend, drugs have been redeemed by the conditions of transcendency and revelation with which they are not uncommonly associated. But qualities such as these are problematic because they tend to maintain drugs on 'this side' of a thinking of experience" (61). Since the sacred is forever on the back side of thought, the expectation that drugs will fully illuminate the sacred is bound to backfire. Where drugs are offered as a means of access to an ecstatic experience of the real, they are offered as an alternative to the impossible experience of altarity. Conceived this way, drugs are a waste free means of getting wasted; they bear no trace of unmanageable remains.

141

However, it turns out drugs *are* linked to unmanageable remains in that we don't quite know how to treat them. Drugs may produce good and bad trips, but, conceptually speaking, they trip us up. Despite medical as well as legal efforts to hold up drug traffic—to monitor the physiological and geographical courses drugs take—it is impossible to regulate their flow perfectly. As Ronell wisely puts it: "Drugs resist conceptual arrest. . . . There is no system that can presently hold or 'take' drugs for long" (51, 61). Though they often provide a rush, though they are often linked to speed, drugs slow down the metabolism of any economic system by making difficult the process of ascribing their value. In this respect, they have offputting effects similar to those generated by Mark Leyner's portrait of a drug-popping, speed-driven, scandalous author. Indeed, Ronell insists that writers and addicts have much in common:

> Obsessed and entranced, narcissistic, private, unable to achieve transference, the writer often resembles the addict. This is why every serious war on drugs comes from a community that is at some level of consciousness also hostile to the genuine writer, the figure of the drifter/dissident, which it threatens to expel. Like the addict, such a writer is incapable of producing real value or stabilizing the truth of a real world. (106)

It is important to note that Ronell's notion of the "genuine writer" does not simply romanticize the writer as a pure embodiment of the marginal, as a trippy hipster getting high in the desert, as a happy wanderer. While it may be true that the writer is addicted to resisting consumer culture's economic and axiological clutches, it is also true that every narrative, no matter how dissident, has built into it an addiction to making meaning, to producing "real value." These competing addictions make the writer a particularly unsettling "drifter/dissident" and make clear how irresponsible are those precepts of political correctness that seek to turn literature into a series of public service announcements. But how then to read literature responsibly? If literature is not drug free, might this responsibility have to include a critically responsible way of doing drugs?

In considering this question, I realize that while I have hit on the way a number of American authors dramatize consumer culture's addiction to waste, I may have left myself open to the charge that the project ultimately backfires because it is addicted to scoring only the most pure form of aesthetic fix on the subject (though it should be stressed that *The Jungle* initially sold as a mass-market phenomenon). In other words, it may look like I am claiming that only high forms of American art deal in or with the abysmal high of virtual waste. To avoid this sort of pedestrian charge, I turn to the most popular, widely distributed drug of them all, television, and, more specifically, to the recent hit HBO series *The Sopranos*. While the show recycles some of the more stereotypically conspicuous waste-related features of mob drama—the murder of a rival or disloyal family member; the black-market traffic in drugs—it also probes under all that spectacular junk to address a more unsettling, virtually inconspicuous form of waste whose score is delivered, in brilliantly halting fashion, by the Soprano family as it goes about fitting uneasily into the upscale world of suburban New Jersey.

The show's remarkable commercial and critical success has something to do with the fact that, despite owning a house in a tony social environment, Tony Soprano's lot remains a rather strange one. A hypermasculine, physically imposing, Leyner-esque version of an underworld figure (he even pumps iron underground, in his basement), he sets up his family on legitimate premises while at the same time challenging the premise of the law of the land (by virtue of his criminal activities) and the premise of the law of the underworld (a mob boss browbeaten by his mother? a mob boss who has panic attacks? a mob boss in therapy?). Like Bartleby, he actively submits to a lawful, productive premise when he copies out such upper-world social rituals as the golf game and the college tour. At times simulating conformity to the rules of cultural assimilation, fast-track mobility, and Hollywood cinema, he nevertheless cuts a stubbornly elusive, subterranean figure. To insist on simply identifying him as a member of the underworld doesn't necessarily help, especially since, as Mircea Eliade points out, cosmogonic myths traditionally describe the underworld as an all-but-unchartable space, a virtual wasteland existing at the limit of the "absolute reality" of bounded, organized, sacred space: "From one point of view, the lower regions can be homologized to the unknown and desert regions that surround the inhabited territory; the underworld, over which the cosmos is firmly established, corresponds to the chaos that extends to its frontiers" (42).

What then is this desert wanderer's lot? It is certainly not identical to the lot of the happy wanderer. As Tony says to his therapist: "I see some guy walking down the street, you know, with a clear head. You know the type. He's always fucking whistling like the happy fucking wanderer. I just want to go up to him and I just want to rip his throat open. I want to fucking grab him and pummel him right there for no reason" ("The Happy Wanderer"). Since he uses the front of waste management consultant, it is not surprising that his lot bears a certain resemblance to a landfill lot in the Arizona desert described by Don DeLillo in his book *Underworld*: "The landfill across the road is closed now, jammed to capacity, but gas keeps rising from the great earthen berm, methane, and it produces a wavering across the land and sky that deepens the aura of sacred work. It is like a fable in the writhing air of some ghost civilization, a shimmer of desert ruin" (809–10). Despite being responsible for some pretty repulsive stuff, Tony Soprano is an underworld figure who inspires reverence (or spurs addiction) among viewers by wavering out there in TV's virtual desert in a steaming, "jammed to capacity" fashion. The comparison with DeLillo's landfill suggests that he too radiates an "aura of sacred work." But given that he is a character who has authorized and carried out any number of hits, how can that be? Given Eliade's assertion that the sacred shows itself as a hierophantic break in the chaotic, profane plane of the underworld, how can that be? These questions presume to make Tony Soprano show up promptly as a profane figure; they assume it is possible to get a good fix on him and from him. However, he not only leads a gang with a habit of showing up late, he also isn't hooked on drugs. In fact, the only pill he pops is the Prozac designed to alleviate the anxiety that is virtually wasting him. The drug is supposed to help him get a better fix on things, but he is hardly an addict. As he admits to his therapist/pusher, Dr. Melfi, he isn't even a consistent user:

Dr. Melfi: I hear depression talking.

Tony: Yeah well, I'm not up on my dosage. Medication, medication, medication. What do I got to show for it? ("House Arrest")

If Tony Soprano isn't sure what he has to show for his habit, then what does the viewer have to show for the habit of watching Tony Soprano? To wrestle with this question, I intend to mimic his move of turning to psychoanalysis for help with the following questions: With what kind of waste is he jammed to capacity? What kind of fix is he in?

To examine this prime time waste fix, I wish to glance at the second-season episode titled "House Arrest" in which Tony tries to escape his underworld lot only to find himself in the position of having to manage both waste and drugs. In the wake of narrowly escaping arrest for a hit on a small-time hood who tried to kill his nephew, he shows up at the office of his lawyer, Neil Mink, with a shit-eating grin and a belief that he can wash his hands of the waste business (the business of murder; the business of eliminating human 'trash') if he simply pays off his counsel. However, he quickly learns that his debt cannot be discharged so easily. Refusing the money, Mink advises his client that if he prefers not to suffer the lot of the apprehended criminal he needs to get his shit together and do a bit of copying. Specifically, his lawyer recommends imitating a virtuous life, a feat Tony can best perform by virtually assuming the duties of waste management consultant: "You have an office at Barone Sanitation. Get your ass out of that strip club and go there." As it turns out, this legal advice looks a bit like a progressive prescription for avoiding meat. It suggests that by agreeing to avoid the strip club (with its erotic display of meat) as well as by agreeing to avoid Satriale's meat market (his gang's other favorite hangout), Tony will be clean. If nothing else, he will avoid a repeat of what Mink calls "that brush with a murder beef."

So, in an effort to save himself, the Home Box Office "hit" man confines himself to two clean, sanitary, lawful lots: his home and his office. However, this decision paradoxically leaves him boxed in by waste. The episode literalizes this predicament in two ways: 1. through the plight of Tony's uncle Junior, who, under actual house arrest for criminal behavior, gets his hand stuck in the garbage disposal; 2. through an exchange that takes place when Tony first arrives at Barone sanitation to mimic the role of waste manager:

> Tony: [jokingly] What the fuck, I don't show up for eight years, all of a sudden you turn my office into a storeroom?
>
> Dick Barone: No, I'm gonna have this shit cleaned right out. . . . [To Connie, his secretary] [L]et's move these boxes out, the books.
>
> Connie DeSapio: What should I do with them?
>
> Dick Barone: I don't know. Make room.
>
> Connie DeSapio: I'll put them by the copy machine. ("House Arrest")

Jammed to capacity with junk, the office is supposed to be a place where Tony can at least make a show of going clean. Yet the strategy seems to backfire, for as soon as he shows up he has to deal with a drug problem. It turns out that cocaine is being sold along the Barone garbage routes, a deal worked out by Junior and Richie Aprile (Tony's brother-in-law-to-be until he gets wasted by Tony's sister in the next episode). When Tony learns that family has gone behind his back, he's furious. He's burning with rage; he's on fire:

> After five years. The cops are finally leaving garbage alone. A drug bust on one of those routes is a different story, you got the FBI, the DEA. Those fucking pricks are gonna be breathing down our necks again. . . . You [Richie] and my uncle, you want to deal drugs, that's your business. You do it on association garbage routes, it's my fucking business. It stops today, you got it? ("House Arrest")

This drug business leaves him strung out not only because it threatens to bring the law down on him but also because it threatens to ruin a fantasy cherished by mobsters and metaphysicians alike: the successful management of remains seemingly not subject to the law ("The cops are finally leaving garbage alone"). A reminder of Auster's white cracks in modernism's aesthetic principles, the cocaine is white stuff that surfaces as a kind of "crack" in an otherwise thoroughly efficient system of waste handling. In Tony's case, this crack appears, dramatically, as a physical disruption. Immediately after he erupts at Richie, his rage backfires on him and he suffers another anxiety attack. There he is, at an official gathering of The Garden State Carting Association, suddenly overcome with what the song in the background refers to as "More Than a Feeling." Thrown out of joint by drugs, he looks wasted. His gaze wanders as his cool deserts him. Not quite a stand-up guy to begin with, his joints now buckle. He shambles . . . he stumbles . . . he suffers a seizure and passes out.

What is this smouldering stuff from which he is taking such hits? It has to be something other than a joint fired up in the storeroom/office. It is surely something other than a cigarette[1] fired up in a restaurant, though Dr. Melfi, struggling with alcohol addiction and admitting to her therapist that she is strung out on her mafioso patient (she receives a prescription as a result), erupts in a rage against nicotine while eating out with her college-aged son:

Dr. Melfi: Excuse me. Could you move your cigarette?

Woman smoking: Pardon me?

Dr. Melfi: It's blowing into my son's face. Thank you.

Woman smoking: We're allowed to smoke.

Dr. Melfi: Unfortunately an area where New Jersey is woefully behind, but could you move it?

Jason Melfi: Mom, it's no big deal.

Dr. Melfi: It's no big deal to move it either.

Woman smoking: No . . .

Dr. Melfi: I'm a physician. Do you know what you're doing to the rest of us? . . . Look, this is silly, could you just move the fucking thing? . . . You bitch.

Woman smoking: She must be drunk. ("House Arrest")

Haunted by a hazardous patient for whom she can offer no clear fix, no final cure (is her complaint "Do you know what you're doing to the rest us" also directed at him?), she calls to mind Melville's lawyer who, haunted by the infinitely reserved Bartleby, "burns to be rebelled against . . ." (24). And just as the lawyer winds up dealing with Bartleby by quitting the premises of his law firm, the therapist winds up the meal by getting thrown out of the joint.

The ethical problem with such an incendiary response to waste—the reason it backfires—is that it smacks of a totalizing sensibility, traces of which actually show up in some of Tony's contraband. While under a self-imposed version of house arrest, he is told over the phone that a recently arrived shipment contains relics from Nazi Germany's quest for a final solution: "Yeah T, it's me. Hey, listen. That container came in. From the other side. . . . It's all original World War II shit. . . . You got to come down here. You'll love this stuff. . . . We got a couple of Herman Göring's personal pearl-handled lugers . . ." ("House Arrest"). At one level, the box from "the other side" would appeal to Tony because, like Macfadden's physical culture package, it includes the totalitarian fantasy of eliminating the other, a fantasy he conveys to Dr. Melfi when asked what he wants out of therapy: "What I want to achieve? I wanna stop passin' out. I wanna stop fuckin' panicking. I want to direct my power and my fuckin' anger against the people in my life that deserve it. I wanna be in total control" ("Big Girls Don't Cry"). At another level, the box would appeal to him because it contains an otherness whose origin-ality appears identifiable and exportable. Yet, as Ronell remarks, this shipment of purist ideology contains its own traces of narcotics: "Göring never went anywhere without his supply; Dr. Hubertus Strughold, father of space medicine, conducted mescaline experiments at Dachau—indeed, it would be difficult to dissociate drugs from a history of modern warfare and genocide" (51–52).

Thus, there is no drug-free delivery of or from unsettling remains, a point Dr. Melfi's therapist makes while listening to his patient deliver the remains of a traumatic crack-up of a dream about Tony Soprano:

> Dr. Melfi: I'm there. I could observe everything. He's driving, he starts to hyperventilate. He grabs for a bottle of prozac, but it's empty. And all the while this is happening that song from *The Wizard of Oz* is playing.

> Elliot: "Over The Rainbow."

> Dr. Melfi: No, that other one: "You're out of the woods, you're out of the woods."

> Elliot: They're in the poppy field.

> Dr. Melfi: "Get into the sun . . ." That one. Anyway, he goes into a full-blown panic attack and he passes out. (Crashing sound) He crashes into this huge truck. ("Big Girls Don't Cry")

Elliot's reference to the poppy field reiterates Auster's insight that one never enters a city of glass without taking a hit. (Significantly, *The Wizard of Oz* also challenges the mystical notion that drugs enable one to see the sacred face to face. Dorothy's opium hit is prelude to the promise that she will gain unmediated access to a divine power, the wizard. Yet the figure who finally emerges—from in *back* of a curtain; from out of a *fire*—turns out to be an imposter.) Dr. Melfi's image of Tony frantically reaching for missing drugs reveals that what comes in to her from the other side (from Tony's side) is, like the gas from DeLillo's landfill, the burning trace of an unreachable Other. Is his inability to reach his Prozac a displaced expression of her anxiety about being unable to reach him, her addiction, even through drugs? Indeed, as she admits, in the course of again employing the metaphor of the crack-up, her patient radiates the dangerous yet fascinating power of a taboo: "Elliot, it's like that thing with watching a train wreck. I'm afraid and repulsed by what he might tell me. But somehow I can't stop myself from wanting to hear it" ("House Arrest"). Put another way, Tony has something of the sacred about him. As Dr. Melfi's patient, he is, in several respects, a forbidden figure, and just as the individual who makes contact with the dangerous charge of a taboo becomes taboo in turn, her contact with her charge leads to infection. For not only is she breaking out in fits of rage, she's swelling up. As her therapist describes it: "You mentioned you've put on a little weight lately. Do you think the overeating has anything to do with your patient?" ("Big Girls Don't Cry").

While traces of an unincorporable Other show up on Dr. Melfi's figure, they also show up, in "House Arrest," on Tony's figure. After his collapse, Tony shows up in the hospital with a lesion on his arm. Unable to make a fast break from waste, he breaks out in a rash.[2] Instead of embodying progressivism's hypermasculine ideal of a toned, self-contained, armored body, Tony, for all his mashismo, displays a body whose meat cracks open and backfires on him. This backfiring is made literal in the second season's final episode when he is wracked by terrific bouts of farting and vomiting. So much for tying up loose ends![3] Though Tony is convinced his fiery physiological expulsions are due to a case of food poisoning, his rash suggests that he suffers from something other than a simple case of autointoxication. The burning trace on his skin is a sign that he is packing a different kind of heat. It is the rem(a)inder of a spectre under his skin, an underworld spook operating in such deep cover as to ruin phallocentric expectations of realizing, in the name of the Father(land), a system in which there are no loose ends, a system in which every body is *tight*, a system in which everybody is, like Göring, both loyal and high, or high on loyalty. Not surprisingly, in the hospital Tony responds to this unidentifiable apparition by trying to frame it as the somatic equivalent of an informant within the family: "I'll be relieved when somebody puts their finger on whatever the fuck it is that's wrong with me. I wish it was physical, so I can have it ripped the fuck out." In a wonderful twist, the nurse responds to his cry about his lot by giving him a dose of his own medicine. Posting the medical system's version of a prescription for keeping things tight, she recommends that Tony tone up a bit: "You know, losing some weight wouldn't hurt" ("House Arrest").[4]

Just getting fit won't do it, though, because what he's got is a parasite so stealthy it can't be confirmed by any systematic analysis. The scandalous thing about the burning mark on his skin is that it is not a moral brand or scarlet letter binding him to the ethical. Instead, it is a debt to which he cannot respond contractually. It a debt that can't be fully discharged by arranging a hit (either pharmacological or murderous). The burning trace bears witness to the Soprano don's reception of what John Caputo, paraphrasing Derrida, refers to as an "impossible gift," a donation made without entrance into a circuit of exchange or return:

> The impossible gift then is one in which no one acquires credit and no one contracts a debt. That in turn requires that neither the donor nor the donee would be able to perceive or recognize the gift as a gift, that the gift not appear as a gift. The gift must "happen" below the plane of phenomenality, too low for the radar of conscious intentionality. The mere consciousness of giving sends the gift back to the giver . . . (163)

Something different even from a debt buried in the unconscious and bound to be remembered later, the impossibly gotten gift—the for-gotten gift—is that which, according to Caputo, "does not leave a trace behind, or which leaves only a trace, an ash, a cinder, which is the 'destruction of memory' . . . which burns the trace of gift-giving behind it . . ." (164).

Let's scratch a little further. Though a reminder of it secretes through a crack in the skin, the impossible gift entails a secrecy and silence so profound that, as the very act of Tony's going to the therapist demonstrates, it cracks open the underworld's ethical code of silence.[5] Buried in a deserted lot on the outskirts of any familiar or familial plot, the gift is bound up with death but only insofar as it revives Blanchot's notion of death as that which unfolds dis-astrously at the limit of every system of philosophical speculation. As one of the sanitation engineers confides to Tony in an ostensible lament about municipal restrictions on how much waste his business can haul at once: "It's not the landfill. The problem is the limit." Or again, since I'm still itching to get at it, since I can't kick the habit, the impossible gift resembles Kristeva's "pseudo-object" (see Chapter Three), the archaic, always already forgotten maternal Other which, in the name of the Father, has been abjected with such intensity that it "does not succeed in differentiating itself as *other* but threatens one's *own and clean* self, which is the underpinning of any organization constituted by exclusions and hierarchies" (Kristeva 65). No wonder Tony's fantasy of being a perfectly self-controlled, hardboiled figure heading up perfectly controlled, hierarchized families (underworld and nuclear) is, as he paradoxically shares with his female therapist, underwritten by a rage to abject the feminine: "Remember the first time I came here? I said the kind of man I admire is Gary Cooper, the strong silent type. And how all Americans, all they're doing is crying and confessing and complaining. A bunch of fucking pussies. Fuck 'em! And now, I'm one of them, a patient" ("The Happy Wanderer"). When not hiding out on the surface of his skin as dermatological cracks, the secret gift hides out on the surface of his families as feminized cracks: the behavior of his wisecracking, increasingly secretive daughter, Meadow (she even secretly scores speed to study for the SATs [see Season 1, Episode 3: "Denial, Anger, Acceptance"]); the behavior of one of his wiseguys, nicknamed "Pussy," who has secretly cracked and turned informant (after getting busted for selling drugs); uncle Junior's secret taste for performing oral sex on women—his habit of taking hits from the crack—which Tony denigrates through a series of wisecracks or wiseguy cracks (see Season 1, Episode 9: "Boca").

Perhaps, then, Tony's cracked skin is a sign that his phallocentric plot is taking hits from a (M)other impossible to address, an Other about which and with which one can never be up front: "An orifice, skin opens to introduce a foreign body, a liquifying phallus" (*Crack Wars* 125). Of course, his angry rash is in part the sign of his having taken hits from his mother, a figure who, subject to her own psychic conflagrations, not only constantly belittles her son but also puts out a hit on him during the first season of the show. Ironically, she functions for Tony as a kind of taboo, a charge described by Ronell as the *"toxic maternal."* As her primary caretaker before the attempted hit, Tony keeps exposing himself to the curse of her sour, scornful personality in the hope of gaining her blessing: "The *toxic maternal* means that while the mother's milk is poison, it still supplies the crucial nourishment that the subject needs. It suggests, moreover, that the maternal is too close, invading orifices and skin with no screen protection, as it were, no intervening law to sever the ever-pumping umbilicus" (*Crack Wars* 118–19). Tony's exclusion of his mother from the family after the attempted hit only confirms the awe-fulness of her charge since, according to Kristeva, traditional rites of defilement and prohibition are dedicated to securing ontological, as well as theological, Oneness at the expense of waste laced with reminders of both the maternal and the sacred:

> The function of these religious rituals is to ward off the subject's fear of his very own identity sinking irretrievably into the mother. . . . [T]he abjected object from which I am separated through abomination, if it guarantees a pure and holy law, turns me aside, cuts me off, and throws me out. The abject tears me away from the undifferentiated and brings me into subjection to a system. In short, the abominate is a response to the sacred, its exhaustion, its ending. (64, 111)

At one level, then, Tony Soprano's response to the hit his mother tries to deliver represents an irresponsible craving to be waste free. By claiming that he has come to expect nothing from her—"She's dead to me"—he's looking for a boost from a posture of pure indifference. In this respect, he's not unlike his son, Anthony, Jr ("A. J."), who has been putting his old man out of joint by inhaling a bit of existential nihilism. For Tony, the mother is dead. For Anthony Jr., God is dead. According to Dr. Melfi, the two may be sharing a habit:

Dr. Melfi: What about your mother? Anthony, I think it's important we talk about your mother and what she tried to do to you.

Tony: No need to. She showed her true colors, that's all.

Dr. Melfi: Has Anthony, Jr. heard you say "She's dead to me"?

Tony: I don't know.

Dr. Melfi: Don't you think that kind of talk could lead a kid to embrace these ideas?

Tony: Oh, so now this is my fault. ("D-Girl")

Father and son embrace these deaths as a way to avoid responding to the divine gift of death. They score the idea of death as total lack or absence in the belief that it will produce the high of an end to expectation, the high of an end to expect(or)ations of waste. So, for instance, at the beginning of "House Arrest" Tony hits on feelings of utter boredom and meaninglessness as proof that he no longer needs to expect anything out of therapy:

Dr. Melfi: So, what's up?

Tony: I don't know, I'm . . . I'm bored or something. I don't want to come here no more.

Dr. Melfi: Well . . . Not the first time we've heard you say that.

Tony: No offense but let's face it, this is starting to feel like a waste of time. I'm sure for the both of us. . . . What's the point? You go to Italy, you lift some weights, you watch a movie. It's all a series of distractions 'til you die.

Anthony Jr. dramatizes nihilism's narcosis when he sneaks out of his confirmation party, goes out back (or down into the garage), and fires up a joint with friends. His response when caught? The "dead" mother is a user too: "What are you yelling at me for? Even grandma says the world has no purpose" ("D-Girl").

And yet . . . what makes Tony Soprano such a compelling figure is that he is ultimately not quite so irresponsible as to expect nothing. His angry response to A. J.'s drug use suggests that he has expectations of his children, while his angry response to his son's philosophical habit suggests that he reads Nietzsche's famous phrase "God is dead" otherwise. In the course of telling A. J. that he expects him to go through the confirmation ceremony, Tony hints at God's death as a kind of gift that one is foolish to believe can be accepted or reciprocated by simply turning one's back:

> Tony: You go to Catholic school and your mother wants it.
>
> A.J.: What does she know?
>
> Tony: She knows that even if God is dead, you're still gonna kiss His ass. ("D-Girl")

Since God never comes out of hiding even when He flames out,[6] since God is a fire hidden in back of all efforts at confirmation, since God is a back fire, since God never shows more than a backside, the best one can do is kiss His ass. This kiss of death seals an impossible deal according to which one expects the arrival of a figure who, held up by death, never shows up at the appointed time. In other words, it carries messianic expectations about a future that, according to the very concept of the Messiah, can never be brought to pass in time, can be glimpsed only in hindsight. As Caputo puts it:

> The very idea of the Messiah is that he is *to* come, *a venir*, someone coming, not that he would ever actually arrive. . . . The messianic idea turns on a certain structural openness, undecidability, unaccomplishment, nonoccurrence, noneventuality, which sees to it that, in contrast to the way things transpire in ordinary time, things are never finished, that the last word is never spoken. Were the Messiah ever to show up, that indiscretion would ruin the whole idea of the messianic. . . . Whatever appearance the Messiah does make must be carefully protected or sheltered by the discretion of a disguise, lest the infinite provocation, the discreet delicacy and lightness, of what is coming be destroyed by its exposure to ordinary time, by its absorption into the grossness of the order of presence. (78–79)

The Messiah shows up only in a shambling disguise, only in hiding, only in hides, only on the hide, only on the skin. On the show, Tony wants to show the doctor what a shambles his skin is in: "Look at it. It's bleeding, for

Chrissake" ("House Arrest"). It's bleeding . . . for Christ's sake. It's bleeding for the sake of a figure whose infinitely cryptic nonappearance throws things out of joint. In Caputo's words again:

> The messianic figure is a little terrifying and unnerving. . . . About "this" (*ça, cela*)—this coming spectral figure, this messianic figure—we can hardly say a thing. We are reduced to apophatic utterances, for the *tout autre* slams against our thought and language, shatters our horizons of expectations, as a being that leaves us groping for words and puts whatever we mean to say to rout. (145)

About Tony's case, "we can hardly say a thing." In Tony's cracked case, there is something slamming "against thought and language" which, as in Paul Auster's cracked case, can be considered and described only as nothing:

Dr. Melfi: What's going on?

Tony: Nothing that I can think of. ("Full Leather Jacket")

Not "I can't think of anything," but "Nothing . . . that I can think of." This apparitional no-thing is even more shady than the ghosts described by Tony's henchman Paulie, who, after visiting a psychic, believes he is haunted by all his past hits: "There's no denying it. I'm dragging a bunch of fucking ghouls around with me" ("From Where to Eternity"). No matter how well Tony keeps an eye out, through his own blinders, for the arrival of this spectral figure, it will not show up as an old gangster looking for revenge; it will not show up, when one peeks between the blinds, as a G-man haunting the corner. So he waits in his house, itching for relief, for a salve for his burning, for salvation, for the kingdom. On her way out of the house to give herself the present of fixing up her eyes, his wife Carmella catches him peeking through the curtain at something never made present to us, something on which we never get a fix:

Carmella: What are you lookin' at?

Tony: Nothin'. Just lookin' out the window.

Carmella: Gettin' my eyebrows done. ("House Arrest")

Tony's self-imposed house arrest backfires precisely because he continues to be haunted by a familiar that cannot be arrested in-house or ghostbusted by family (hence his 'trips' to therapy). This "Nothin'" is, like the cause of Tony's skin condition, like the impossible gift of God's death, like the messiah, something missing but active, something actively missing, something missing in action.

Not surprisingly, his eventual response to this backfire is to return, against his lawyer's wishes, to the butcher shop. After all, one of the effects of his having boxed himself in to home and office is that, despite having been drawn into drug deals, he feels like he is *hors de combat* or missing in action. As he explains earlier to Dr. Melfi when rationalizing his professional use of violence, he believes the mob is like the army: "We're soldiers. Soldiers don't go to hell. It's war ("From Where to Eternity"). When he enters the back room at Satriale's, he is welcomed back by Christopher's teasing reassurance of his military rank—"Hey, our long lost leader"—and the suggestion that he has reentered an economy in which his presence insures repayment of all gifts: "Somebody must owe him money." In fact, looked at one way, the meat market is a more efficient waste management operation than the sanitation business. After Richie Aprile is shot to death by Tony's sister, his body is chopped up on the site as part of the thorough dispatch of remains. Enabling the Soprano clan to make sure Richie is gone for good, the pork store appears to post one safely beyond the double dealings of the flesh.

In the end, however, the meat market is not exactly where the action is. In fact it seems somewhat more like Pynchon's shadowy W.A.S.T.E. postal system than a waste-free postal system.[7] While Pynchon's acronym alludes to an underground service defined by unrelieved expectancy (W[e] A[wait] S[ilent] T[rystero's] E[mpire]), Satriale's harbors underworld figures who seem to be just waiting around. Even Tony's arrival does little to fulfill their expectancy. The pork store is a lot where virtually nothing is happening, except that one wiseguy is offering another tips on how to treat cracked, burning skin:

Tony: So what else is going on?

Christopher: Nothing.

Paulie: I'm having good luck with Swiss Basics Moisturizing Formula.

Sylvio: Maybe I'll try it. ("House Arrest")

In a move reminiscent of Upton Sinclair's decision to hit on the slaughterhouse, *The Sopranos* hits on the meat market as a site of unmanageable remains. Satriale's may bear traces of a carnivalesque space where the unruly behavior of the low is sanctioned; the storefront sign actually bears an emblem of the pig, a figure often sacralized during traditional carnival.

Yet even in this respect things are not all they are cracked up to be, which explains why the gang rushes outside at the sound of an automobile crack-up to chew out the perpetrator but good. In their virtual shambles, they are still somehow missing out on the action, so they rage to reduce others to a shambles. As Sylvio says to the speeding driver: "C'mon, you hurt? That's too bad. You should be fucking crippled, you fucking asshole." Tired of sitting still, desperate to see some action, they race to curse someone for moving too fast. In Tony's words: "He drives too fast, and he's always fucking hitting shit."

As this project has tried to argue, to hit on shit is always, in some fashion, to attempt to seize on an ungraspable alterity. The episode of *The Sopranos* on which I've been hitting says as much when it concludes with Tony getting accosted in front of the market by a detective who wants to introduce his partner. His response to the law is at once a shitty, racist dig and an acknowledgment that his lot constitutes, like Pynchon's W.A.S.T.E. system, a shady alternative to the official postal service:

> **Agent Harris:** I was in the neighborhood. I wanted to introduce you to my new partner. Joe Marquez, Tony Soprano.
>
> **Tony:** What's the matter, no openings in the post office? ("House Arrest")

Or, finally, maybe Tony's lot is best articulated through a remark he makes at a restaurant called The Stockyard Inn, where he and Pussy go after delivering a gruesome hit on the kid who tried to kill Christopher. It is a meaty remark, for it can be read a number of ways: as the indicator of a guilty recoil or backfire during which the mob boss begins to acknowledge the shittiness of his murderous act; as a veiled threat to a figure, Pussy, who is doing the shitty work of informing or backfiring on him; as a meditation on the inscrutability of the sacred. Regardless, it is remark delivered while he is eating meat: "Do you believe in God?"[8]

Notes

Backfire I

1 Two classic examples of this argument are Daniel J. Boorstin, *The Image: A Guide to Pseudo-Events in America* (New York: Macmillan, 1961) and Allan Bloom, *The Closing of the American Mind: How Higher Education has Failed Democracy and Impoverished the Souls of Today's Students* (New York: Simon & Schuster, 1987).

2 The identification of the sacred with backfire is a cross-cultural phenomenon. A particularly striking example of this identification occurs in various Hindu myths concerning the figure of Agni, the god of fire. As Wendy Doniger O'Flaherty points out, Agni is a slippery, tricky, treacherous figure alternately portrayed as fleeing from the demonic and fleeing from the divine. She cites a passage from the Vrtra cycle in the Rg Veda in which Agni begins as an offspring of evil only to betray his parentage by backing out of this affiliation and allying himself with the divine: "In one hymn, Indra invites Agni to come to him; Agni replies, 'Leaving the nongod secretly and by hidden ways, as a god I go to immortality. Deserting him, I go from my natural friends to a strange household'" (*Origins* 114). O'Flaherty goes on to point out that in other stories Agni is originally a divine figure who nevertheless has a tendency to run around in back of the gods and ally himself with the demonic: "The role of Agni as traitor may also be viewed in the context of the many Rg Veda myths in which Agni treacherously flees from the gods and must be bribed to come back. In the *Mahābhārata*, this theme is embroidered with another betrayal: Agni betrays his wife to the demons (Rāksasas) and is cursed for this, whereupon he flees from the sacrifice until the gods seek him out and bring him back" (Wendy Doniger O'Flaherty, *The Origins of Evil in Hindu Mythology*, [Berkeley: University of California Press, 1976], 115).

Chapter 1

1 The *Blade Runner* script reinforces this identification of replicant and abattoir. In an early scene not included in the film, a replicant, presumably Batty, is introduced as follows: "We are looking at the bright image of a NAKED MAN in a white tiled room with a white floor... an abbatoir [*sic*] without blood. The naked

157

man is very athletic" (Hampton Fancher and David Peoples, writ. *Blade Runner*, [BladeZone 21 June 1999 <http://www.bladezone.com/>], 1981).

2   Another contemporary cinematic example of a cybernetic figure threatening to abate the system of humanist mimetic production while haunting the streets of Los Angeles is the liquid alloy cybernetic organism named "T2" in James Cameron's film *Terminator 2: Judgment Day*. As Cohen points out, this figure assaults humanism's "legal machinery of mimetic production" by morphing like mad. Its slippery self-figurations terminate the notion of a neatly representable subjectivity: "So here then is the secret inversion: 'T2' manifests himself not only as an invading 'real,' but as a figure—opposed to Arnold, whose non-humanity is now avuncular, paternal, and fuzzy warm by comparison—whose primary trope is anamorphosis and who burns relentlessly through the empty commodity images of mimetic reality. Indeed he performs this demolition of representation by exceeding it, exploding it, and replicating anything he touches" (Cohen 261).

3   The image of limping in the face of the sacred is powerfully drawn in the Biblical story of Jacob's nocturnal tussle with a nameless adversary: "And Jacob was left alone, and a man wrestled with him until the break of dawn" (Genesis: 32:25). In his translation of Genesis, Robert Alter makes it clear that Jacob's grappling with the sacred involves a struggle with an irreducibly pre-figural figure. In a footnote, he argues that since the anonymous "man" pleas with Jacob to be released with the coming light—"'Let me go, for dawn is breaking'" (32:27)—the figure is not a transparent representation of the divine but is rather, like a replicant, a figure that imitates the human while resisting classification: "The temporal limitation of activity suggests that the 'man' is certainly not God Himself and probably not an angel in the ordinary sense. . . . [T]he real point, as Jacob's adversary himself suggests when he refuses to reveal his name, is that he resists identification" (n. 27). Moreover, if by virtue of wrestling in the dark Jacob has "'seen God face to face'" (32:31), what he carries away from the encounter, staggeringly, is the imprint of the pre-figural. The man's touch permanently marks him—whose Hebraic name, as Alter points out, bears a trace of the crooked ['*aqob*]—with a shambling gait: "And the sun rose upon him as he passed Penuel and he was limping on his hip" (32:32) (*Genesis*, trans. Robert Alter, [New York: W. W. Norton & Co., 1996.], 180–83).
    Jacob's identically crooked twin is perhaps the African mythological figure of Èsù. A messenger of the gods like Hermes, Èsù is a figure who bears the traces of an absent theological presence. A trickster like Jacob, he is disfigured by his ability to straddle the sacred and secular realms. As Henry Louis Gates puts it: "Èsù is guardian of the crossroads, master of style and the stylus, phallic god of generation and fecundity, master of the mystical barrier that separates the divine from the profane world. In Yoruba mythology, Èsù always limps, because his legs are of different lengths: one is anchored in the realm of the gods, the other rests in the human world" ("The Blackness of Blackness: A Critique of the Sign and the Signifying Monkey," ed. Henry Louis Gates, *Black Literature and Literary Theory*, [New York: Methuen, 1984], 287).

4   Dennis Hollier, in his book *Against Architecture*, sketches out the history of the shambles' architectural conversion from shambling figure to upstanding figure. Drawing on Bataille's theory of *dépense*, he argues that slaughterhouse violence is a radically unproductive, "harsh" form of expenditure whose wastefulness appears, by the nineteenth century, terribly hazardous to bourgeois culture's

conservative, utilitarian values. As a result, the slaughterhouse get transformed, often literally, into sites promoting what he calls "soft" expenditure, the passing (or wasting) of leisure time in a productive, nonsubversive fashion. Stressing that a disciplinary "logic of the modernization of urban space" informs the modern history of the slaughterhouse, Hollier recounts how, by the nineteenth century, stockyards get replaced by the museum and the park:

> The small neighborhood slaughterhouses were recycled into green spaces, urban parks, just as the central slaughterhouses of La Villette are being recycled, a century later, into a park of science and industry. Thanks to this conversion a nice, clean expenditure takes the place of a dirty one and the visitor takes over for the worker. Doing in the slaughterhouses makes room for educational parks, spaces where workers on holiday see demonstrated the meaning of their work. At the park of science and industry they celebrate Labor Day by looking at their work. (*Against Architecture: The Writings of Georges Bataille*, trans. Betsy Wing, [Cambridge, MA: MIT Press, 1989], xv).

In place of the abattoir's atrocity exhibition, the museum's edifying exhibit. In place of the dirty shambles, a clean and proper Sunday stroll.

5 For a fictional satire of Kellogg's shit fits, see T. Coraghessan Boyle, *The Road To Wellville: A Novel* (Viking, 1993).

6 The all-white uniform might be considered a progressivist fashion statement of sorts in that it is also adopted by John Harvey Kellogg and Horace Fletcher.

7 Much of the garbage brought to treatment plants to be reduced, through a process of steaming, yielded grease which was then clarified to make soap. The conversion of refuse into an agent of cleanliness corresponds neatly to Waring's project of converting otherwise disorderly subjects into agents of order.

8 Perhaps the most bizarre weapons employed in the progressive war on social waste are the Juvenile Street-Cleaning Leagues set up to supervise potentially subversive elements of the population while promoting awareness of public health. In addition to attending mass meetings, singing songs, and taking a pledge, the working class children recruited into these organizations are given incentives to assume the posts of sanitation inspectors, pubescent pollution police encouraged to file complaint reports identifying those guilty of littering. David Willard, Waring's Supervisor of Street Cleaning, makes clear the connection between sanitary awareness, moral improvement, and social conformity in describing the benefits of this education: "He [the child] is cleaner in his person and habits, to which the report of many a school-teacher bears witness. And he cannot fail to grow up with an increased love for his city, the result of that knowledge which will make him the sturdy, upright citizen which the times demand in great measure" (Colonel George E. Waring, Jr., *Street Cleaning and the Disposal of a City's Wastes: Methods and Results and the Effects upon Public Health, Public Morals, and Municipal Prosperity*, [New York, 1898], 186).

9 In an ostensibly postmodern apology for adipose titled *Eat Fat*, Richard Klein actually recycles naturalism's accusation of an obscene linkage between information technology and obesity: "Modern machines are spare and efficient; postmodern machines are fat and all-consuming, excessive, luxurious, ill-defined. . . .

We are growing sicker and more unhealthy as civilization produces more garbage and toxins in order to fabricate the machines that give us the leisure to grow fatter and sicker. And in the meantime, we are being sold an increasingly distant ideal of desirable weight" (*Eat Fat*, [New York: Pantheon, 1996], 24, 108).

10 Sinclair's connection between obesity and spiritual shambling is reprised in the work of a contemporary Christian evangelist named, appropriately enough, Gwen Shamblin. A best-selling author and founder of the Remnant Fellowship, she preaches a fundamentalist brand of self-help that equates trimness with transcendence: "Shamblin promises followers of her diet that, in addition to losing weight, they will be granted eternal life. . . . Shamblin's core contention is that the fatness of America is the symptom of spiritual crisis: overweight people have mistaken a spiritual emptiness for a hunger for food" (Rebecca Mead, "Slim for Him," [*New Yorker* 15 January 2001], 48).

11 Fashioning a surface without soft spots or crevices, this modern form of self-flagellation applies to the body the same principles applied to the bathroom by modern domestic engineering. As Ellen Lupton and J. Abbott Miller illustrate in their analysis of early twentieth-century interior design, the modern bathroom—now stripped of the folded drapes and thick carpets constituting so much Victorian flab—emerges as a space defined by seamless, hard, and, not coincidentally, white surfaces:

> It was at the turn of the century that the bathroom was more strictly defined as a site of sanitary care. As promotional images show, aesthetically and technically coordinated fixtures replaced the loose accumulation of chamber pots, portable tubs, washstands, and "running water appliances." White porcelain and bright, polished metals were favored because they revealed the presence of dirt: they were proof of their own cleanliness. ("Hygiene, Cuisine, and the Product World of Early Twentieth-Century America," *Incorporations*, ed. Jonathan Crary and Sanford Kwinter, [New York: Urzone, Inc., 1992], 499).

Like Waring's white duck, the bathroom's white surfaces act as panoptic instruments designed to make visible "the presence of dirt."

12 One of the most outspoken, flamboyant supporters of what Seltzer refers to as "the 'naturalist' project of making men" (*Bodies* 152) is Bernarr Macfadden. In addition to marketing a macho health-food cereal he calls Strengtho, Macfadden fashions a macho signature for himself, literally changing his given name from Bernard McFadden to Bernarr Macfadden with the rationale that the extra "r" makes him sound more fearless and that the "Mac" re-creates the image of toughness and power projected by the "Mac" truck. A cross between Teddy Roosevelt and P. T. Barnum, he promotes the virtues of what Seltzer refers to as "the male natural body" in a number of ways: by performing feats of physical strength in public; by peddling exercise equipment (everything from Indian clubs to a genital enlarger called the "peniscope"); by establishing a short-lived Physical Culture City; by repeatedly publishing photographs of himself in nearly nude, flexed postures. On Macfadden's life, see William R. Hunt, *Body Love: The Amazing Career of Bernarr Macfadden* (Bowling Green State University Popular Press, 1989); Robert Ernst, *Weakness is a Crime: The Life of Bernarr Macfadden* (Syracuse University Press, 1991).

13 It should be noted that *The Jungle* is not the only example of a progressive health reformer seeking to put the shambles to shame. See John Harvey Kellogg, *Shall We Slay to Eat?* (Good Health Publishing Co., 1899).

14 Sinclair's anxiety about linguistic figuration is later expressed, in dramatic fashion, through his obsession with telepathy, a form of communication in which, ideally, there are no figures to slow or corrupt the transmission of meaning. See Upton Sinclair, *Mental Radio*, intro. William McDougall, (Pasadena: The Author, 1930). His use of the term "mental radio" to describe telepathy reflects how the naturalist idealization of immediacy is consistently mediated by an investment in the mechanical.

15 The phrase "blank fiction" has been used recently to describe postmodern fictions that depict and, to some extent, embrace the excesses of 1980s American consumer culture: yuppie decadence, rampant greed, brand-name fetishism, explicit sexuality, gratuitous violence. See James Annesley, *Blank Fictions: Consumerism, Culture, and the Contemporary American Novel* (London: Pluto Press, 1998). Sinclair's proletarian project ostensibly stands in opposition to such texts, though the author's quest for blankness problematizes the book's politics.

16 Another author drawn to fashioning a literary posterity in accordance with the principles of progressive health reform is Henry James, for a time a devoted Fletcherite. For an analysis of the connection between James' Fletcherism and his revision of his corpus for the New York Edition of his work, see Tim Armstrong, *Modernism, Technology, and the Body: A Cultural Study* (Cambridge: Cambridge UP, 1998), 42–58.

BACKFIRE II

1 See, for example, Gillian Brown, "The Empire of Agoraphobia," *Representations*, 20 (Fall 1987), 134–57; Michael T. Gilmore, "'Bartleby, the Scrivener' and the Transformation of the Economy," *American Romanticism and the Marketplace* (Chicago: U of Chicago P, 1985), 132–45; Michael Paul Rogin, *Subversive Genealogy: The Politics and Art of Herman Melville* (Berkeley: U of California P, 1985), 192–201.

CHAPTER 2

1 All references to *City of Glass*, *Ghosts*, and *The Locked Room* are to Paul Auster's *New York Trilogy* and will be cited hereafter as *City*, *Ghosts*, and *Locked* respectively.

2 For an examination of Macfadden's significant success as publisher of pulp magazines, see Ann Fabian, "Making a Commodity of Truth: Speculations on the Career of Bernarr Macfadden," *American Literary History* 5 (Spring 1993), 51–76.

3 The concept of *levity* informs much of Auster's novel *Mr. Vertigo*, a story about a young orphan trained in the art of levitation. A reminder of the unbearable

lightness of being, Walt the Wonder Boy is a literally floating signifier who hovers in and over the void. Defying the law of gravity, a law that defines being as a grounded presence, his remarkable routines are, above all, performances on the plane of nothing: "It wasn't a matter of first going up and then going out, it was a matter of going up and out at the same time, of launching myself in one smooth, uninterrupted gesture into the arms of the great ambient nothingness" (*Mr. Vertigo*, [New York: Viking, 1994], 85).

4   According to Kristeva, the "logic of distribution" that structures both society and subjectivity by setting up formal systems of oppositions—pure/impure, holy/defiling etc.—is nowhere more in evidence than in the prohibitions and divisions constructed with regard to food: "Food loathing is perhaps the most elementary and most archaic form of abjection" (2). Like the impossible memory of mother's plenitude, which Kristeva names "the *hallucination of nothing*" (42), food, which first issues from mother, is a constant reminder of the fragility of every subject's integrity.

5   An example, from Auster, of this exhausted opening is the first line of his own dystopian vision titled *In the Country of Last Things*, which begins: "These are the last things, she wrote" (1).

6   For a reading of modernism's anorexic look as symptomatic of a masculinist rage to fashion texts purged of the feminine, see Leslie Heywood, *Dedication to Hunger: The Anorexic Aesthetic in Modern Culture* (Berkeley: U of California P, 1996).

7   For more on the dis-figuring principles of modernist architecture, see Mark C. Taylor, *Disfiguring: Art, Architecture, Religion* (Chicago: U of Chicago P, 1992).

8   The call is an example of what Avital Ronell refers to as the "toxic invasions waged by the telephone" (10), toxic because, like the consumption of food, the telephone call represents a transaction with an other that constantly calls into question the address of a proper subject: "It [the telephone] destabilizes the identity of self and other, subject and thing, it abolishes the originariness of site; it undermines the authority of the Book and constantly menaces the existence of literature" (*The Telephone Book: Technology, Schizophrenia, Electric Speech*, [Lincoln: U of Nebraska P, 1989], 9).

9   The threat these calls pose recalls the case of another literary double and recluse in quest of ascetic bliss. In a lust-filled attempt to transcend the world of want, Humbert Humbert, Vladimir Nabokov's infamous pedophile, twice roams across the American landscape in a plot to preserve the innocence he abuses by making a hermetically sealed environment for his beloved Lolita out of an endless series of roadside hotels. Despite working to the max to preserve his errant bliss, he lives in dread of the ladies' room and the line out—the head and the horn—both of which offer ungovernable opportunities for escape: "I felt instinctively that toilets—as also telephones—happened to be, for reasons unfathomable, the points where my destiny was liable to catch" (*The Annotated Lolita*, ed. and intro. Alfred Appel, Jr., [New York: Vintage, 1970], 211).

10 Compare this account of the ascetic with Melville's account of Bartleby, a figure who also traces marks at a desk for a living: "Bartleby was an eminently deco-

rous person. He would be the last man to sit down to his desk in any state approaching to nudity" ("Bartleby, the Scrivener," 27).

CHAPTER 3

1 Indeed, DeLillo believes the most serious kind of writing is defined by its commitment to addressing the unanswerable question of death. As he indicates in an interview with *The Paris Review*: "'If writing is a concentrated form of thinking, then the most concentrated writing probably ends in some kind of reflection on dying. This is what we eventually confront if we think long enough and hard enough'" ("Don DeLillo: The Art of Fiction CXXXV," 298).

2 For an analysis of the normalizing and recuperative mechanisms governing traditional disaster narratives, particularly science fiction film narratives, see Susan Sontag, "The Imagination of Disaster," *Science Fiction: A Collection of Critical Essays*, ed. Mark Rose, (Englewood Cliffs, NJ: Prentice-Hall, Inc., 1976), 116–31.

3 An astro-logic pursued much more dramatically in the partially Trek-influenced suicides committed by members of the Heaven's Gate cult. Inspired by an astral sign—the approach of the Halle-Bopp comet—this disastrous decision to transcend death was informed by an idealism expressed by the cult in several different ascetic ways: the choice made by several males to be castrated; the belief that their bodies were "containers" to be discarded and then recycled; the decision to leave their estate (or plot) in a remarkably uncluttered, empty state; the fact that the members departed wearing all black and Nike shoes (sprinting for the stars to avoid life's disaster).

4 In this latter respect, the character bears a comic resemblance to his historical namesake, the Flemish geographer Gerhardus Mercator (1512–1594), a figure famous for his contribution to cartographic reduction of territorial waste through invention of a map projection designed to make the globe a total package. The "mercator projection" renders parallels and meridians as straight lines spaced so as to produce at any point an accurate ratio of latitude and longitude.

5 Cf. the uncertain noise of revelation/annihilation described in the famous opening line of *Gravity's Rainbow*: "A screaming comes across the sky" (Thomas Pynchon, *Gravity's Rainbow*, [New York: Viking, 1973], 3).

6 DeLillo's interest in the problem of forgetfulness extends beyond his own work. He has created a writing program in New York City for people in the early stages of Alzheimer's disease. The intent of the program is two-fold: to help patients combat and come to terms with the disastrous forgetfulness that marks the disease by encouraging them "to express, through written passages, memories that will soon fossilize, or to unlock ones that reside just beyond awareness" (Gardner, C1+.)

7 *White Noise* can be read, of course, as a satire skewering the contemporary culture of simulation for its refusal to put this belief to question. The novel dramatizes a devotion to simulation in the form of the public's "spiritual surrender" to photographs of "THE MOST PHOTOGRAPHED BARN IN AMERICA," souvenirs so invested with an "aura" of the Real as to make the barn itself "impossible to see" (12).

CHAPTER 4

1   I use this enlarging "shadow" font throughout the essay to represent the flashy
    and hypertrophic author portrayed in *Et Tu, Babe* and thereby to distinguish
    him from the 'real' author Mark Leyner. However, in writing the essay I found
    it was not easy to maintain a clear distinction between these two authorial fig-
    ures. It became difficult to choose, in places, which signifier—Mark Leyner or
    Mark Leyner—would be more appropriate to use. The point is that the reader
    of the essay, like the reader of *Et Tu, Babe*, should always be aware that Mark
    Leyner continually threatens to collapse into, or to become overshadowed by,
    Mark Leyner.

2   See Mark Leyner, "Hulk Couture," *Tooth Imprints on a Corn Dog*, (New York:
    Harmony, 1995), 96–102.

3   The closest real-life counterpart to **Mark Leyner** is undoubtedly Tony Little, the
    ponytailed, muscle-bound fitness guru who sells exercise equipment, workout
    wear, and shape-up videos (his own, of course) through infomercials and on the
    Home Shopping Network. A former Mr. America contender and a gung-ho,
    hypermotivated "selling machine," Little grossed $100 million dollars from the
    sale of his products in 1994. As with **Mark Leyner**, the key to his success is the
    way he sells his own personality or markets his own image:

> A stickler for detail and a master of self-promotion, he has so completely entwined
> his image with that of his product line that the shrewdest concept developed by Mr.
> Little may not be the tapes or the books or the plans for a chain of rehabilitation
> clinics, but Tony Little himself. (Peter Marks, "Perfect Pitch: Tony Little's
> Infomercials Keep the Fitness Gear Moving," [*New York Times* 9 May 1994], B4)

4   For a good discussion of the compression of time in postmodern culture, see
    David Harvey, *The Condition of Postmodernity* (Cambridge MA: Blackwell,
    1990).

5   See Herman Melville, "Poor Man's Pudding and Rich Man's Crumbs," *The
    Piazza Tales and Other Prose Pieces 1839–1860*, ed. Harrison Hayford, Hershel
    Parker, G. Thomas Tanselle et al., [Evanston: Northwestern-Newberry, 1987),
    289–302.

6   Marcel Duchamp's attempt to exhibit his *Fountain* (1917)—a "ready-made,"
    mass-produced urinal—is perhaps the most famous example of this impulse to
    subvert the notion of image as waste by flushing out an image of waste.

7   A magazine advertisement for Ford Motor Company graphically demonstrates
    this homogenizing logo-rrhea. The ad displays a map of the world dotted
    throughout by the blue Ford logo (the United States is literally almost hidden
    behind a blizzard of these signs), each logo supposedly marking a site where a
    Ford-sponsored or Ford-built vehicle won a racing event in the last year. The
    text reads: "And you thought the earth's surface was dominated by water. There
    are oceans. And then there's something that's really big and blue. Once again,
    the Ford Oval has made its mark across the world. . . . Looks like we have every-
    thing covered" (*Time*, 20 February 1995, 74–75).

8 There is a certain symmetry achieved by invoking Pynchon here since the trajectory of his career constitutes a real-life variation on **Mark Leyner's** career. The former is an author who has created, through his disappearance and dis-figurement, the same kind of commodified persona **Leyner** eagerly creates for himself by disappearing into his disfigured figure. The notion that the author's "death" does not simply result in art's escape from economy is addressed by Don DeLillo in his novel *Mao II*. DeLillo's fictional author, Bill Gray, has been in hiding for many years, successfully removing his image from circulation. Ironically, the very image of his absence—his image as a "gray," nearly dis-figured figure—only serves to promote his work; the iconoclastic author assumes the stature of an icon: "'In our world we sleep and eat the image and pray to it and wear it too. The writer who won't show his face is encroaching on holy turf. He's playing God's own trick'" (*Mao II*, [New York: Viking, 1991], 37).

BACKFIRE III

1 Not coincidentally, in the process of revealing to Tony that Tony's father also experienced anxiety attacks, Hesh Rabkin, the ex-record producer and sometime family business adviser, connects this psychological crack in the Soprano background with cigarettes: "He cracked his head open once on a cigarette machine" ("Big Girls Don't Cry").

2 Tony's skin condition makes him resemble the character from another critically acclaimed television series, Dennis Potter's *The Singing Detective*. A writer of detective fiction (like Auster's Daniel Quinn), Potter's Philip Marlow is a figure who, like Chandler's Philip Marlowe, like Tony Soprano, like Daniel Quinn, tries to embody a tough, thick-skinned, hardboiled identity. However, he suffers from a dramatic, debilitating dermatological affliction; the whole surface of his body is cracking open with a case of acute, raging psoriasis. It is a fire whose origin is so obscure that it would at best only be banked by the drugs he refuses from his hospital bed. At one level, then, the Soprano mobster and the Singing Detective are similarly marked.

3 The relay between cracking and excremental backfiring is also made manifest in the case of one of Christopher's sub-gang who, every time he is on a safecracking job, has to take a shit. As Christopher puts it: "The adrenaline effects everybody differently. Big Pussy Bompensiero, he started out as a cat burglar. One time he left a load so big, cop thought a bear was in the place" ("Full Leather Jacket").

4 The subtle thread connecting cultural pressures about fashioning a toned body, about fitting into a tony social environment, and about running a perfectly tight family weaves its way marvelously through the background of a scene in which Carmella is expressing to Tony her anxiety about which college their daughter Meadow will attend. As the scene opens, the television in the background emits a burst of white noise about the virtues of toning. Call it a backfire of sorts:

> (**Male voice**): The profile toner is a wonderful, affordable, easily used alternative to undergoing facelift surgery. (Female voice) The profile toner is great for any age and any body type, even for those hereditary . . . you've probably given up on.

> **Tony:** Carm. Why don't you take a xanax or something?

> Carmella: What is this obsession with Berkeley? What, is she trying to get away from us?
>
> Tony: Absolutely, that's her job.
>
> Carmella: Go ahead, laugh. What are you gonna do if she gets into Berkeley and not into Notre Dame or Georgetown?
>
> Tony: She's in the national honor society, for chrissake. ("Full Leather Jacket")

Carmella is burning to keep Meadow close to the family (and the Catholic tradition) and yet is also burning to have Meadow's college experience facilitate removal of those unsightly hereditary 'wrinkles' in the family. Tony's solution is to offer Carmella drugs.

5 The traditional underworld dynamics of gift giving are at stake in an earlier episode titled "Full Leather Jacket." In this instance, Richie Aprile makes Tony the gift of a leather jacket with the assumption that the donation of this supple skin or soft hide places the boss in his debt. However, Tony enrages Richie by simultaneously canceling and capitalizing on the debt. He donates the jacket to the Soprano family maid's husband, effectively acquiring credit at Richie's expense.

6 I invoke, with a forked tongue, the idea of God's "flame out," intending to catch both of the following meanings of the phrase: 1. to expire; to cease; to go cold; 2. to burst forth; to express a heretofore secret identity in spectacular fashion; to come all the way out (of the closet). In his poem "God's Grandeur," Gerard Manley Hopkins engages in just such double talk of the divine: "The world is charged with the grandeur of God./ It will flame out, like shining from shook foil" (Gerard Manley Hopkins, *Poems and Prose of Gerard Manley Hopkins*, selected and intro. W. H. Gardner, [New York: Penguin, 1953], 27).

7 The connection between the butcher shop and the postal service is made explicit in Pynchon's novel through the name of the lawyer ("Metzger") who is supposed to help Oedipa Maas execute Pierce Inverarity's will, though he spends more time trying to score with her. As J. Kerry Grant points out in his book *A Companion to The Crying of Lot 49*:

> Nicholson cites Mendelson's note that the name [Metzger] is German for butcher and then adds his own observation: "Because of the peripatetic nature of their trade, German butchers in the Middle Ages were given letters to carry from village to village: Metzger hence came to signify 'temporary postman'" (94). The "butcher post" was by no means an exclusively medieval phenomenon, however: "In the course of time the Butchers' Guild formed a regular postal organization. A patent of the Emperor Rudolf II in 1597 mentions the butcher post as an established institution to promote communication. Even in 1622, after the beginning of the Thirty Years' War, a special Post and Butcher Regulation issued by Duke Johann Friedrich of Wurttemburg shows that in remote localities where there was no regular mail service the butchers were still in the habit of carrying letter bags. (J. Kerry Grant, *A Companion to The Crying of Lot 49*, [Athens: U of Georgia P, 1994], 11).

8 At the beginning of the third season, Tony discovers, with Dr. Melfi's help, that, for complicated psychological reasons, his physiological backfires—his panic attacks—are triggered by the sight of meat. See "Fortunate Son," writ. Todd A. Kessler, dir. Henry J. Bronchtein, *The Sopranos*, (HBO, 11 March 2001).

Bibliography

Agger, Ben. *Fast Capitalism: A Critical Theory of Significance*. Urbana, IL: University of Illinois Press, 1989.

Anderson, Mark. "Anorexia and Modernism, or How I Learned to Diet in All Directions." *Discourse* 11.1 (1988–89): 28–41.

Auster, Paul. "The Art Of Hunger." *The Art of Hunger: Essays, Prefaces, Interviews*. Los Angeles: Sun and Moon Press, 1992. 9–20.

———. "Book of the Dead: An Interview with Edmond Jabès." *The Sin of the Book: Edmond Jabès*. Lincoln: University of Nebraska Press, 1985. 3–25.

———. *Disappearances: Selected Poems*. Woodstock, NY: The Overland Press, 1988.

———. *In the Country of Last Things*. New York: Viking, 1987.

———. *Moon Palace*. New York: Viking, 1989.

———. *The Music of Chance*. New York: Viking, 1990.

———. *The New York Trilogy*. New York: Penguin, 1990.

———. "White Spaces." *Ground Work: Selected Poems and Essays: 1970–1979*. London: Faber and Faber, 1990. 81–88.

Banta, Martha. *Taylored Lives: Narrative Productions in the Age of Taylor, Vehlen, and Ford*. Chicago: University of Chicago Press, 1993.

Barthelme, Donald. "Nothing: A Preliminary Account." *Sixty Stories*. New York: E.P. Dutton, 1981. 245–48.

Barthes, Roland. "The Death of the Author." 1968. *The Rustle of Language*. Trans. Richard Howard. New York: Hill and Wang, 1986. 49–55.

———. "The Jet-man." *Mythologies*. Trans. Annette Lavers. New York: Farrar, Strauss & Giroux, 1972. 71–73.

Bataille, Georges. "The Sacred." *Visions of Excess: Selected Writings, 1927–1939*. Ed. and Intro. Allan Stoekl. Trans. Allan Stoekl, Carl R. Lovitt, Donald

M. Leslie, Jr. Theory and History of Literature Vol. 14. Minneapolis: University of Minnesota Press, 1985. 240–45.

———. "Slaughterhouse." *October* 36 (1986): 14.

Baudrillard, Jean. "Absolute Advertising, Ground-Zero Advertising." *Simulacra and Simulation*. Trans. Sheila Faria Glaser. Ann Arbor: University of Michigan Press, 1994. 87–94.

———. "The Ecstasy of Communication." *The Anti-Aesthetic: Essays on Postmodern Culture*. Ed. Hal Foster. Seattle: Bay Press, 1983. 126–34.

———. "The Obese." *Fatal Strategies*. Ed. Jim Fleming. Trans. Philip Beitchman and W. G. Niewsluchowski. New York: Semiotext(e), 1990. 27–34.

Beckett, Samuel. *Endgame: A Play in One Act*. New York: Grove, 1958.

"Big Girls Don't Cry." *The Sopranos*. Writ. Terence Winter. Dir. Tim Van Patten. HBO. 13 Feb. 2000.

Blanchot, Maurice, "Interruptions." Trans. Rosmarie Waldrop and Paul Auster. *The Sin of the Book: Edmond Jabès*. Lincoln: University of Nebraska Press, 1985. 43–54.

———. *The Space of Literature*. Trans. and Intro. Ann Smock. Lincoln: University of Nebraska Press, 1982.

———. *The Writing of the Disaster*. Trans. Ann Smock. Lincoln: University of Nebraska Press, 1995.

Brown, Norman O. *Love's Body*. New York: Vintage, 1966.

Caputo, John D. *The Prayers and Tears of Jacques Derrida: Religion without Religion*. Bloomington, Indiana University Press, 1997.

Cassell's French-English English-French Dictionary. 1981.

Cohen, Tom. *Anti-Mimesis from Plato to Hitchcock*. Cambridge: Cambridge University Press, 1994.

Connor, Steven. "Absolute Rubbish: Cultural Economies of Loss in Freud, Bataille, and Beckett." *Theory and Cultural Value*. Oxford: Blackwell, 1992. 57–101.

DeLillo, Don. *Americana*. New York: Penguin, 1971.

———. "Don DeLillo: The Art of Fiction CXXXV." *The Paris Review* 35 (1993): 274–306.

———. *End Zone*. New York: Penguin, 1972.

———. *The Names*. New York: Vintage, 1982.

———. *Ratner's Star*. New York: Vintage, 1976.

———. *Underworld*. New York: Scribner, 1997.

———. *White Noise*. New York: Penguin, 1984.

Derrida, Jacques. *Cinders*. Trans. and Ed. Ned Lukacher. Lincoln: University of Nebraska Press, 1991.

———. "Plato's Pharmacy." *Dissemination*. Trans. Barbara Johnson. Chicago: University of Chicago Press, 1981. 61–171.

———. "White Mythology: Metaphor in the Text of Philosophy." *Margins of Philosophy*. Trans. Alan Bass. Chicago: University of Chicago Press, 1982. 207–271.

"D-Girl." *The Sopranos*. Writ. Todd A. Kessler. Dir. Allen Coulter. HBO. 27 Feb. 2000.

Dixon, Thomas. *A Dreamer in Portugal: The Story of Bernarr Macfadden's Mission to Continental Europe*. New York: Covici Friede, Inc., 1934.

Douglas, Mary. *Purity and Danger: An Analysis of the Concepts of Pollution and Taboo*. London: Routledge & Kegan Paul Ltd., 1966.

Eliade, Mircea. *The Sacred and the Profane: The Nature of Religion*. Trans. Willard R. Task. New York: Harcourt Brace Jovanovich, 1957.

Eliot, T. S. *The Complete Poems and Plays 1909–1950*. New York: Harcourt, Brace & World, Inc., 1971. 21–23.

Ellmann, Maud. *The Hunger Artists: Starving, Writing, and Imprisonment*. Cambridge, MA: Harvard University Press, 1993.

Ellsworth, William W. "Colonel Waring's 'White Angels': A Sketch of the Street-Cleaning Department of New York." *The Outlook* 27 June 1896, 1191–94.

Ernst, Robert. *Weakness is a Crime: The Life of Bernarr Macfadden*. Syracuse: Syracuse University Press, 1991.

Folsom, Michael Brewster. "Upton Sinclair's Escape from The Jungle: The Narrative Strategy and Suppressed Conclusion of America's First Proletarian Novel." *Prospects* 4 (1979): 237–66.

Fletcher, Horace. *The New Glutton or Epicure*. New York: Fredrick A. Stokes Co., 1906.

"From Where to Eternity." *The Sopranos*. Writ. Michael Imperioli. Dir. Henry J. Bronchtein. HBO. 12 March 2000.

"Full Leather Jacket." *The Sopranos*. Writ. Robin Green and Mitchell Burgess. Dir. Allen Coulter. HBO. 5 March 2000.

Freud, Sigmund. *The Standard Edition of the Complete Psychological Works of Sigmund Freud*. Trans. James Strachey. Vol. 10. London: Hogarth Press, 1955.

———. *Totem and Taboo: Some Points of Agreement between the Mental Lives of Savages and Neurotics*. Trans. and Ed. James Strachey. New York: W. W. Norton & Co., 1950.

Girard, René. *Violence and the Sacred*. Trans. Patrick Gregory. Baltimore: Johns Hopkins University Press, 1977.

Grimes, William. "The Ridiculous Vision of Mark Leyner." *New York Times Magazine* 13 September 1992: 34+.

Haase, Andrew. "Panic Art." *Panic Encyclopedia: The Definitive Guide to the Postmodern Scene.* Eds. Arthur Kroker, Marilouise Kroker, David Cook. New York: St. Martin's, 1989. 18–25.

"The Happy Wanderer." *The Sopranos.* Writ. Frank Renzulli. Dir. John Patterson. HBO. 20 Feb. 2000.

Harpham, Geoffrey Galt. *The Ascetic Imperative in Culture and Criticism.* Chicago: University of Chicago Press, 1987.

Herbert, Christopher. "Rat Worship and Taboo in Mayhew's London." *Representations* 23 (1988): 1–24.

"House Arrest." *The Sopranos.* Writ. Terence Winter. Dir. Tim Van Patten. HBO. 26 March 2000.

Irigaray, Luce. *This Sex Which is Not One.* Trans. Catherine Porter, with Carolyn Burke. Ithaca, NY: Cornell University Press, 1985.

Jabès, Edmond. *The Book of Margins.* Trans. Rosemarie Waldrop. Chicago: University of Chicago Press, 1993.

———. *The Book of Questions: Yaël Elya Aely.* Trans. Rosmarie Waldrop. Middletown, CT: Wesleyan University Press, 1983.

———. *The Book of Resemblances, Vol. 2: Intimations The Desert.* Trans. Rosmarie Waldrop. Hanover NH: Wesleyan University Press, 1991.

———. *The Book of Resemblances, Vol. 3: The Ineffaceable The Unperceived.* Trans. Rosmarie Waldrop. Hanover NH: Wesleyan University Press, 1991.

James, William. *The Varieties of Religious Experience.* Ed. Martin Marty. New York: Penguin, 1982.

Jay, Gregory. *America the Scrivener: Deconstruction and the Subject of Literary History.* Ithaca: Cornell University Press, 1990.

Kellogg, John Harvey. *Colon Hygiene.* Battle Creek, Mich: Good Health Publishing Co., 1916.

Kristeva, Julia. *Powers of Horror: An Essay on Abjection.* Trans. Leon S. Roudiez. New York: Columbia University Press, 1982.

Leyner, Mark. *Et Tu, Babe.* New York: Vintage, 1992.

———. *My Cousin, My Gastroenterologist.* New York: Harmony, 1990.

———. "Great Pretenders." *Tooth Imprints on a Corn Dog.* New York: Harmony, 1995. 125–30.

Lingis, Alphonso. *Foreign Bodies.* New York: Routledge, 1994.

Lyotard, Jean-Francois. *The Postmodern Condition: A Report on Knowledge.* Trans. Geoff Bennington and Brian Massumi. Theory and History of Literature Vol. 10. Minneapolis: University of Minnesota Press, 1984.

Macfadden, Bernarr. "Clean Dirt—Filthy Dirt." *Physical Culture* Nov. 1910: 435–36.

———. "The Editor's Viewpoint." *Physical Culture* May 1910: 413–18.

————. "The Editor's Viewpoint." *Physical Culture* Sept. 1911: 233–38.

Melville, Herman. "Bartleby, the Scrivener: A Story of Wall-Street." *The Piazza Tales and Other Prose Pieces 1839–1860*. Ed. Harrison Hayford, Hershel Parker, G. Thomas Tanselle et al. Evanston: Northwestern-Newberry, 1987. 13–45.

————. *Moby-Dick or The Whale*. Ed. Harrison Hayford, Hershel Parker, G. Thomas Tanselle et al. Evanston: Northwestern-Newberry, 1988.

Michael, George. "Freedom '90." *Listen Without Prejudice, Vol. 1*. Columbia, CK 46898, 1990.

Michaels, Walter Benn. *The Gold Standard and the Logic of Naturalism*. Berkeley: University of California Press, 1987.

Morgan, Thomas B. *Italian Physical Culture Demonstration: A Report of the Visit Training and Accomplishments of the Forty Italian Students Who Were Guests of Bernarr Macfadden during a Stay of Six Months in the United States Studying His Methods of Physical Culture*. New York: Macfadden, 1932.

Norris, Frank. "Novelists of the Future: The Training They Need." *Novels and Essays*. Ed. Donald Pizer. New York: The Library of America, 1986.

The Oxford English Dictionary. 2nd ed. 1989.

Pynchon, Thomas. *The Crying of Lot 49*. New York: Harper & Row, 1966.

————. "Nearer, My Couch, to Thee." *New York Times Book Review* 6 June 1993: 3+.

Rideout, Walter B. *The Radical Novel in the United States, 1900–1954: Some Interrelations of Literature and Society*. New York: Hill and Wang, 1956.

Ronell, Avital. *Crack Wars: Literature Addiction Mania*. Lincoln: University of Nebraska Press, 1992.

Seltzer, Mark. *Bodies and Machines*. New York: Routledge, 1992.

————. "Serial Killers (1)." *differences: A Journal of Feminist Cultural Studies* 5 (1993): 92–128.

Serres, Michel. *The Parasite*. Trans., with notes, Lawrence R. Schehr. Baltimore: Johns Hopkins University Press, 1982.

Sinclair, Upton. *The Book of Life: Mind and Body*. New York: MacMillan, 1921.

————. "Divorce and Public Health." *Physical Culture* March 1911: 316–20.

————. "Exercise for Brain Workers." *Physical Culture* Sept. 1911: 279–85.

————. *The Fasting Cure*. Los Angeles: Mitchell Kennerley, 1911.

————. *The Jungle*. Intro. Ronald Gottesman. New York: Penguin, 1985.

————. "Living on Raw Foods: The Advantages in Strength, Economy, and Health of an Uncooked Diet." *Collier's* 16 Apr. 1910: 37–38.

————. "My Cause." 1903. *Upton Sinclair Anthology*. Intro. Irving Stone and Lewis Browne. Murray & Gee: Culver City, 1947.

——. "The Raw Food Table." *Physical Culture* Feb. 1910: 137–40.

——. "Returning to Nature." *Physical Culture* June 1911: 623–28.

——. "Starving for Health's Sake." *Cosmopolitan* 48 (1909–10): 739–46.

——. "Wheat—The King of Foods." *Physical Culture* Sept. 1910: 223–38.

Smock, Ann. "Quiet." *Qui Parle: Literature, Philosophy, Visual Arts, History.* 1988 (Fall), 2:2, 68–100.

Stallybrass, Peter, and Allon White. *The Politics and Poetics of Transgression.* Ithaca: Cornell University Press, 1986.

Stevens, Wallace. "The Snow Man." *The Collected Poems of Wallace Stevens.* New York: Vintage, 1982. 9–10.

Taylor, Mark C. *Altarity.* Chicago: University of Chicago Press, 1987.

——. *Erring: A Postmodern A/theology.* Chicago: University of Chicago Press, 1984.

——. *Hiding.* Chicago: University of Chicago Press, 1997.

Theweleit, Klaus. *Male Fantasies, Vol. 1: Floods, Bodies, History.* Trans. Stephen Conway. Theory and History of Literature Vol. 22. Minneapolis: University of Minnesota Press, 1987.

——. *Male Fantasies, Vol. 2: Male Bodies: Psychoanalyzing the White Terror.* Trans. Erica Carter and Chris Turner. Theory and History of Literature Vol. 23. Minneapolis: University of Minnesota Press, 1989.

Thomas, Calvin. *Male Matters: Masculinity, Anxiety, and the Male Body on the Line.* Urbana, IL: University of Illinois Press, 1996.

Tierney, John. "Recycling is Garbage." *New York Times Magazine* 30 June 1996: 24+.

Trachtenberg, Alan. "White City." *The Incorporation of America: Culture and Society in the Gilded Age.* New York: Hill and Wang, 1982.

Veblen, Thorstein. *The Theory of the Leisure Class.* Intro. Robert Lekachman. New York: Penguin, 1979.

Waring, George E., Jr. "The Cleaning of a Great City." *McClure's Magazine* 9 (Sept. 1897): 1911–24.

Weber, Max. *The Protestant Ethic and the Spirit of Capitalism.* Trans. Talcott Parsons. New York: Routledge, 1930.

Webster's Third New International Dictionary of the English Language. Springfield, MA: Merriam Webster Inc., 1981.

Wigley, Mark. *White Walls, Designer Dresses: The Fashioning of Modern Architecture.* Cambridge, MA: MIT Press, 1995.

Wilson, Christopher P. "American Naturalism and the Problem of Sincerity." *American Literature* 54 (1982): 511–527.

Index

abattoir. *See* slaughterhouse
addiction, 1, 24, 33, 114, 120,
    141–42
Agger, Ben, 124–25
altar, 9, 15, 107–09
altarity, 9, 27, 70, 116
Anderson, Mark, 75–77
anxiety:
    about figuration, 26–27, 35, 45,
        51–52, 87, 161n14
    about immigration, 40
    about masculinity, 10, 82
    about mechanical reproduction, 33
    about slaughterhouse, 15
    ontological, 2, 4–6, 16–19, 26, 75,
        99
asceticism, 36, 43, 57, 76–77, 112–13
    and consumer culture and, 130,
        132, 136
    and hyperconsumption and, 101,
        122
    and modernism and, 80, 131
    and progressivism and, 18, 22, 23
    and speculative philosophy and, 32
    and speed and, 121
    and writing and, 43, 46, 52–53,
        83–85, 88, 124–25, 129
Auster, Paul, 11, 99, 110, 148, 153,
        161n3
    "The Art of Hunger," 74–75
    City of Glass, 66–69, 71, 73–74,
        80–81, 83–91, 101, 109

Ghosts, 65–66, 72, 89–90
In the Country of Last Things, 67,
        78
The Locked Room, 66–67, 72
Moon Palace, 77–78
The Music of Chance, 79–80
authenticity, 5, 46, 52
autointoxication, 19–21, 26, 31, 33,
        40, 48, 81

backfire, 6, 8–12, 55–56, 60, 63, 88,
        90, 108–09, 115, 146, 148,
        152–53, 157n1, 165n4,
        166n8
Banta, Martha, 43–44
Barthelme, Donald, 69
Barthes, Roland, 121–22, 137
Bataille, Georges, 14–16, 115, 119,
        125
Baudrillard, Jean, 35, 123–24, 133,
        136
Beckett, Samuel, 76, 118
Blade Runner, 13–14, 16, 71, 157n1
Blanchot, Maurice, 56–57, 62–63, 68,
        94–96, 98–100, 108, 113,
        115, 149
blankness, 27, 79–80, 81, 88, 90. *See
        also* whiteness
body:
    alteration, 120
    and language, 32, 73, 80
    and machine, 16, 22–23, 43

and masculinity, 10, 36–38, 82,
   126, 160n12
and waste, 11, 18, 20–25, 76, 109,
   130
and writing, 76, 80, 123, 132–33
boundaries of, 6, 34–36, 73, 101,
   104, 148
liberation from, 76–78
bodybuilding, 66, 82, 132, 134–35
Brown, Norman O., 73, 111

Caputo, John, 149, 152–53
Cohen, Tom, 14–16, 158n2
Connor, Steven, 118, 126–27, 137
consumption, 40, 111
   and commodification of the aesthet-
      ic, 56–57, 117
   conspicuous, 2, 5, 20, 44
   food, 20–27, 107
      and self-realization, 95, 99
   See also cyberconsumption
   See also hyperconsumption
   See also writing
conversion:
   and narrative, 17, 24, 42–43, 46,
      52, 84
   architectural, 158n4
   dietary, 25, 36
   economic, 124–27, 159n7
   of waste, 4, 61
currents:
   electronic, 22, 85, 120, 124–25,
      133
   monetary, 47–48, 51, 120, 124–25
   physiological, 47, 85
cyberconsumption, 23–26, 44, 81,
   113

DeLillo, Don, 11, 50, 165n8
   End Zone, 101–05
   The Names, 111
   Ratner's Star, 98, 112
   Underworld, 6–7, 143
   White Noise, 93–102, 105–11,
      113–16
Derrida, Jacques, 9, 31–32, 88,
   108–09, 114–15, 121
diet. *See* consumption

difference, 3, 60, 62, 79, 110, 123
   aesthetic, 57, 119, 125, 129, 138
   and identity, 75, 95, 99, 121–22,
      135, 137
   and language, 71, 80, 87, 131
   metaphysical, 8, 31, 69
   social, 9, 95, 138
Dixon, Thomas, 38, 40
Douglas, Mary, 3, 6–7, 21, 104

Eliade, Mircea, 7–8, 68, 143
Eliot, T. S., 87
Ellmann, Maud, 75, 80–81, 88
Ellsworth, William W., 28–31
end, 58, 69, 154
   eschatological, 9, 61, 75, 94, 103,
      151
   narrative, 60, 71, 134, 141
   physiological, 23, 148
errancy, 24, 31, 42–43, 46, 52, 70–72,
   74, 82, 84, 87, 90, 114
excrement, 19, 21–24, 28, 47,
   103–05, 108, 112, 165n3
expectoration, 4, 6, 10, 23, 48, 51–52

faith, 2, 59, 61, 96, 97, 113, 116, 119
fascism, 38–41, 101
fasting, 18, 24–25, 36–38, 62, 74,
   75–78, 86, 88
fat, 34–35, 76, 159–60n9, 160n10
feminine, the:
   and the sacred, 10
   repression of, 11, 38, 82, 105, 150,
      162n6
figuration, 14–17, 27, 51–52, 68, 80,
   89, 131, 136, 161n14
fitness, 10, 23, 32, 87, 95
fix, 1–3, 7–8, 10, 12, 15, 57, 59, 115,
   137, 142, 144, 153
Fletcher, Horace, 20, 22–24, 38, 81,
   113, 159n6, 161n16
Freud, Sigmund, 8–9, 47–49, 104

Girard, René, 105–08
God, 2–3, 18, 70, 74, 90, 96, 104,
   107, 111, 130, 151–52, 155,
   166n6
Grimes, William, 123–24

Haase, Andrew, 125
Harpham, Geoffrey Galt, 42–43, 46,
    52–53, 84
Herbert, Christopher, 48
Hollier, Dennis, 158n4
Hopkins, Gerard Manley, 166n6
humanism, 14–15, 56–57, 68–69, 72,
    158n2
hyperconsumption, 101, 122, 131
hyperfiction, 123–25, 137

imitation, 5, 7–9, 31, 44–43, 45, 46,
    51, 62, 158n2, 158n3
Irigaray, Luce, 9–10

Jabès, Edmond, 68–70, 73, 87–90
James, William, 18–19
joint:
    architectural, 15, 51–53
    physiological, 20, 42, 146
joint anxiety, 16–17, 43, 47, 87

Kellogg, John Harvey, 21–22, 25, 81,
    159n5, 159n6
Klein, Richard, 159–60n9
Kristeva, Julia, 75, 104–07, 110–12,
    149–50, 162n4

Lears, T. J. Jackson, 5
Leyner, Mark, 11, 36, 102
    Et Tu, Babe, 117–30, 132–37, 139
    My Cousin, My Gastroenterologist,
        121, 126, 137
    Tooth Imprints on a Corn Dog, 132
Lingis, Alphonso, 134–35
logo, 129–37, 164n7
Lyotard, Jean-François, 96

Macfadden, Bernarr, 18, 21, 38–40,
    66, 78, 81, 101, 160n12
marginal, the, 68, 69, 105, 127–28,
    142
meat:
    avoidance of, 22, 144
    body as, 14, 27, 148, 154
    consumption of, 48, 80, 155, 166n8
    language as, 14, 77

mechanical reproduction of, 14–15,
    27
Melville, Herman, 128, 164n5
    "Bartleby, the Scrivener, a Story of
        Wall-Street," 12, 41, 55–63,
        68, 85, 89, 111, 141, 143,
        146, 162n10
    Moby-Dick, 59
Michael, George, 126
Michaels, Walter Benn, 51
modernism:
    and abstract representation, 51,
        75–77, 80–81, 83, 89–90,
        100, 131, 136
Morgan, Thomas B., 40

Nabokov, Vladimir, 162n9
naturalism, 16–17, 22, 36, 40–41, 47,
    51, 53, 81, 161n14
Norris, Frank, 36
nothing, 23, 57, 61, 63, 65–66, 69,
    72–75, 79, 81, 83, 86, 90,
    98, 153, 162n3, 162n4
nothing, 66, 68–74, 79–80, 84–86,
    88–90

Other, the, 6, 9–10, 19, 41, 49, 63,
    69, 84–85, 90, 96, 104–05,
    119, 148–49, 150

parasite, 49–50, 59, 90, 149
patriarchy, 9–10, 68, 110
physical culture, 18, 32, 38–40, 82
plot, 7–8, 11, 42, 95–97, 99–100,
    105, 107, 110, 149, 162n9
pop art, 130–31
post:
    architectural, 7, 31, 53
    as transmission, 16, 24, 27, 50, 52,
        65–66, 149, 154
    as station, 23, 30–31, 38, 44, 50,
        52–53, 66, 85–86, 89
postal system, 24, 56, 60, 89, 129,
    137–38, 154–55, 166n7
posthuman, 14, 51, 71
postmodernism:
    and culture, 4, 13, 33, 97, 107

and modernism, 131, 136–37
and narrative, 11, 55, 68–69, 71,
    88, 118, 161n15
posture:
  critical, 115, 119, 151
  fascist, 38–40
  literary, 36–38
  physical, 22, 31, 35–40, 56, 66, 98,
    160n12
  self-effacing, 98, 100, 125
progressivism, 17–22, 30, 32, 35, 38,
    144, 159n8, 161n13, 161n16
Puritanism, 2–3
Pynchon, Thomas, 163n5, 165n8
  The Crying of Lot 49, 137–38,
    154–55, 166n7
  "Nearer, My Couch, to Thee,"
    137–38

Real, the, 5, 9, 33–35, 45, 80, 114,
    130, 131
recycling, 4–5, 30, 87, 163n3
refuse. *See* waste
resistance, 11, 57, 63, 72, 77, 82, 96,
    119, 129, 136, 138–39
Rideout, Walter B., 45
Ronell, Avital, 41–42, 147, 150,
    162n8

sacred, the, 6–11, 16–17, 48, 50, 63,
    68, 104, 106–110, 141, 144,
    150, 157n1, 158n3
salvation:
  and narrative, 44, 50, 52, 71
  and self-denial, 26, 78, 99
  expectation of, 2, 10, 23, 87, 96,
    120, 130, 153
seizure, 6, 30, 57, 97, 115, 119, 146,
    155
self-realization, 6, 74, 95, 100, 121
self-starvation. *See* fasting
Seltzer, Mark, 16, 22, 26, 33
serialization, 33, 35, 40, 43–44
serial killing, 14, 27, 35, 41, 43, 44
Serres, Michel, 49–51, 96
sham, the, 45–46, 50–52, 55, 85
shambles:
  narrative, 11, 68

philosophical, 94
physical, 14, 17–18, 20
spiritual, 20, 42
See also slaughterhouse
shambling, 17, 42, 52–53, 66, 85,
    160n10
  and locomotion, 31, 42, 51, 58, 89,
    146, 158n3
  and representation, 15–16, 42, 51,
    73, 114, 152, 158n4
shit. *See* excrement
Sinclair, Upton, 10–11, 122, 141, 154
  "Divorce and Public Health," 34
  "Exercise for Brain Workers," 36
  The Fasting Cure, 25–27
  The Jungle, 10–11, 17, 22–23,
    40–52
  "Living on Raw Foods," 34
  "The Raw Food Table," 22, 32–34
  relationship with Bernarr
    Macfadden, 17–18, 22
  "Starving for Health's Sake,"
    24–25, 36–38
  "Wheat—The King of Foods,"
    25–26
slaughterhouse, 13, 14–16, 19, 27, 30,
    35, 41–42, 47, 49–51,
    158n4, 161n13
Smock, Ann, 60–61
Sopranos, The, 12, 142–55
Stallybrass, Peter, 34
Stevens, Wallace, 89
system, 95, 142, 149
  alternative, 138, 155
  and totalism, 62, 68, 119, 124–26,
    128–29, 148
  and waste management, 3–6, 16,
    23–24, 57, 60, 124, 145

taboo, 8, 48, 75, 148, 150
Taylor, Frederick Winslow, 23, 26, 99
Taylor, Mark C., 8–9, 42, 68, 71, 73,
    106, 100, 129–32
Theweleit, Klaus, 38, 40
Trachtenberg, Alan, 30

uselessness, 2, 23, 57–58, 61, 97, 118

Veblen, Thorstein, 1–3, 6
virtual, the, 1, 4–5, 7–8, 11, 14, 30,
        33, 55, 100
virtual waste, 6–7, 9–11, 17, 90, 97,
        109, 113
    and asceticism, 46
    and the sacred, 9, 63
    as chaos, 7
    Bartleby as, 58
    death as, 94–95, 103
    God as, 70, 111
    relationship to bodily waste, 24
    resistance to, 17
    slaughterhouse as, 50
    white noise as, 111
    writing as, 114

Waring, Colonel George E., 28–31,
        40, 56, 159n7, 159n8,
        160n11
waste:
    and art, 57, 118, 125, 127, 129
    and death, 14, 94
    and drugs, 1, 141, 144–45
    and forgetting, 113
    and identity, 3–6, 11, 18, 20, 26,
        34, 43, 46, 77, 83, 95, 99,
        100, 104, 120, 130, 144,
        148, 151
    and image, 1, 131, 164n6
    and imitation, 31, 33, 61
    and language, 73, 77, 86–87
    and narrative, 7, 11, 19, 42, 44, 50,
        58, 71, 76, 119, 124, 141
    and philosophy, 6, 9, 19, 32, 41,
        58, 69, 94, 96, 103, 112
    and ruin, 14, 20, 46, 58, 61, 70, 97,
        146
    and the sacred, 7, 9, 16, 50, 63,
        102, 104–07, 150
    and the slaughterhouse, 15, 27,
        41–42, 48, 158n4
    and time, 2–3, 25–27, 56, 61–62,
        103, 117–22, 124–25,
        128–30 136–38, 159n4
    and writing, 12, 26, 53, 136
    as primordial chaos, 7

    consumption of, 2, 19, 93–94, 97,
        101–02, 122, 127–28
    elimination of, 3, 18, 27, 28, 43,
        86, 99–100, 128, 147, 163n4
        from body, 38, 53, 68, 98,
        113–14
        from text, 52–53, 68, 76
    management, 4, 5, 11, 23–24, 28,
        30, 41, 43, 60, 95, 98, 106,
        143–45, 149, 154, 159n8
wasteland, 1, 5, 52, 87, 97
Weber, Max, 2–3, 62
White, Allon, 34
whiteness:
    and Columbian Exposition, 30
    and fascism, 40–41
    and modernist architecture, 81–83,
        145
    and progressive reform, 28–29,
        159n6, 160n11
    and the sacred, 62, 80, 90–91, 106,
        109
Wigley, Mark, 81–83
Wilson, Christopher, 47
writing:
    and celebrity, 117, 120, 126,
        132–34
    and consumption, 26, 52–53, 74,
        76, 117–18, 120–22
    and forgetting, 114
    and the sacred, 110–11
    See also asceticism

For Product Safety Concerns and Information please contact our EU
representative GPSR@taylorandfrancis.com
Taylor & Francis Verlag GmbH, Kaufingerstraße 24, 80331 München, Germany